CALIGUL

CROSS PURF

THE JUST

THE POSSESSED

Albert Camus was born in Algeria in 1913. His childhood was poor although not unhappy. He studied philosophy at the University of Algiers, and became a journalist as well as organizing the *Théâtre de l'équipe*, a young avant-garde dramatic group. His early essays were collected in *L'Envers et l'endroit* (*The Wrong Side and the Right Side*) and *Noces* (*Nuptials*). He went to Paris, where he worked on the newspaper *Paris Soir* before returning to Algeria. His play *Caligula* appeared in 1939. His first two important books, *L'Etranger* (*The Outsider*) and the long essay *Le Mythe de Sisyphe* (*The Myth of Sisyphus*), were published when he returned to Paris. After the occupation of France by the Germans in 1941, Camus became one of the intellectual leaders of the Resistance movement. He edited and contributed to the underground newspaper *Combat*, which he had helped to found. After the war he devoted himself to writing and established an international reputation with such books as *La Peste* (*The Plague*) (1947), *Les Justes* (*The Just*) (1949) and *La Chute* (*The Fall*) (1956). During the late 1950s, Camus renewed his active interest in the theatre, writing and directing stage adaptations of William Faulkner's *Requiem for a Nun* and Dostoyevsky's *The Possessed*. He was awarded the Nobel Prize for Literature in 1957. He was killed in a road accident in 1960.

Sartre paid tribute to him in his obituary notice: 'Camus could never cease to be one of the principal forces in our cultural domain, nor to represent, in his own way, the history of France and of this century.'

Albert Camus

CALIGULA
CROSS PURPOSE
THE JUST
THE POSSESSED

PENGUIN BOOKS
in association with Hamish Hamilton

PENGUIN BOOKS

Published by the Penguin Group
Penguin Books Ltd, 27 Wrights Lane, London W8 5TZ, England
Penguin Books USA Inc., 375 Hudson Street, New York, New York 10014, USA
Penguin Books Australia Ltd, Ringwood, Victoria, Australia
Penguin Books Canada Ltd, 2801 John Street, Markham, Ontario, Canada L3R 1B4
Penguin Books (NZ) Ltd, 182–190 Wairau Road, Auckland 10, New Zealand

Penguin Books Ltd, Registered Offices: Harmondsworth, Middlesex, England

Le Malentendu and *Caligula* first published in France 1944
Copyright 1947 by Éditions Gallimard
This translation first published by Hamish Hamilton 1948

Les Justes first published in France 1950
Copyright 1950 by Éditions Gallimard
This translation copyright © Hamish Hamilton Ltd, 1965

Les Possédés first published in France 1959
Copyright © Éditions Gallimard, 1959
This translation copyright © Alfred A. Knopf Inc., 1960

Le Malentendu and *Caligula* first published together in Penguin Books 1965
Les Justes and *Les Possédés* published together in Penguin Books 1970
This collection published with an Introduction in Penguin Books 1984
5 7 9 10 8 6 4

Introduction copyright © John Cruickshank, 1984
All rights reserved

Printed in England by Clays Ltd, St Ives plc
Set in Monotype Baskerville

Contents

Introduction

Albert Camus, whose name is one of the best known in post-war France, was what we have learned to call a *pied-noir*. In other words, he was a European born in French Algeria. His father's family originated in the Bordeaux region (and not in Alsace as Camus himself believed), while his mother's family came from the Spanish island of Minorca. Both families had settled in Algeria well before 1870 and lived the relatively impoverished lives of agricultural workers who also had connections with the wine trade. Within a year of Camus's birth – at Mondovi, in the Constantine department of Algeria, on 7 November 1913 – his father was killed in France during the first battle of the Marne. Camus's mother moved with her two small sons to the home of her own widowed mother in the Belcourt district of Algiers. She worked as a charwoman to help support the family, and during their early years Albert and his brother were looked after by their somewhat tyrannical grandmother. Camus's first published collection of essays, *L'Envers et l'endroit*, describes the poverty in which he grew up and contains portraits of his mother, his grandmother and an uncle.

In 1918 Camus entered the primary school serving the Belcourt district. He was fortunate enough to be taught by Louis Germain, who saw his intellectual promise and helped him to win a scholarship to secondary school, the Lycée d'Alger, in 1923. Thirty-five years later he dedicated the published version of his Nobel Prize acceptance speech, *Discours de Suède* (1958), to Germain. Between

1923 and 1930 he proved a gifted schoolboy and acquired the literary and sporting interests which he was to retain throughout his life. By 1930 he was reading Gide, Montherlant and Malraux as well as the classics. From 1928 to 1930 he kept goal for Racing Universitaire d'Alger and showed much enthusiasm for swimming and boxing. The year 1930 proved a critical one, however, since he experienced the first of several severe attacks of tuberculosis. His educational career was interrupted and his footballing activities had to stop. For the same health reasons he had to move out of the small, dark, two-roomed apartment which had been his home for fifteen years. After a short period spent with an uncle who was a butcher by trade and a Voltairean by conviction, he decided to live on his own. He supported himself with a variety of jobs and registered as a philosophy student at the University of Algiers.

One of Camus's university teachers, Jean Grenier, was another important influence on his intellectual development, and Camus recognized the fact by dedicating *L'Envers et l'endroit* to him. Before this, in 1933, Camus had married Simone Hié, the daughter of an Algiers doctor, but she proved to have a severe drug problem and the marriage was tragically dissolved in the following year. In 1935, despite Grenier's scepticism concerning party orthodoxy, Camus joined the Algerian Communist Party. However, this was another relatively short-lived affair which ended with his expulsion in 1937. The outcome is not surprising since it seems that he had not read Marx before 1935, and was unconvinced by many of Marx's arguments when he later became familiar with them.

In the meantime Camus had completed his *licence* at the university, and in 1936 had obtained a postgraduate *diplôme d'études supérieures* for a thesis on the relations between

8

Hellenism (Plotinus) and Christianity (St Augustine). A year later he had a further attack of tuberculosis. He was prevented from taking the *agrégation*, and his university career came to an end. He had to rest in the French Alps (his first visit to Europe), and he returned to Algeria via Florence, Pisa and Genoa.

It was during his student days that Camus's lifelong love of the theatre first found active expression. With a number of young left-wing intellectuals he helped to found the Théâtre du Travail in Algiers. The group's aim, according to its manifesto, was to create a popular theatre which would prove itself a 'school of values'. The intention was to bring good plays to the working population and to a small *élite* of progressive intellectuals. The Théâtre du Travail was above all a theatre of ideology. Following his expulsion from the Communist Party, Camus and his friends replaced it by a theatre of ideas, the Théâtre de l'Équipe, which still proclaimed a social mission but also recognized the importance of the best contemporary plays, encouraged a new look at classical plays and emphasized theatrical teamwork. A number of plays and adaptations of novels were performed, including Malraux's *Le Temps du mépris*, Gide's *Le Retour de l'Enfant Prodigue*, Vildrac's *Le Paquebot 'Tenacity'*, Pushkin's *The Stone Guest*, Ben Jonson's *The Silent Woman*, Aeschylus's *Prometheus* and Copeau's adaptation of *The Brothers Karamazov*. This was a particularly exhilarating period in Camus's life. Among his many activities he directed his own adaptation of *Prometheus* and played Ivan in *The Brothers Karamazov* and the Prodigal Son in Gide's play.

By 1938 Camus was involved in the additional career of journalism. He accepted Pascal Pia's offer of a post as *rédacteur-reporter* with the newly founded newspaper *Alger-Républicain*. This paper was anti-colonialist, supported the ideals of the Popular Front and campaigned for social justice in Algeria. In the course of a valuable apprenticeship Camus acted variously as leader-writer, sub-editor, social and political reporter and book reviewer. Among the books he reviewed were Sartre's *La Nausée* and *Le Mur*, while the most impressive of his social reports was a series of articles on the deprivation of the Moslems of the Kabylia region of Algeria. This experience was very valuable when he later undertook the editorship of the Parisian daily, *Combat*, from its first clandestine appearance in 1943 until his resignation from the post in 1947.

When the Second World War broke out in 1939 Camus had published two collections of essays – *L'Envers et l'endroit* (1937) and *Noces* (1939) – and a 'collective' play written with the cooperation of friends under the title *Révolte dans les Asturies* (1936). The subject of this 'essai de création collective, dédié aux victimes de répression' was the capture of Oviedo by the Asturian miners in 1934, their later defeat and the executions which followed. In fact Camus had written a second play, *Caligula*, by 1939, but it was neither performed nor published at this time. He also began writing *L'Étranger* (*The Outsider*), and in 1940 completed his first long essay on ideas, *Le Mythe de Sisyphe* (*The Myth of Sisyphus*). Both books were published in France in 1942 but were not widely noticed at the time. A year later, after periods spent alternately in Algeria and France, and his marriage to Francine Faure late in 1940, he joined Pascal Pia and others in the 'Combat' resistance group and worked for the underground press.

After the Liberation, and in addition to his editorial responsibilities, Camus quickly resumed his work in the theatre. In May 1944, before the actual liberation of Paris, the Théâtre des Mathurins put on *Le Malentendu*

(*Cross Purpose*) and it was published along with *Caligula* shortly afterwards. Maria Casarès and Marcel Herrand played Martha and Jan, but despite their talents *Le Malentendu* did not have a good press. It was perhaps too unusual, as well as too abstract, to be quickly understood and accepted, though it was given a more favourable reception when produced later in the same year. In September 1945 *Caligula* was put on at the Théâtre Hébertot with Gérard Philipe in the title role. This time Camus scored a success and the play had a long run. There were, of course, critics ready to attribute the success to Gérard Philipe rather than Camus. And in fact Camus's subsequent career as a playwright was a chequered one. In 1948 he completed a play, *L'État de siège*, on the theme of a plague, symbolically interpreted. It was a failure despite Jean-Louis Barrault's resourceful production at the Marigny and a brilliant cast which included Barrault himself, Madeleine Renaud, Maria Casarès and Pierre Brasseur. On the other hand, *Les Justes*, with Serge Reggiani and Casarès, was well received at the Hébertot in December 1949 and ran for over 400 performances.

Camus wrote no further plays, but between 1953 and 1959 he produced six translations or adaptations for the stage, culminating in *Les Possédés*. This was a version for the theatre of Dostoyevsky's novel known variously in English as *The Possessed* or *The Devils*, and Camus's adaptation was given its first performance at the Théâtre Antoine in January 1959.

During this post-war period Camus also maintained a fairly steady output of novels, essays and political articles. In fiction he followed *L'Étranger* with *La Peste* (*The Plague*) in 1947, *La Chute* (*The Fall*) in 1956 and a collection of striking short stories, *L'Exil et le royaume* (*Exile and the Kingdom*), in 1957. In 1945 his four *Lettres à un ami allemand* (*Letters to a German Friend*) had been published in one small volume. They were followed by a work of political philosophy, *L'Homme révolté* (*The Rebel*), in 1951, *L'Été* in 1954 and *Réflexions sur la peine capitale* (his book against capital punishment written with Arthur Koestler) in 1957.

In the same year, 1957, at the early age of forty-four, Camus was awarded the Nobel Prize for Literature. His speech of acceptance, together with a lecture on the social responsibility of the writer which he gave at the University of Uppsala four days later, was published as *Discours de Suède* in 1958. Camus reacted to the award with characteristic modesty, saying that had he been a member of the committee he would have voted for Malraux. The event was widely welcomed both in France and overseas, yet it also provided an occasion for a number of Camus's French critics to attack him, largely because of his anti-Marxist views and his attitude to the burning question of Algeria. On the face of it, it seemed surprising that he should not have expressed himself more specifically and publicly on such notorious matters as the torture of Djamila Boupacha, the murder of Maurice Audin and indeed the whole conception and use of torture and physical violence by elements in the French army. On the other hand there are several facts which go some way towards explaining Camus's cautious and often negative attitude. For one thing, he belonged by birth and upbringing to the underprivileged section of the European population of Algeria and well understood the anti-Moslem feelings of this group even though he did not share them himself. He was inevitably critical of the often highly abstract and ill-informed liberalism of certain left-bank intellectuals in Paris. Again, his aged and ailing mother lived in Algiers; his fears for her well-being seem to have been exploited and used against him for purposes of blackmail. He made it clear that in any conflict between devotion to ideology and devotion to his mother he would choose his mother. It should also be said that Camus, unlike virtually all his critics, had actually drawn attention to the injustices practised against the Arab population as early as 1939, though he never saw the problems of his country in simple and straightforward 'colonialist' terms. He believed French technical and economic aid to be essential to its well-being and wanted what he called 'an Algerian Algeria . . . not an Egyptian Algeria'. He visited Algeria in 1956, appealed for a truce, and supported the 'truce committees' formed in several parts of the country afterwards. These committees proved ineffectual, of course, and his whole attitude to the Algerian war was regarded by many as little more than an expression of innocuous moral generalizations. He appeared to be confirming the accusations of political otherworldliness levelled against him by Sartre in the course of their famous quarrel of 1951 following the publication of *L'Homme révolté*.

Camus did not live to see either the achievement of Algerian independence in 1962 or its aftermath. On Monday 4 January 1960, travelling at speed between Sens and Paris in a Facel-Véga driven by his friend and publisher Michel Gallimard, he met sudden death when the car skidded, hit two plane trees and was virtually cut in half. He was forty-six. Part of the irony lies in the fact that he disliked cars and had intended to travel to Paris by train until Gallimard persuaded him to change his mind (the return half of a rail ticket to Paris was found in his pocket). Part of the tragedy is suggested by what he had recently written in the preface to a new edition of *L'Envers et l'endroit*: 'I continue to be convinced that my work hasn't even been begun.'

*

13

Much was written immediately after Camus's death about the appropriateness of its arbitrary circumstances for a writer so closely identified with the idea of 'the absurd'. In the early part of his life (when he wrote *Caligula*, *Le Malentendu* and *L'Étranger*, for example) he was certainly very much preoccupied with this concept. By 'the absurd' he meant what is inexplicable in terms of human reason: those experiences that defy rational explanation or seem to confound and controvert our sense of fair play, our desire for happiness, our need to find pattern and purpose in human existence. He wrote in *Le Mythe de Sisyphe* of such evidence of the absurd as this questioning of the purpose of existence and the meaning of the lives we lead; the inexorable, mathematical certainty of death; the consciousness of human transience in contrast to the endurance of inanimate nature; the 'otherness' of people and even of an element within ourselves; the waste of so much human potential in apparently arbitrary death or protracted suffering (flood, famine, earthquake, etc.).

To the extent to which Camus observed some such outlook among his contemporaries, and partly shared it himself, he became for a time both spokesman and symptom of a widespread nihilistic element in the intellectual climate of the age. Consent to this state of affairs, or that form of consent called indifference, both plays its part in *Caligula* and finds expression in the hedonism, the instinctualism, or the tragic stoicism of the early collections of essays. Hence the balancing of physical affirmation and intellectual negation in such phrases as 'there is no love of life without despair about life' (*L'Envers et l'endroit*) or 'my whole horror of death is derived from my anxious appetite for life' (*Noces*). But Camus's fundamental humanity, together with his persistent search for an elusive happiness, led him before long to attempt to replace indifference by rebellion and consent by refusal. It is the tension between these terms that gives much of its dramatic impetus to *Le Malentendu*. Rebellion and refusal meet defeat in this particular play, but Camus was soon to move beyond this discouragement to a more positive position. In the twenty-five years of his adult life he travelled the road from nihilism to positive humanism, from a largely self-indulgent paganism to a passionate defence of the claims of justice and human solidarity. He did this with great modesty and integrity, avoiding both fashionable posturing and sectarian bias. One of his essays in *L'Été* outlines the task which he set himself and the path which he followed:

I do not believe firmly enough in reason to subscribe to the idea of progress or some philosophy of history. But at least I believe that men have not ceased to make progress in becoming aware of their own situation. We have not risen above our human condition, but we understand it better. We know that we are the victims of a dilemma; that we must refuse to accept it and do what is necessary to eradicate it. Our task as men is to find some formulas to pacify the great anguish of human kind. We must put together what has been torn apart, make justice a possibility in an obviously unjust world, render happiness meaningful to peoples poisoned by the sufferings of our age.* This is of course a superhuman task, yet one simply calls 'superhuman' those tasks which men take a very long time to accomplish.

On the face of it there seems to be a considerable intellectual difficulty about progressing beyond the absurd if one does not explicitly deny it. Camus did not go this far, but as early as 1939 he had written in *Alger-Républicain* that 'to establish the absurdity of life cannot be an end

---

* In *Actuelles II* Camus wrote: 'Do you know that over a period of twenty-five years, between 1922 and 1947, 70 million Europeans – men, women and children – have been uprooted, deported and killed?'

but only a beginning'. This remark makes the next stage in his thinking both interesting and complex. What seems to have happened is that the circumstances of war, together with his experience of Occupation and Resistance in France from 1942 onwards, presented him with a disturbing emotional and intellectual challenge and also provided a possible clue to the solution of the problem. In the closing pages of *Le Mythe de Sisyphe* the emphasis fell on the moral equivalence of all actions and the need to live each passing moment to the full. These are consequences which Camus drew from his analysis of the absurd. But in the concrete reality of occupation and resistance such attitudes, while apparently coherent in 'logic', were not emotionally tenable for a person of his natural humanity and integrity. A personal, self-indulgent ethic could not be sustained in circumstances where moral choices and practical decisions meant life or death to others (both unknown individuals and close friends and colleagues). At the same time Camus had thought a great deal about the phenomenon of Nazism. He became convinced that Nazi doctrine, as certainly as his own conclusions in *Le Mythe de Sisyphe*, was the outcome of modern nihilism. This proposition is set out in the *Lettres à un ami allemand* (written between 1943 and 1945). Camus admits that he accepted, at one stage, the diagnosis of the absurdity of human existence made by various German thinkers. He shared their sceptical attitude to moral absolutes and could sympathize, at least in an abstract way, with their resolve to escape from the apparent senselessness of life by means of force, hardness, cunning, national self-aggrandizement. In war, however, despite a common starting-point, he found that he was on one side of a moral argument (symbolized by the French Resistance) while the Nazis took their stand on the opposite side (symbolized by the Occupation and the Final Solution). He found the explanation of this in one important fact apparently overlooked by German nihilism. A nihilistic approach ought not to make human beings and human life valueless. On the contrary, it demands that one place particular value on these things. The argument is that because man is 'the one creature whose desire [for value and meaning] is constantly thwarted in the world', it follows that 'man himself possesses value and meaning'. It is precisely by reference to value and meaning that he judges his human condition to be valueless and meaningless. As it stands, this assertion is no doubt open to logical objections, but the actual context of Camus's argument makes it clear that he is not at this point claiming objective and absolute meaning for man. What he is saying is that man has value and meaning *for other men*. Three separate but related lines of argument have therefore led to this position. First, a purely selfish, quantitative ethic proves inadequate in the face of human suffering and human need (e.g. the Resistance). Second, an abstract interpretation of the absurd can lead to terrible human disasters (e.g. Nazi ideology). Third, a closer scrutiny of the absurd shows that such a concept is inseparable from some implied standard of coherence. Now this standard is manifestly of human origin. It therefore represents a foothold, however tenuous, on the sheer cliff-face of nihilism. It provides a starting-point for Camus's exploration of a possible route from nihilism to a form of humanism.

Because he charted the main features of twentieth-century nihilism with clarity and considerable sympathy, Camus's attempt to fashion what he called 'an art of living in times of catastrophe' was much more persuasive to his contemporaries than would otherwise have been the case. The fact that he accepted the worst before attempting to outline some positive reaction to it increased his readers' respect. He confirmed or made articulate many of their feelings: their sense of the failure of nineteenth-century scientific rationalism, their suspicion of such great rallying words as 'freedom', 'justice' and 'truth', and their awareness of the breakdown of so much religious and political idealism. As a result many were disposed to see him not only as a spokesman but, once he had begun to reject nihilism, as a potential guide. Camus himself denied any desire to play such a role. His modesty, together with his sense of the depth and complexity of the twentieth century's malaise, made him resist suggestions of this kind. In fact, when he rejected nihilism and moved away from the absurd to revolt against it, he had little to offer in the way of detailed, practical advice. It is probably true to say that the most persuasive aspects of his thought remained general and negative rather than specific and positive.

Revolt against the absurd and a positive reaction to nihilism are themes of *La Peste* and the main topic of *L'Homme révolté*. In the latter work Camus is looking for a strict humanism – strict in the sense that it rejects any form of revolt involving the idea of transcendence. He regards religious forms of transcendence – belief in eternal life – as a leap into irrationality. Put in another way, he sees religious faith as a major attempt to negate the absurd (he asserts that Christianity and Marxism are the only serious attempts to do so), yet one which can only do so by denying that same limited human reason which revealed and affirmed the absurd in the first place. Camus is even more critical of Marxism with its doctrine of historical inevitability which he regards as horizontal transcendence, 'the only transcendence of men without God'. This deification of history he shows to have led to intellectual abstraction of the worst kind. It leads to what Yeats called 'the thoughts men think in the mind alone' – ideas that lack all human warmth and which eventually imprison and exploit individuals rather than serving or liberating them. Hence the attacks on the revolutionary theory and practice of communism in *L'Homme révolté*. Hence, also, Camus's clear distinction between political revolution and his own particular conception of moral revolt or rebellion.

This idea of revolt is obviously both non-Christian and non-Marxist. It emphasizes nature rather than history or God, moderation rather than extremism, human concern rather than divine law, the dialogue rather than the directive. A genuine humanism – one which refuses to bend human nature to the demands of an *a priori* intellectual framework – presides over all these attitudes. Camus, the Algerian, locates them in a humane, Mediterranean tradition which is in marked contrast to our 'nordic dreams' of intemperance. It is no doubt obvious that the guide in Camus, as distinct from the spokesman, is vague about details and sometimes has recourse to a lyrical, personal language that uses such terms as *pensée solaire* and *esprit méditerranéen*. Nevertheless, he brought much benefit to his contemporaries by locating and exploring the major problems of his age. The kind of exploration which he carries out, with its emphasis on the needs of individual men and its exposure of murderous ideologies, is an essential step towards any ultimate solution of these problems. The writings on revolt offer us the only kind of humanism we should ask for – a humanism honest in its temper, modest in its claims and as free from illusions as one man can make it. It points to a possible justification for Miguel de Unamuno's claim, made in *The Tragic Sense of Life*, that 'uncertainty and doubt, perpetual wrestling with the mystery of our fatal destiny, mental despair and the lack of any solid and stable dogmatic foundation, may be the basis of an ethic'.

*

It is not my intention to discuss in any great detail the four plays which follow. Readers will make their own judgements. Nevertheless a few general observations, followed by brief comments on each play, may be useful.

It is clear that Camus, in common with a number of his French contemporaries, used the theatre primarily as a medium for the expression and dramatization of serious ideas – philosophical problems and moral dilemmas of the kind discussed in the previous pages. This characteristic, particularly noticeable in the immediate post-war French theatre, has a great deal to do with the existentially inclined ideas of such dramatists as Sartre, Simone de Beauvoir, Gabriel Marcel and Camus. Despite important differences between them, all had in common the conviction that moral and philosophical ideas must be approached from a concrete, human, 'existential' standpoint – as a living individual might encounter them. The result is that the theatre, insofar as it works through individuals towards ideas, was held (along with the novel) to be an ideal vehicle for the expression of philosophical ideas. This also explains why many of these plays, including those of Camus, offer what Sartre called a theatre of situation rather than a theatre of deep psychological penetration. The characters are not mainly portrayed for their intrinsic interest as individuals but because they can embody certain philosophical ideas or act out certain moral problems involving humanity at large. It is this concern to explore aspects of 'the human condition' that requires Anglo-Saxon audiences to make some effort of adjustment before judging Camus's plays.

Caligula and *Cross Purpose* belong to the early, predominantly negative and nihilistic phase of Camus's thought. In the case of *Caligula*, and in keeping with the point made above, Camus's aim was not to study the psychology of a monster in human form but to investigate the consequences of taking nihilism to its logical conclusions. However, since he claimed that Nazi doctrine responded to nihilism in exactly this way, it would be possible to interpret his play as a dramatic symbol, in the person of Caligula himself, of the 'mad emperor' who derived his political logic from the absurd and plunged the world into violent bloodshed between 1939 and 1945.

Originally written in 1938, the play was reworked to some extent both in 1945 and in 1958, though the first version underwent no fundamental alteration. Camus drew his material directly from Suetonius's *Lives of the Twelve Caesars* and claimed to have followed the Latin historian faithfully. He naturally interprets the original material in accordance with his own ideas, but he invented none of the main scenes such as the worship of Caligula dressed as Venus and the 'poetic contest' on the theme of death. We also find in Suetonius accounts of Caligula's scheme to contrive a famine and his plan to open brothels as a source of private income, while there are references to his restlessless and insomnia, his apparent madness, his grimacing in front of the mirror and his wooing of the moon. The historical facts appear to be that Caius Caesar Caligula, third of the twelve Caesars, came to power in A.D. 37 at the age of twenty-five and reigned for four years until his assassination in A.D. 41. For the first eight months of his reign he proved a relatively enlightened and generous ruler, but about this time he conceived an incestuous love for his sister Drusilla and announced his intention of marrying her. Drusilla suddenly died, however, and Caligula's character apparently changed completely so that Suetonius speaks of him as having become 'rather a monster than a man'. He killed or tortured many of his subjects so the patricians finally rebelled openly and assassinated him.

The one point at which Camus gives us a distinctly personal gloss on Caligula's behaviour is his explanation of the emperor's abrupt reversal of character and apparent madness after Drusilla's death. Suetonius speaks of epilepsy, or a philtre given to Caligula by his mistress Caesonia which had the effect of driving him mad. Camus, however, treats Drusilla's death as an experience which suddenly reveals the nature of the absurd to Caligula and the truth that 'men die and are not happy'. It is this feature of our human condition which Caligula presses to its logical conclusion. He does so in the belief that this will confer freedom upon him, yet in the course of the play he learns that one cannot be free *against* other people. Camus's own explanation of the play's meaning is contained in a note included in the programme for the Hébertot production:

. . . if his integrity consists of his denial of the gods, his fault is to be found in his denial of men. One cannot destroy everything without destroying oneself. This is why Caligula depopulates the world around him and then, in keeping with his own logic, does what is necessary to arm against himself those who will ultimately kill him. Caligula's story is that of a high-minded type of suicide. It is an account of the most human and most tragic of mistakes. Caligula is faithless towards humanity in order to keep faith with himself. He consents to die, having learned that no man can save himself alone and that one cannot be free by working against mankind. But at least he will have rescued some souls, including his own and that of his friend Scipio, from the dreamless sleep of mediocrity.

The sombre material of *Cross Purpose* is briefly mentioned in the second part of Camus's novel *L'Étranger*. Meursault finds a yellowed piece of newspaper sticking to the underside of the mattress in his prison cell. This scrap of paper reports the story of a man who returned to his native Czechoslovakia after many years abroad and stayed at an inn run by his mother and sister without revealing his identity to them. Only after they have murdered him for gain – as they had done in the case of previous guests – do the mother and her daughter realize the exact nature of their crime. Having done so, both commit suicide. Meursault's comment is that in one way he finds the story improbable yet in another it is quite natural. He adds that the son was guilty because 'one should never fool around'.

This news item naturally provides the basis for a deeply pessimistic play. In *Caligula* Camus portrayed what he considered to be one individual's mistaken reaction to his discovery of the absurd. In *Cross Purpose* it is the injustice and misunderstanding built into the world as we experience it – the absurd fabric of existence itself – that frustrates and confounds the characters. In this aspect at least *Cross Purpose* is much the more gloomy of the two plays. It emphasizes human experience of the absurd by stressing the failure of human beings to communicate adequately, the obstacles lying in the path of a direct and simple desire for happiness, and the sense of solitude or exile which affects the main characters. Jan seeks happiness through integration, solidarity, spontaneous recognition. Martha wants to escape to the sea and the sunlight and plans to use the money stolen from murdered guests for this purpose. Both reactions meet inevitable failure in a universe where inexplicable, arbitrary, cruel things happen alike to those who have chosen crime and those who have chosen innocence. Ironically, too, what seem like morally regenerative actions can seal and confirm an individual's 'condemnation'. Thus when Jan manages to appeal to the small human residue in Martha's almost inhumanly harsh nature he makes his own death inevitable. Martha explains that when he evoked a response from her by speaking of the sun-drenched country of which she had always dreamt he provided her with weapons against himself. He unwittingly renewed her reasons for killing him and she says bitterly: 'That is how innocence is rewarded.'

The absurdity or incoherence of life is not merely implicit in the subject matter of *Cross Purpose*. It is directly referred to in the text on a number of occasions. In the third act, for example, the mother speaks of 'this earth where nothing's sure' and asserts that 'this world we live in doesn't make sense'. Similarly Martha says to the wife of the brother she has murdered:

neither for him nor for us, neither in life nor in death, is there any peace or homeland. For you'll agree one can hardly call it a home, that place of clotted darkness underground, to which we go from here, to feed blind animals.

Hence her final piece of advice to Maria:

Pray your God to harden you to stone. It's the happiness He has assigned Himself, and the one true happiness. Do as He does, be deaf to all appeals, and turn your heart to stone while there still is time.

This seems to be the final, despairing message of the play, yet Camus was reported as saying as early as 1944 that this apparent pessimism hid a deeper optimism in the sense that 'man, freed from his illusions and his gods, can find in action and revolt the only liberty which he can bear'. This is certainly not the impression conveyed by a performance of the play, and it leans rather heavily on a positive interpretation of Jan's negative behaviour. Camus revealed this himself when he stated shortly afterwards:

> Finally it comes down to saying that everything would have been different if the son had said: 'It's me, this is my name'. It comes down to saying that in an unjust and indifferent world, man can still achieve his own salvation and that of other people by the use of the simplest sincerity and the most precise language.

This statement probably expresses in very concentrated form the attitude towards which Camus was working at the time of his transition from an acceptance of the absurd to an assertion of revolt. Action and revolt in the name of liberty are central features of his next play, *The Just*. But this is surely not the burden of *Cross Purpose*. On the contrary, *Cross Purpose* suggests that human effort cannot really change anything, and it is in its exploration of this belief that its real interest lies.

The point has already been made that Camus wrote what is essentially a theatre of ideas. This is again borne out by *The Just* and is perhaps one reason why Anglo-Saxon critics have sometimes been cautious in their judgements and lukewarm in their praise, writing as they do from a very different theatrical tradition. Furthermore, *The Just* contains an idealistic political rhetoric which was not unique in post-war France but which translates rather uneasily into English. Also, the claim that the play is 'abstract and academic', which some have made, is hard to justify. The problem at the centre of the play – the question of whether it is right to kill in pursuit of a political ideal, whether the use of assassination in securing social justice can be justified – is, far from being merely 'academic', even more real and pressing in the 1980s than it was in the late 1950s. Increased political terrorism in many parts of the world has seen to that.

The play is based on an actual event which took place in Moscow in 1905. In that year the Grand Duke Sergei Alexandrovitch was assassinated by a young terrorist, Ivan Kaliayev. Kaliayev belonged to a 'combat organization' which the Revolutionary Socialist Party had formed in 1903 and which killed a number of politicians, government officials and police in a wave of terrorism. As in Camus's play, Kaliayev refused to throw a bomb on the first planned occasion because the Grand Duke was accompanied by two young children – his niece and nephew – but he carried out the assassination a couple of days later and was hanged by the authorities. We also know from Savinkov's memoirs, translated into French as *Souvenirs d'un terroriste* in 1931 and used by Camus, that on another occasion Savinkov himself refused to sanction a bomb attack in a train because innocent passengers would almost certainly have been killed. Again, in history as in the play, Kaliayev and the other members of the group (apart from the invented character, Stepan, who is said to represent the attitude of such terrorists as Bakunin, Nechayev and Shigalev) sought to redeem murder in pursuit of their political aims by accepting their own execution. Each was prepared to sacrifice his own life for a life he destroyed. This is why Camus termed them 'meurtriers délicats' or 'scrupulous assassins'.

It was this idealism and high moral sense which aroused Camus's interest in the terrorists of 1905. They acknowledged certain limits beyond which terrorism must not go. Their killing was reluctant, not pathological. They attempted to purify the means employed to attain 'just' ends. This is the feature of their political action which forms the central theme of the play and gives it its title. The other members of the group argue this moral position against one of their number, Stepan, who has suffered humiliation in a Czarist prison. The conflict is put succinctly in the second act when Annenkov says: 'thousands of us have died to prove that everything is *not* justifiable'. Stepan retorts: 'Nothing that can serve our cause should be ruled out.' Kaliayev represents scrupulousness when he insists: 'killing children is a crime against a man's honour, and if the revolution should ever break with honour . . . then I should break with revolution'. Stepan expresses the contrary terrorist doctrine when he insists that 'squeamishness has no place in terrorism' and adds: 'We are murderers and that's what we've chosen to be.'

This irreducible conflict between political idealism and political realism recalls Camus's statement, in his Athens lecture of 1955 on 'The Future of Tragedy', that tragedy arises from 'the clash of two irreconcilable forces equal in power and legitimacy'. There is little doubt that he intended *The Just* to be a modern tragedy in this sense. He conceived of tragedy as a balancing of equally persuasive ideas or attitudes in which 'Antigone is right, but Creon is not wrong'. And he added that drama is different from tragedy in the vital sense that only one of the two contending elements is legitimate or acceptable.

Using Camus's own terms, there is little doubt that *The Just* is a drama rather than a tragedy. It is true that Stepan scores some points against Kaliayev in their quarrel in the first act. Also, at the end of the play, Dora seems to move from the idealism of Kaliayev towards the realism of Stepan. She suffers so intensely from Kaliayev's death that she asks to throw the next bomb and Stepan says: 'Let her . . . She's . . . like me . . . now.'

Nevertheless, Camus's admiration and preference for the 'scrupulous assassins' comes through clearly in the play. He admitted in his *Notebooks* that to pay for one life with another is at best 'a false but respectable' moral position. But he is far from saying that 'Kaliayev is right, but Stepan is not wrong'. He rejects Stepan's realism and greatly admires the high moral idealism of Kaliayev and his friends. It is this moral position, this didacticism, which undermines that irreducible antithesis between virtue and killing which tragedy would have required.

In the end, however, it is difficult to avoid the view, especially when one sees the play on the stage, that Kaliayev and Stepan simply take different routes towards the same negative goal. Kaliayev may claim that he loves mankind and Stepan that he hates it, yet they are united by the fact that all they have to offer is the destruction of others and of themselves. The true tragedy of revolt lies in the fact that, when it takes the form of political revolution, it intensifies the very inhumanity which it seeks to overcome.

This is also a major theme of *The Possessed*, Camus's adaptation of Dostoyevsky's novel. Dostoyevsky's title, *The Possessed* or *The Devils*, is a reference to the New Testament story in which Jesus drove the demons out of a demented man at Gadara and allowed them to enter a herd of pigs which then rushed down a cliffside and drowned in the Lake of Galilee (St Luke 8, 26–39. Also St Matthew 8, 28–34 and St Mark 5, 1–20). For Dostoyevsky, nineteenth-century Russia had become a body inhabited by the demons of liberalism and radicalism – atheism, nihilism, revolutionary socialism, etc. In the final scene of Camus's adaptation (and in keeping with Part III, Chapter 7 of *The Devils*), Stepan Verkhovensky expresses the central meaning of the play:

Those devils who depart from the sick man, *chère*, you see – well, you recognize them . . . They are our defects, our impurities, of course, and the sick man is Russia . . . But the impurities leave him, they enter into the swine. I mean us, my son, the others, and we run violently down a steep place as if possessed of the devil, and we shall perish. But the sick man will be cured and he will sit at the feet of Jesus and all will be cured . . . Yes, Russia will be cured some day!

Camus goes further in his foreword to the play by underlining the present-day application of Dostoyevsky's novel. He describes *The Devils* as a 'prophetic book' and continues: 'this is not only because it prefigures our nihilism, but also because its protagonists are torn or dead souls unable to love and suffering from that inability, wanting to believe and yet unable to do so – like those who people our society and our spiritual world today'.

In the same foreword Camus speaks of having visualized Dostoyevsky's characters on the stage 'for almost twenty years'. He also refers to Dostoyevsky's theatrical technique – a maximum use of dialogue with minimal indications of place and action. This encouraged him to begin work on a stage adaptation in 1953 or 1954. Initially progress was slow and rehearsals of the completed play did not begin until the autumn of 1958. It is said that Camus gave a lot of latitude to his actors, listened to their suggestions, provided them with notes on Dostoyevsky and even, on one occasion, produced vodka and records of Russian folksongs to help them catch the very Slav mood on which the story of the play depends. It was generally well received when it opened in January 1959 for what proved to be a six-month run. It was on tour in the provinces when the cast received news of Camus's sudden death.

Despite many obvious difficulties, Camus kept surprisingly close to Dostoyevsky's novel. By using a narrator and dividing his play into twenty-two scenes spread over three parts he managed to simplify the novel considerably while retaining the essence of its spirit and meaning. His main deviation from the original is in his use of Stavrogin's confession (scene 14). The version which Dostoyevsky originally wrote was omitted from his published novel but is printed as an appendix in the Penguin translation of *The Devils*. In fact, Camus used Stavrogin as the focus of his play. In this way he managed to give an impressive degree of coherence to his adaptation of the 700-page novel.

One of the major actions of both novel and play is the murder of Shatov by the revolutionary group as a means of creating group identity and group solidarity through the binding power of shed blood (scene 19). This is based on the actual murder in Moscow, on 21 November 1869, of a student named Ivanov by a small group of terrorists led by Nechayev. Historical reality is also reflected in the fact that suicide exists side by side with political murder. In the play Kirilov kills himself after writing, a false confession to the murder of Shatov (scene 21), while Stavrogin commits suicide because he can no longer live with his own guilty past (scene 22). Suicide and murder are to be seen, in fact, as two manifestations of a common sickness – the despair of those who cannot believe in moral imperatives and the cynicism of those who disguise their megalomania as social liberation, reject all limitations and believe that 'everything is permitted'. Camus interprets such an attitude as having facilitated, indeed made inevitable, the transition from individual revolutionary terrorism to state terrorism. In his play (as also in Part III of *The Rebel* and in Dostoyevsky's novel) state terrorism is represented by Shigalov's social system. In scene 12 of *The Possessed* Shigalov is quite frank about his plan for society. What is envisaged is a 'society of sheep' in which one tenth of the population will have totally unrestrained freedom and authority over the other nine tenths who must be kept in complete subjection. Shigalov sums up his social blueprint: 'Starting from unlimited freedom, I end up in fact with unlimited despotism.' He argues that people of superior gifts must be suppressed and equality imposed so that 'all men are slaves and equal in their slavery'. He adds: 'They can't be equal otherwise. Hence it is essential to level. For instance, the level of education and talent will be lowered. Since men of talent always tend to rise, Cicero's tongue will have to be torn out, Copernicus's eyes gouged out, and Shakespeare stoned. There is my system.'

It is clear that *The Possessed* is as much a dramatization of Camus's own argument in *The Rebel* as it is an adaptation of Dostoyevsky's novel. This indicates something of the distance which he travelled in his theatre – in political as well as in moral and philosophical terms – from the bare nihilism of *Cross Purpose* to this severe criticism of the demons of power-seeking through rationalized inhumanity. The type of revolutionary action which deliberately disregards human dignity and surrenders to the (Marxist) absolute of history wholly betrays his conception of 'revolt'. He argued on a number of occasions before his death that the secularization of life and the deification of man, which he associated with revolutionary politics, ignored or even positively rejected exactly those humane limits which the moral doctrine of revolt had revealed and affirmed. He insisted on the need to establish new values 'identified with the entire human race' – values which could not be created by the short cuts of physical violence or political dictatorship. And so in his plays he gave unique dramatic expression to the conviction that one point of view is not as valid as another; that the end does not always justify the means and is ultimately affected by the means used to secure it; that the world of men is neither absurd nor valueless, but that men are also capable of great evil in their dealings with one another. These may be negative sentiments, but only such negation can clear the way for the positive response of revolt with its recognition of limits. If they have their way, the 'totalitarian theocrats' of revolutionary movements will deny the limits which revolt demands and thus destroy the very ideal which it seeks to make active in the world.

CALIGULA

Characters

CALIGULA, *aged from twenty-five to twenty-nine*
CAESONIA, *Caligula's mistress, aged thirty*
HELICON, *Caligula's intimate friend, aged thirty*
SCIPIO, *aged seventeen*
CHEREA, *aged thirty*
THE OLD PATRICIAN, *aged seventy-one*
MEREIA, *aged sixty*
MUCIUS, *aged thirty-three*
THE INTENDANT, *aged fifty*
FIRST PATRICIAN
SECOND PATRICIAN } *aged from forty to sixty*
THIRD PATRICIAN
KNIGHTS, PALACE GUARDS, SERVANTS

The scene of the First, Third and Fourth Acts is a State Room in the Imperial Palace. In it are a mirror (man's height), a gong, and a couch. The scene of the Second Act is CHEREA's dining-room.

ACT ONE

A number of PATRICIANS, *one a very old man, are gathered in a State Room of the Palace. They are showing signs of nervousness.*

FIRST PATRICIAN: Still no news.

THE OLD PATRICIAN: None last night, none this morning.

SECOND PATRICIAN: Three days without news. Strange indeed!

THE OLD PATRICIAN: Our messengers go out, our messengers return. And always they shake their heads and say, 'Nothing'.

SECOND PATRICIAN: They've combed the whole countryside. What more can be done?

FIRST PATRICIAN: We can only wait. It's no use meeting trouble half way. Perhaps he'll return as abruptly as he left us.

THE OLD PATRICIAN: When I saw him leaving the Palace, I noticed a queer look in his eyes.

FIRST PATRICIAN: Yes, so did I. In fact I asked him what was amiss.

SECOND PATRICIAN: Did he answer?

FIRST PATRICIAN: One word. 'Nothing.'

[*A short silence.* HELICON *enters. He is munching onions.*]

SECOND PATRICIAN [*in the same nervous tone*]: It's all very perturbing.

FIRST PATRICIAN: Oh, come now! All young fellows are like that.

THE OLD PATRICIAN: You're right there. They take things hard. But time smooths everything out.

SECOND PATRICIAN: Do you really think so?

THE OLD PATRICIAN: Of course. For one girl dead, a dozen living ones.

HELICON: Ah? So you think that there's a girl behind it?

FIRST PATRICIAN: What else should there be? Anyhow – thank goodness! – grief never lasts for ever. Is any one of us here capable of mourning a loss for more than a year on end?

SECOND PATRICIAN: Not I, anyhow.

FIRST PATRICIAN: No one can do that.

THE OLD PATRICIAN: Life would be intolerable if one could.

FIRST PATRICIAN: Quite so. Take my case. I lost my wife last year. I shed many tears, and then I forgot. Even now I feel a pang of grief at times. But, happily, it doesn't amount to much.

THE OLD PATRICIAN: Yes, Nature's a great healer.

[CHEREA *enters*.]

FIRST PATRICIAN: Well . . . ?

CHEREA: Still nothing.

HELICON: Come, gentlemen! There's no need for consternation.

FIRST PATRICIAN: I agree.

HELICON: Worrying won't mend matters – and it's lunchtime.

THE OLD PATRICIAN: That's so. We mustn't drop the prey for the shadow.

CHEREA: I don't like the look of things. But all was going too smoothly. As an emperor, he was perfection's self.

SECOND PATRICIAN: Yes, exactly the emperor we wanted; conscientious and inexperienced.

FIRST PATRICIAN: But what's come over you? There's no reason for all these lamentations. We've no ground for assuming he will change. Let's say he loved Drusilla. Only natural; she was his sister. Or say his love for her was something more than brotherly; shocking enough, I grant you. But it's really going too far, setting all Rome in a turmoil because the girl has died.

CHEREA: Maybe. But, as I said, I don't like the look of things; this escapade alarms me.

THE OLD PATRICIAN: Yes, there's never smoke without fire.

FIRST PATRICIAN: In any case, the interests of the State should prevent his making a public tragedy of . . . of, let's say, a regrettable attachment. No doubt such things happen; but the less said the better.

HELICON: How can you be sure Drusilla is the cause of all this trouble?

SECOND PATRICIAN: Who else should it be?

HELICON: Nobody at all, quite likely. When there's a host of explanations to choose from, why pick on the stupidest, most obvious one?

[*Young* SCIPIO *enters.* CHEREA *goes towards him.*]

CHEREA: Well?

SCIPIO: Still nothing. Except that some peasants think they saw him last night not far from Rome, rushing through the storm.

[CHEREA *comes back to the Patricians,* SCIPIO *following him.*]

CHEREA: That makes three days, Scipio, doesn't it?

SCIPIO: Yes . . . I was there, following him as I usually do. He went up to Drusilla's body. He stroked it with two fingers, and seemed lost in thought for a long while. Then he swung round and walked out, calmly enough. . . . And ever since we've been hunting for him – in vain.

CHEREA [*shaking his head*]: That young man was too fond of literature.

SECOND PATRICIAN: Oh, at his age, you know . . .

CHEREA: At his age, perhaps; but not in his position. An

37

artistic emperor is an anomaly. I grant you we've had one or two; misfits happen in the best of empires. But the others had the good taste to remember they were public servants.

FIRST PATRICIAN: It made things run more smoothly.

THE OLD PATRICIAN: One man, one job – that's how it should be.

SCIPIO: What can we do, Cherea?

CHEREA: Nothing.

SECOND PATRICIAN: We can only wait. If he doesn't return, a successor will have to be found. Between ourselves – there's no shortage of candidates.

FIRST PATRICIAN: No, but there's a shortage of the right sort.

CHEREA: Suppose he comes back in an ugly mood?

FIRST PATRICIAN: Oh, he's a mere boy; we'll make him see reason.

CHEREA: And what if he declines to see it?

FIRST PATRICIAN [*laughing*]: In that case, my friend, don't forget I once wrote a manual of revolutions. You'll find all the rules there.

CHEREA: I'll look it up – if things come to that. But I'd rather be left to my books.

SCIPIO: If you'll excuse me . . . [*Goes out.*]

CHEREA: He's huffed.

THE OLD PATRICIAN: Scipio is young, and young folk always hang together.

HELICON: Scipio doesn't count, anyhow.

[*Enter a member of the Imperial Bodyguard.*]

THE GUARDSMAN: Caligula has been seen in the Palace Gardens.

[*All leave the room. The stage is empty for some moments. Then* CALIGULA *enters stealthily from the left. His legs are caked with mud, his garments dirty; his hair is wet, his look dis-*

traught. He brings his hand to his mouth several times. Then he approaches a mirror, stopping abruptly when he catches sight of his reflected self. After muttering some unintelligible words, he sits down on the right, letting his arms hang limp between his knees. HELICON *enters, left. On seeing Caligula, he stops at the far end of the stage and contemplates him in silence.* CALIGULA *turns and sees him. A short silence.*

HELICON [*across the stage*]: Good morning, Caius.

CALIGULA [*in quite an ordinary tone*]: Good morning, Helicon. [*A short silence.*]

HELICON: You're looking tired.

CALIGULA: I've walked a lot.

HELICON: Yes, you've been away for quite a while. [*Another short silence.*]

CALIGULA: It was hard to find.

HELICON: What was hard to find?

CALIGULA: What I was after.

HELICON: Meaning?

CALIGULA [*in the same matter-of-fact tone*]: The moon.

HELICON: What?

CALIGULA: Yes, I wanted the moon.

HELICON: Ah . . . [*Another silence.* HELICON *approaches Caligula.*] And why did you want it?

CALIGULA: Well . . . it's one of the things I haven't got.

HELICON: I see. And now – have you fixed it up to your satisfaction?

CALIGULA: No. I couldn't get it.

HELICON: Too bad!

CALIGULA: Yes, and that's why I'm tired. [*Pauses. Then*] Helicon!

HELICON: Yes, Caius?

CALIGULA: No doubt, you think I'm crazy.

HELICON: As you know well, I never think.

CALIGULA: Ah yes . . . Now, listen! I'm not mad; in fact

I've never felt so lucid. What happened to me is quite simple; I suddenly felt a desire for the impossible. That's all. [*Pauses.*] Things as they are, in my opinion, are far from satisfactory.

HELICON: Many people share your opinion.

CALIGULA: That is so. But in the past I didn't realize it. *Now* I know. [*Still in the same matter-of-fact tone*] Really, this world of ours, the scheme of things as they call it, is quite intolerable. That's why I want the moon, or happiness, or eternal life — something, in fact, that may sound crazy, but which isn't of this world.

HELICON: That's sound enough in theory. Only, in practice one can't carry it through to its conclusion.

CALIGULA [*rising to his feet, but still with perfect calmness*]: You're wrong there. It's just because no one *dares* to follow up his ideas to the end that nothing is achieved. All that's needed, I should say, is to be logical right through, àt all costs. [*He studies Helicon's face.*] I can see, too, what you're thinking. What a pother over a woman's death! But that's not it. True enough, I seem to remember that a woman died some days ago; a woman whom I loved. But love, what is it? A side-issue. And I swear to you her death is not the point; it's no more than the symbol of a truth that makes the moon essential to me. A childishly simple, obvious, almost silly truth, but one that's hard to come by and heavy to endure.

HELICON: May I know what it is, this truth that you've discovered?

CALIGULA [*his eyes averted, in a toneless voice*]: Men die; and they are not happy.

HELICON [*after a short pause*]: Anyhow, Caligula, it's a truth with which one comes to terms, without much trouble. Only look at the people over there. This truth of yours doesn't prevent them from enjoying their meal.

CALIGULA [*with sudden violence*]: All it proves is that I'm surrounded by lies and self-deception. But I've had enough of that; I wish men to live by the light of truth. And I've the power to make them do so. For I know what they need and haven't got. They're without understanding and they need a teacher; someone who knows what he's talking about.

HELICON: Don't take offence, Caius, if I give you a word of advice ... But that can wait. First, you should have some rest.

CALIGULA [*sitting down. His voice is gentle again*]: That's not possible, Helicon. I shall never rest again.

HELICON: But – why?

CALIGULA: If I sleep, who'll give me the moon?

HELICON [*after a short silence*]: That's true.

CALIGULA [*rising to his feet again, with an effort*]: Listen, Helicon ... I hear footsteps, voices. Say nothing – and forget you've seen me.

HELICON: I understand.

CALIGULA [*looking back, as he moves towards the door*]: And please help me, from now on.

HELICON: I've no reason not to do so, Caius. But I know very few things, and few things interest me. In what way can I help you?

CALIGULA: In the way of ... the impossible.

HELICON: I'll do my best.

[CALIGULA *goes out.* SCIPIO *and* CAESONIA *enter hurriedly.*]

SCIPIO: No one! Haven't you seen him?

HELICON: No.

CAESONIA: Tell me, Helicon. Are you quite sure he didn't say anything to you before he went away?

HELICON: I'm not a sharer of his secrets, I'm his public. A mere onlooker. It's more prudent.

CAESONIA: Please don't talk like that.

HELICON: My dear Caesonia, Caius is an idealist as we all know. He follows his bent, and no one can foresee where it will take him . . . But, if you'll excuse me, I'll go to lunch. [*Exit.*]

CAESONIA [*sinking wearily on to a divan*]: One of the Palace Guards saw him go by. But all Rome sees Caligula everywhere. And Caligula, of course, sees nothing but his own idea.

SCIPIO: What idea?

CAESONIA: How can I tell, Scipio?

SCIPIO: Are you thinking of Drusilla?

CAESONIA: Perhaps. One thing is sure; he loved her. And it's a cruel thing to have someone die today whom only yesterday you were holding in your arms.

SCIPIO [*timidly*]: And you . . . ?

CAESONIA: Oh, I'm the old, trusted mistress. That's my role.

SCIPIO: Caesonia, we must save him.

CAESONIA: So you, too, love him?

SCIPIO: Yes. He's been very good to me. He encouraged me; I shall never forget some of the things he said. He told me life isn't easy, but it has consolations: religion, art, and the love one inspires in others. He often told me that the only mistake one makes in life is to cause others suffering. He tried to be a just man.

CAESONIA [*rising*]: He's only a child. [*She goes to the glass and scans herself.*] The only god I've ever had is my body, and now I shall pray this god of mine to give Caius back to me.

[CALIGULA *enters. On seeing Caesonia and Scipio he hesitates, and takes a backward step. At the same moment several men enter from the opposite side of the room:* PATRICIANS *and the* INTENDANT *of the Palace. They stop short when they see Caligula.* CAESONIA *turns. She and* SCIPIO *hurry towards Caligula, who checks them with a gesture.*

INTENDANT [*in a rather quavering voice*]: We . . . we've been looking for you, Caesar, high and low.

CALIGULA [*in a changed, harsh tone*]: So I see.

INTENDANT: We . . . I mean . . .

CALIGULA [*roughly*]: What do you want?

INTENDANT: We were feeling anxious, Caesar.

CALIGULA [*going towards him*]: What business had you to feel anxious?

INTENDANT: Well . . . er . . . [*He has an inspiration.*] Well, as you know, there are points to be settled in connexion with the Treasury.

CALIGULA [*bursting into laughter*]: Ah, yes. The Treasury! That's so. The Treasury's of prime importance.

INTENDANT: Yes, indeed.

CALIGULA [*still laughing, to Caesonia*]: Don't you agree, my dear? The Treasury is all-important.

CAESONIA: No, Caligula. It's a secondary matter.

CALIGULA: That only shows your ignorance. We are extremely interested in our Treasury. Everything's important: our fiscal system, public morals, foreign policy, army equipment, and agrarian laws. Everything's of cardinal importance, I assure you. And everything's on an equal footing: the grandeur of Rome and your attacks of arthritis. . . . Well, well, I'm going to apply my mind to all that. And, to begin with . . . Now listen well, Intendant.

INTENDANT: We are listening, sir.

[*The* PATRICIANS *come forward.*]

CALIGULA: You're our loyal subjects, are you not?

INTENDANT [*in a reproachful tone*]: Oh, Caesar! . . .

CALIGULA: Well, I've something to propose to you. We're going to make a complete change in our economic system. In two moves. Drastic and abrupt. I'll explain, Intendant . . . when the Patricians have left. [*The*

43

PATRICIANS *go out.* CALIGULA *seats himself beside Caesonia, with his arm round her waist.*] Now mark my words. The first move's this. Every Patrician, everyone in the Empire who has any capital – small or large, it's all the same thing – is ordered to disinherit his children and make a new will leaving his money to the State.

INTENDANT: But Caesar . . .

CALIGULA: I've not yet given you leave to speak. As the need arises, we shall have these people die; a list will be drawn up by us fixing the order of their deaths. When the fancy takes us, we may modify that order. And, of course, we shall step into their money.

CAESONIA [*freeing herself*]: But – what's come over you?

CALIGULA [*imperturbably*]: Obviously the order of their going has no importance. Or, rather, all these executions have an equal importance – from which it follows that none has any. Really all those fellows are on a par, one's as guilty as another. [*To the Intendant, peremptorily*] You are to promulgate this edict without a moment's delay and see it's carried out forthwith. The wills are to be signed by residents in Rome this evening; within a month at the latest by persons in the provinces. Send out your messengers.

INTENDANT: Caesar, I wonder if you realize . . .

CALIGULA: Do I realize . . . ? Now, listen well, you fool! If the Treasury has paramount importance, human life has none. That should be obvious to you. People who think like you are bound to admit the logic of my edict and, since money is the only thing that counts, should set no value on their lives or anyone else's. I have resolved to be logical, and I have the power to enforce my will. Presently you'll see what logic's going to cost you; I shall eliminate contradictions and contradictors. If necessary, I'll begin with you.

INTENDANT: Caesar, my good will can be relied on, that I swear.

CALIGULA: And mine, too; that I guarantee. Just see how ready I am to adopt your point of view, and give the Treasury the first place in my programme. Really you should be grateful to me; I'm playing into your hand, and with your own cards. [*He pauses, before continuing in a flat, unemotional tone.*] In any case there is a touch of genius in the simplicity of my plan – which clinches the matter. I give you three seconds in which to remove yourself. One . . .

[*The* INTENDANT *hurries out.*]

CAESONIA: I can't believe it's you! But it was just a joke, wasn't it? – all you said to him.

CALIGULA: Not quite that, Caesonia. Let's say, a lesson in statesmanship.

SCIPIO: But Caius, it's . . . it's impossible!

CALIGULA: That's the whole point.

SCIPIO: I don't follow.

CALIGULA: I repeat – that is my point. I'm exploiting the impossible. Or, more accurately, it's a question of making the impossible possible.

SCIPIO: But that game may lead to – to anything! It's a lunatic's pastime.

CALIGULA: No, Scipio. An emperor's vocation. [*He lets himself sink back wearily amongst the cushions.*] Ah, my dears, at last I've come to see the uses of supremacy. It gives impossibilities a run. From this day on, so long as life is mine, my freedom has no frontier.

CAESONIA [*sadly*]: I doubt if this discovery of yours will make us any happier.

CALIGULA: So do I. But, I suppose, we'll have to live it through.

[CHEREA *enters.*]

45

CHEREA: I have just heard of your return. I trust your health is all it should be.

CALIGULA: My health is duly grateful. [*A pause. Then, abruptly*] Leave us, Cherea. I don't want to see you.

CHEREA: Really, Caius, I'm amazed . . .

CALIGULA: There's nothing to be amazed at. I don't like literary men, and I can't bear lies.

CHEREA: If we lie, it's often without knowing it. I plead Not Guilty.

CALIGULA: Lies are never guiltless. And yours attribute importance to people and to things. That's what I cannot forgive you.

CHEREA: And yet – since this world is the only one we have, why not plead its cause?

CALIGULA: Your pleading comes too late, the verdict's given . . . This world has no importance; once a man realizes that, he wins his freedom. [*He has risen to his feet.*] And that is why I hate you, you and your kind; because you are not free. You see in me the one free man in the whole Roman Empire. You should be glad to have at last amongst you an emperor who points the way to freedom. Leave me, Cherea; and you, too, Scipio, go – for what is friendship? Go, both of you, and spread the news in Rome that freedom has been given her at last, and with the gift begins a great probation.

[*They go out.* CALIGULA *has turned away, hiding his eyes.*]

CAESONIA: Crying?

CALIGULA: Yes, Caesonia.

CAESONIA: But, after all, what's changed in your life? You may have loved Drusilla, but you loved many others – myself included – at the same time. Surely that wasn't enough to set you roaming the countryside for three days and nights and bring you back with this . . . this cruel look on your face?

CALIGULA [*swinging round on her*]: What nonsense is this?
Why drag in Drusilla? Do you imagine love's the only
thing that can make a man shed tears?

CAESONIA: I'm sorry, Caius. Only I was trying to understand.

CALIGULA: Men weep because . . . the world's all wrong.
[*She comes towards him.*]

CALIGULA: No, Caesonia.
[*She draws back.*]

CALIGULA: But stay beside me.

CAESONIA: I'll do whatever you wish. [*Sits down.*] At my
age one knows that life's a sad business. But why deliberately set out to make it worse?

CALIGULA: No it's no good; you can't understand. But
what matter? Perhaps I'll find a way out. Only, I feel a
curious stirring within me, as if undreamt-of things were
forcing their way up into the light – and I'm helpless
against them. [*He moves closer to her.*] Oh, Caesonia, I knew
that men felt anguish, but I didn't know what that word,
anguish, meant. Like everyone else I fancied it was a sickness of the mind – no more. But no, it's my body that's in
pain. Pain everywhere, in my chest, in my legs and arms.
Even my skin is raw, my head is buzzing, I feel like
vomiting. But worst of all is this queer taste in my mouth.
Not blood, or death, or fever, but a mixture of all three.
I've only to stir my tongue, and the world goes black, and
everyone looks . . . horrible. How hard, how cruel it is,
this process of becoming a man!

CAESONIA: What you need, my dear, is a good, long sleep.
Let yourself relax and, above all, stop thinking. I'll stay
by you while you sleep. And when you wake, you'll find
the world's got back its savour. Then you must use your
power to good effect – for loving better what you still find
lovable. For the possible, too, deserves to be given a chance.

CALIGULA: Ah, but for that I'd need to sleep, to let myself go – and that's impossible.

CAESONIA: So one always thinks when one is over-tired. A time comes when one's hand is firm again.

CALIGULA: But one must know where to place it. And what's the use to me of a firm hand, what use is the amazing power that's mine, if I can't have the sun set in the east, if I can't reduce the sum of suffering and make an end of death? No, Caesonia, it's all one whether I sleep or keep awake, if I've no power to tamper with the scheme of things.

CAESONIA: But that's madness, sheer madness. It's wanting to be a god on earth.

CALIGULA: So you, too, think I'm mad. And yet – what is a god that I should wish to be his equal? No, it's something higher, far above the gods, that I'm aiming at, longing for with all my heart and soul. I am taking over a kingdom where the impossible is king.

CAESONIA: You can't prevent the sky from being the sky, or a fresh young face from ageing, or a man's heart from growing cold.

CALIGULA [with rising excitement]: I want ... I want to drown the sky in the sea, to infuse ugliness with beauty, to wring a laugh from pain.

CAESONIA [facing him with an imploring gesture]: There's good and bad, high and low, justice and injustice. And I swear to you these will never change.

CALIGULA [in the same tone]: And I'm resolved to change them ... I shall make this age of ours a kingly gift – the gift of equality. And when all is levelled out, when the impossible has come to earth and the moon is in my hands – then, perhaps, I shall be transfigured and the world renewed; then men will die no more and at last be happy.

CAESONIA [*with a little cry*]: And love? Surely you won't go
back on love!

CALIGULA [*in a wild burst of anger*]: Love, Caesonia! [*He
grips her shoulders and shakes her.*] I've learnt the truth about
love; it's nothing, nothing! That fellow was quite right –
you heard what he said, didn't you? – it's only the
Treasury that counts. The fountain-head of all. Ah, now
at last I'm going to live, really *live*. And living, my dear,
is the opposite of loving. I know what I'm talking about –
and I invite you to the most gorgeous of shows, a sight for
gods to gloat on, a whole world called to judgement. But
for that I must have a crowd – spectators, victims,
criminals, hundreds and thousands of them. [*He rushes to
the gong and begins hammering on it, faster and faster.*] Let the
accused come forward. I want my criminals, and they all
are criminals. [*Still striking the gong*] Bring in the condemned men. I must have my public. Judges, witnesses,
accused – all sentenced to death without a hearing. Yes,
Caesonia, I'll show them something they have never seen
before, the one free man in the Roman Empire.

[*To the clangour of the gong the Palace has been gradually
filling with noises; the clash of arms, voices, footsteps slow or
hurried, coming nearer, growing louder. Some soldiers enter,
and leave hastily.*]

CALIGULA: And you, Caesonia, shall obey me. You must
stand by me to the end. It will be marvellous, you'll see.
Swear to stand by me, Caesonia.

CAESONIA [*wildly, between two gong-strokes*]: I needn't swear.
You know I love you.

CALIGULA [*in the same tone*]: You'll do all I tell you.

CAESONIA: All, all, Caligula – but do, please, stop . . .

CALIGULA [*still striking the gong*]: You will be cruel.

CAESONIA [*sobbing*]: Cruel.

CALIGULA [*still beating the gong*]: Cold and ruthless.

49

CAESONIA: Ruthless.

CALIGULA: And you will suffer, too.

CAESONIA: Yes, yes – oh, no, please . . . I'm – I'm going mad, I think!

[*Some* PATRICIANS *enter, followed by members of the Palace staff. All look bewildered and perturbed.* CALIGULA *bangs the gong for the last time, raises his mallet, swings round, and summons them in a shrill, half-crazy voice.*]

CALIGULA: Come here. All of you. Nearer. Nearer still. [*He is quivering with impatience.*] Your Emperor commands you to come nearer.

[*They come forward, pale with terror.*]

CALIGULA: Quickly. And you, Caesonia, come beside me. [*He takes her hand, leads her to the mirror and with a wild sweep of his mallet effaces a reflection on its surface. Then gives a sudden laugh.*] All gone. You see, my dear? An end of memories; no more masks. Nothing, nobody left. Nobody? No, that's not true. Look, Caesonia. Come here, all of you, and look . . . [*He plants himself in front of the mirror in a grotesque attitude.*]

CAESONIA [*staring, horrified, at the mirror*]: Caligula!

[CALIGULA *lays a finger on the glass. His gaze steadies abruptly and when he speaks his voice has a new, proud ardour.*]

CALIGULA: Yes . . . Caligula.

CURTAIN

ACT TWO

A room in Cherea's house where the Patricians have met in secret.

FIRST PATRICIAN: It's outrageous, the way he's treating us.

THE OLD PATRICIAN: He calls me 'darling'! In public, mind you – just to make a laughing-stock of me. Death's too good for him.

FIRST PATRICIAN: And fancy making us run beside his litter when he goes into the country.

SECOND PATRICIAN: He says the exercise will do us good.

THE OLD PATRICIAN: Conduct like that is quite inexcusable.

THIRD PATRICIAN: You're right. That's precisely the sort of thing one can't forgive.

FIRST PATRICIAN: He confiscated your property, Patricius. He killed your father, Scipio. He's taken your wife from you, Octavius, and forced her to work in his public brothel. He has killed your son, Lepidus. I ask you, gentlemen, can you endure this? I, anyhow, have made my mind up. I know the risks, but I also know this life of abject fear is quite unbearable. Worse than death, in fact. Yes, as I said, my mind's made up.

SCIPIO: He made my mind up for me when he had my father put to death.

FIRST PATRICIAN: Well? Can you still hesitate?

A KNIGHT: No. We're with you. He's transferred our stalls at the Circus to the public, and egged us on to fight with the rabble – just to have a pretext for punishing us, of course.

THE OLD PATRICIAN: He's a coward.

SECOND PATRICIAN: A bully.

THIRD PATRICIAN: A buffoon.

THE OLD PATRICIAN: He's impotent – that's his trouble, I should say.

[*A scene of wild confusion follows, weapons are brandished, a table is overturned, and there is a general rush towards the door. Just at this moment* CHEREA *strolls in, composed as usual, and checks their onrush.*]

CHEREA: What's all this about? Where are you going?

A PATRICIAN: To the Palace.

CHEREA: Ah, yes. And I can guess why. But do you think you'll be allowed to enter?

THE PATRICIAN: There's no question of asking leave.

CHEREA: Lepidus, would you kindly shut that door?

[*The door is shut.* CHEREA *goes to the upturned table and seats himself on a corner of it. The others turn towards him.*]

CHEREA: It's not so simple as you think, my friends. You're afraid, but fear can't take the place of courage and deliberation. In short, you're acting too hastily.

A KNIGHT: If you're not with us, go. But keep your mouth shut.

CHEREA: I suspect I'm with you. But make no mistake. Not for the same reasons.

A VOICE: That's enough idle talk.

CHEREA [*standing up*]: I agree. Let's get down to facts. But, first, let me make myself clear. Though I am *with* you, I'm not *for* you. That, indeed, is why I think you're going about it the wrong way. You haven't taken your enemy's measure; that's obvious, since you attribute petty motives to him. But there's nothing petty about Caligula, and you're riding for a fall. You'd be better placed to fight him if you would try to see him as he really is.

A VOICE: We see him as he is – a crazy tyrant.

CHEREA: No. We've had experience of mad emperors. But this one isn't mad enough. And what I loathe in him is this: that he knows what he wants.

FIRST PATRICIAN: And we, too, know it; he wants to murder us all.

CHEREA: You're wrong. Our deaths are only a side-issue. He's putting his power at the service of a loftier, deadlier passion; and it imperils everything we hold most sacred. True, it's not the first time Rome has seen a man wielding unlimited power; but it's the first time he sets no limit to his use of it, and counts mankind, and the world we know, for nothing. That's what appals me in Caligula; that's what I want to fight. To lose one's life is no great matter; when the time comes I'll have the courage to lose mine. But what's intolerable is to see one's life being drained of meaning, to be told there's no reason for existing. A man can't live without some reason for living.

FIRST PATRICIAN: Revenge is a good reason.

CHEREA: Yes, and I propose to share it with you. But I'd have you know that it's not on your account, or to help you to avenge your petty humiliations. No, if I join forces with you, it's to combat a big idea – an ideal, if you like – whose triumph would mean the end of everything. I can endure your being made a mock of, but I cannot endure Caligula's carrying out his theories to the end. He is converting his philosophy into corpses and – unfortunately for us – it's a philosophy that's logical from start to finish. And where one can't refute, one strikes.

A VOICE: Yes. We must *act*.

CHEREA: We must take action, I agree. But a frontal attack's quite useless when one is fighting an imperial madman in the full flush of his power. You can take arms against a vulgar tyrant, but cunning is needed to fight down disinterested malice. You can only urge it on to

follow its bent, and bide your time until its logic founders
in sheer lunacy. As you see, I prefer to be quite frank, and
I warn you I'll be with you only for a time. Afterwards, I
shall do nothing to advance your interests; all I wish is to
regain some peace of mind in a world that has regained
a meaning. What spurs me on is not ambition but fear,
my very reasonable fear of that inhuman vision in which
my life means no more than a speck of dust.

FIRST PATRICIAN [*approaching him*]: I have an inkling of
what you mean, Cherea. Anyhow, the great thing is that
you, too, feel that the whole fabric of society is threatened.
You, gentlemen, agree with me, I take it, that our ruling
motive is of a moral order. Family life is breaking down,
men are losing their respect for honest work, a wave of
immorality is sweeping the country. Who of us can be
deaf to the appeal of our ancestral piety in its hour of
danger? Fellow-conspirators, will you tolerate a state of
things in which patricians are forced to run, like slaves,
beside the Emperor's litter?

THE OLD PATRICIAN: Will you allow them to be addressed
as 'darling'?

A VOICE: And have their wives snatched from them?

ANOTHER VOICE: And their money?

ALL TOGETHER: No!

FIRST PATRICIAN: Cherea, your advice is good, and you
did well to calm our passion. The time is not yet ripe for
action; the masses would still be against us. Will you join us
in watching for the best moment to strike – and strike hard?

CHEREA: Yes – and meanwhile let Caligula follow his
dream. Or, rather, let's actively encourage him to carry
out his wildest plans. Let's put method into his madness.
And then, at last, a day will come when he's alone, a
lonely man in an empire of the dead and kinsmen of the dead.

[*A general uproar. Trumpet-calls outside. Then silence, but for whispers of a name: 'Caligula!'* CALIGULA *enters with* CAESONIA, *followed by* HELICON *and some soldiers. Dumb-show.* CALIGULA *halts and gazes at the conspirators. Without a word he moves from one to the other, straightens a buckle on one man's shoulder, steps back to contemplate another, sweeps them with his gaze, then draws his hand over his eyes and walks out, still without a word.*]

CAESONIA [*ironically, pointing to the disorder of the room*]: Were you having a fight?

CHEREA: Yes, we were fighting.

CAESONIA [*in the same tone*]: Really? Might I know what you were fighting about?

CHEREA: About . . . nothing in particular.

CAESONIA: Ah? Then it isn't true.

CHEREA: What isn't true?

CAESONIA: You were *not* fighting.

CHEREA: Have it your own way. We weren't fighting.

CAESONIA [*smiling*]: Perhaps you'd do better to tidy up the place. Caligula hates untidiness.

HELICON [*to the Old Patrician*]: You'll end by making him do something out of character.

THE OLD PATRICIAN: Pardon . . . I don't follow. What have we done to him?

HELICON: Nothing. Just nothing. It's fantastic being futile to that point; enough to get on anybody's nerves. Try to put yourselves in Caligula's place. [*A short pause.*] I see; doing a bit of plotting, weren't you now?

THE OLD PATRICIAN: Really, that's too absurd. I hope Caligula doesn't imagine . . .

HELICON: He doesn't imagine. He *knows*. But, I suppose, at bottom, he rather wants it. . . . Well, we'd better set to tidying up.

[*All get busy.* CALIGULA *enters and watches them.*]

CALIGULA [*to the Old Patrician*]: Good day, darling. [*To the others*] Gentlemen, I'm on my way to an execution. But I thought I'd drop in at your place, Cherea, for a light meal. I've given orders to have food brought here for all of us. But send for your wives first. [*A short silence.*] Rufius should thank his stars that I've been seized with hunger. [*Confidentially*] Rufius, I may tell you, is the knight who's going to be executed. [*Another short silence.*] What's this? None of you asks me why I've sentenced him to death? [*No one speaks. Meanwhile slaves lay the table and bring food.*] Good for you! I see you're growing quite intelligent. [*He nibbles an olive.*] It has dawned on you that a man needn't have done anything for him to die. [*He stops eating and gazes at his guests with a twinkle in his eye.*] Soldiers, I am proud of you. [*Three or four women enter.*] Good! Let's take our places. Anyhow. No order of precedence today. [*All are seated.*] There's no denying it, that fellow Rufius is in luck. But I wonder if he appreciates this short reprieve. A few hours gained on death, why, they're worth their weight in gold! [*He begins eating; the others follow suit. It becomes clear that Caligula's table manners are deplorable. There is no need for him to flick his olive stones on to his neighbours' plates, or to spit out bits of gristle over the dish, or to pick his teeth with his nails, or to scratch his head furiously. However, he indulges in these practices throughout the meal, without the least compunction. At one moment he stops eating, stares at Lepidus, one of the guests, and says roughly*] You're looking grumpy, Lepidus. I wonder, can it be because I had your son killed?

LEPIDUS [*thickly*]: Certainly not, Caius. Quite the contrary.

CALIGULA [*beaming on him*]: 'Quite the contrary!' It's always nice to see a face that hides the secrets of the heart. Your face is sad. But what about your heart? Quite the contrary – isn't that so, Lepidus?

LEPIDUS [*doggedly*]: Quite the contrary, Caesar.

CALIGULA [*more and more enjoying the situation*]: Really,

Lepidus, there's no one I like better than you. Now let's have a laugh together, my dear friend. Tell me a funny story.

LEPIDUS [*who has overrated his endurance*]: Please . . .

CALIGULA: Good! Very good! Then it's I who'll tell the story. But you'll laugh, won't you, Lepidus? [*With a glint of malice*] If only for the sake of your other son. [*Smiling again*] In any case, as you've just told us, you're not in a bad humour. [*He takes a drink, then says in the tone of a teacher prompting a pupil*] Quite . . . quite the . . .

LEPIDUS [*wearily*]: Quite the contrary, Caesar.

CALIGULA: Splendid! [*Drinks again.*] Now listen. [*In a gentle, far-away tone*] Once upon a time there was a poor young emperor whom nobody loved. He loved Lepidus and, to root out of his heart his love for Lepidus, he had his youngest son killed. [*In a brisker tone*] Needless to say, there's not a word of truth in it. Still it's a funny story, eh? But you're not laughing. Nobody's laughing. Now listen! [*In a burst of anger*] I insist on everybody's laughing. You, Lepidus, shall lead the chorus. Stand up, every one of you, and laugh. [*He thumps the table.*] Do you hear what I say? I wish to see you laughing, all of you.

[*All rise to their feet. During this scene all the players, Caligula and Caesonia excepted, behave like marionettes in a puppet-play.* CALIGULA *sinks back on his couch, beaming with delight, and bursts into a fit of laughter.*]

CALIGULA: Oh, Caesonia! Just look at them! The game is up; honour, respectability, the wisdom of the nations, gone with the wind! The wind of fear has blown them all away. Fear, Caesonia – don't you agree? – is a noble emotion, pure and simple, self-sufficient, like no other; it draws its patent of nobility straight from the guts. [*He strokes his forehead and drinks again. In a friendly tone*] Well, well, let's change the subject. What have you to say, Cherea? You've been very silent.

CHEREA: I'm quite ready to speak, Caius. When you give me leave.

CALIGULA: Excellent. Then – keep silent. I'd rather have a word from our friend Mucius.

MUCIUS [*reluctantly*]: As you will, Caius.

CALIGULA: Then tell us something about your wife. And begin by sending her to this place, on my right.

[MUCIUS' WIFE *seats herself beside Caligula.*]

CALIGULA: Well, Mucius? We're waiting.

MUCIUS [*hardly knowing what he says*]: My wife . . . but . . . I'm very fond of her.

[*General laughter.*]

CALIGULA: Why, of course, my friend, of course. But how ordinary of you! So unoriginal! [*He is leaning towards her, tickling her shoulder playfully with his tongue.*] By the way, when I came in just now, you were hatching a plot, weren't you? A nice bloody little plot?

OLD PATRICIAN: Oh Caius, how can you . . . ?

CALIGULA: It doesn't matter in the least, my pet. Old age will be served. I shan't take it seriously. Not one of you has the spunk for an heroic act . . . Ah, it's just come to my mind, I have some affairs of state to settle. But, first, I've a little natural craving to relieve.

[*He rises and leads Mucius' Wife into an adjoining room.* MUCIUS *starts up from his seat.*]

CAESONIA [*amiably*]: Please, Mucius. Will you pour me out another glass of this excellent wine.

[MUCIUS *complies; his movement of revolt is quelled. Everyone looks embarrassed. Chairs creak noisily. The ensuing conversation is in a strained tone.* CAESONIA *turns to Cherea.*]

CAESONIA: Now, Cherea, suppose you tell me why you people were fighting just now?

CHEREA [*coolly*]: With pleasure, my dear Caesonia. Our

quarrel arose from a discussion whether poetry should be blood-thirsty or not.

CAESONIA: An interesting problem. Somewhat beyond my feminine comprehension, of course. Still it surprises me that your passion for art should make you come to blows.

CHEREA [*in the same rather stilted tone*]: That I can well understand. But I remember Caligula's telling me the other day that all true passion has a spice of cruelty.

CAESONIA [*helping herself from the dish in front of her*]: There's truth in that. Don't you agree, gentlemen?

THE OLD PATRICIAN: Ah, yes. Caligula has a rare insight into the secret places of the heart.

FIRST PATRICIAN: And how eloquently he spoke just now of courage!

SECOND PATRICIAN: Really he should put his ideas into writing. They would be most instructive.

CHEREA: And, what's more, it would keep him busy. It's obvious he needs something to occupy his leisure.

CAESONIA [*still eating*]: You'll be pleased to hear that Caligula shares your views; he's working on a book. Quite a big one, I believe.

[CALIGULA *enters, accompanied by* MUCIUS' WIFE.]

CALIGULA: Mucius, I return your wife, with many thanks. But excuse me, I've some orders to give. [*He hurries out.*]

[MUCIUS *has gone pale and risen to his feet.*]

CAESONIA [*to Mucius, who is standing*]: This book of his will certainly rank amongst our Latin classics. Are you listening, Mucius?

MUCIUS [*his eyes still fixed on the door by which Caligula went out*]: Yes. And what's the book about, Caesonia?

CAESONIA [*indifferently*]: Oh, it's above my head, you know.

CHEREA: May we assume it deals with the murderous power of poetry?

CAESONIA: Yes, something of that sort, I understand.

THE OLD PATRICIAN [*cheerfully*]: Well anyhow, as our friend Cherea said, it will keep him busy.

CAESONIA: Yes, my love. But I'm afraid there's one thing you won't like quite so much about this book, and that's its title.

CHEREA: What is it?

CAESONIA: 'Cold Steel.'

[CALIGULA *hurries in.*]

CALIGULA: Excuse me, but I've some urgent public work in hand. [*To the Intendant*] Intendant, you are to close the public granaries. I have signed a decree to that effect; you will find it in my study.

INTENDANT: But, sire . . .

CALIGULA: Famine begins tomorrow.

INTENDANT: But . . . but heaven knows what may happen – perhaps a revolution.

CALIGULA [*firmly and deliberately*]: I repeat; famine begins tomorrow. We all know what famine means – a national catastrophe. Well, tomorrow there will be a catastrophe, and I shall end it when I choose. After all, I haven't so many ways of proving I am free. One is always free at someone else's expense. Absurd perhaps, but so it is. [*With a keen glance at Mucius*] Apply this principle to your jealousy – and you'll understand better. [*In a meditative tone*] Still, what an ugly thing is jealousy! A disease of vanity and the imagination. One pictures one's wife . . .

[MUCIUS *clenches his fists and opens his mouth to speak. Before he can get a word out,* CALIGULA *cuts in.*]

CALIGULA: Now, gentlemen, let's go on with our meal . . . Do you know, we've been doing quite a lot of work, with Helicon's assistance? Putting the final touches to a little monograph on execution – about which you will have much to say.

HELICON: Assuming we ask your opinion.

CALIGULA: Why not be generous, Helicon, and let them into our little secrets? Come now, give them a sample. Section Three, first paragraph.

HELICON [*standing, declaims in a droning voice*]: 'Execution relieves and liberates It is universal, tonic, just in precept and in practice. A man dies because he is guilty. A man is guilty because he is one of Caligula's subjects. Now all men are Caligula's subjects. Ergo, all men are guilty and shall die. It is only a matter of time and patience.'

CALIGULA [*laughing*]: There's logic for you, don't you agree? That bit about 'patience' was rather neat, wasn't it? Allow me to tell you, that's the quality I most admire in you . . . your patience. Now, gentlemen, you can disperse. Cherea doesn't need your presence any longer. Caesonia, I wish you to stay. You too, Lepidus. Also our old friend Mereia. I want to have a little talk with you about our National Brothel. It's not functioning too well; in fact, I'm quite concerned about it.

[*The others file out slowly.* CALIGULA *follows Mucius with his eyes.*]

CHEREA: At your orders, Caius. But what's the trouble? Are the staff unsatisfactory?

CALIGULA: No, but the takings are falling off.

MEREIA: Then you should raise the entrance fee.

CALIGULA: There, Mereia, you missed a golden opportunity of keeping your mouth shut. You're too old to be interested in the subject, and I don't want your opinion.

MEREIA: Then why ask me to stay?

CALIGULA: Because, presently, I may require some cool, dispassionate advice.

[MEREIA *moves away.*]

CHEREA: If you wish to hear my views on the subject, Caius, I'd say, neither coolly nor dispassionately, that it would be a blunder to raise the scale of charges.

CALIGULA: Obviously. What's needed is a bigger turnover. I've explained my plan of campaign to Caesonia, and she will tell you all about it. Personally, I've had too much wine, I'm feeling sleepy. [*He lies down, and closes his eyes.*]

CAESONIA: It's very simple. Caligula is creating a new order of merit.

CHEREA: Sorry, I don't see the connexion.

CAESONIA: No? But there is one. It will be called the Badge of Civic Merit and awarded to those who have patronized Caligula's National Brothel most assiduously.

CHEREA: A brilliant idea!

CAESONIA: I agree. Oh, I forgot to mention that the Badge will be conferred each month, after checking the admission tickets. Any citizen who has not obtained the Badge within twelve months will be exiled, or executed.

CHEREA: Why 'or executed'?

CAESONIA: Because Caligula says it doesn't matter which – but it's important he should have the right of choosing.

CHEREA: Bravo! The Public Treasury will wipe out its deficit in no time.

[CALIGULA *has half-opened his eyes and is watching old Mereia who, standing in a corner, has produced a small flask and is sipping its contents.*]

CALIGULA [*still lying on the couch*]: What's that you're drinking, Mereia?

MEREIA: It's for my asthma, Caius.

[CALIGULA *rises and, thrusting the others aside, goes up to Mereia and sniffs his mouth.*]

CALIGULA: No, it's an antidote.

MEREIA: What an idea, Caius! You must be joking. I have choking fits at night and I've been in the doctor's hands for months.

CALIGULA: So you're afraid of being poisoned?

MEREIA: My asthma . . .

CALIGULA: No. Why beat about the bush? You're afraid I'll poison you. You suspect me. You're keeping an eye on me.

MEREIA: Good heavens, no!

CALIGULA: You suspect me. I'm not to be trusted, eh?

MEREIA: Caius!

CALIGULA [*roughly*]: Answer! [*In a cool, judicial tone*] If you take an antidote, it follows that you credit me with the intention of poisoning you. Q.E.D.

MEREIA: Yes ... I mean ... no!

CALIGULA: And thinking I intend to poison you, you take steps to frustrate my plan. [*He falls silent.*]

[*Meanwhile* CAESONIA *and* CHEREA *have moved away, back stage.* LEPIDUS *is watching the speakers with an air of consternation.*]

CALIGULA: That makes two crimes, Mereia, and a dilemma from which you can't escape. *Either* I have no wish to cause your death; in which case you are unjustly suspecting me, your emperor. *Or else* I desire your death; in which case, vermin that you are, you're trying to thwart my will. [*Another silence.* CALIGULA *contemplates the old man gloatingly.*] Well, Mereia, what have you to say to my logic?

MEREIA: It ... it's sound enough, Caius. Only it doesn't apply to the case.

CALIGULA: A third crime. You take me for a fool. Now sit down and listen carefully. [*To Lepidus*] Let everyone sit down. [*To Mereia*] Of these three crimes only one does you honour; the second one – because by crediting me with a certain wish and presuming to oppose it you are deliberately defying me. You are a rebel, a leader of revolt. And that needs courage. [*Sadly*] I've a great liking for you, Mereia. And that is why you'll be condemned for crime number two, and not for either of the others. You shall die nobly, a rebel's death.

[*While he talks* MEREIA *is shrinking together on his chair.*]

CALIGULA: Don't thank me. It's quite natural. Here. [*Holds out a phial. His tone is amiable.*] Drink this poison. [MEREIA *shakes his head. He is sobbing violently.* CALIGULA *shows signs of impatience.*]

CALIGULA: Don't waste time. Take it.

[MEREIA *makes a feeble attempt to escape. But* CALIGULA *with a wild leap is on him, catches him in the centre of the stage and after a brief struggle pins him down on a low couch. He forces the phial between his lips and smashes it with a blow of his fist. After some convulsive movements* MEREIA *dies. His face is streaming with blood and tears.* CALIGULA *rises, wipes his hands absentmindedly, then hands Mereia's flask to Caesonia.*]

CALIGULA: What was it? An antidote?

CAESONIA [*calmly*]: No, Caligula. A remedy for asthma. [*A short silence.*]

CALIGULA [*gazing down at Mereia*]: No matter. It all comes to the same thing in the end. A little sooner, a little later . . .

[*He goes out hurriedly, still wiping his hands.*]

LEPIDUS [*in a horrified tone*]: What . . . what shall we do?

CAESONIA [*coolly*]: Remove that body to begin with, I should say. It's rather a beastly sight.

[CHEREA *and* LEPIDUS *drag the body into the wings.*]

LEPIDUS [*to Cherea*]: We must act quickly.

CHEREA: We'll need to be two hundred.

[*Young* SCIPIO *enters. Seeing Caesonia, he makes as if to leave.*]

CAESONIA: Come.

SCIPIO: What do you want?

CAESONIA: Come nearer. [*She pushes up his chin and looks him in the eyes. A short silence. Then, in a calm, unemotional voice*] He killed your father, didn't he?

SCIPIO: Yes.

CAESONIA: Do you hate him?

SCIPIO: Yes.

CAESONIA: And you'd like to kill him?

SCIPIO: Yes.

CAESONIA [*withdrawing her hand*]: But – why tell me this?

SCIPIO: Because I fear nobody. Killing him or being killed – either way out will do. And anyhow you won't betray me.

CAESONIA: That's so. I shan't betray you. But I want to tell you something – or, rather, I'd like to speak to what is best in you.

SCIPIO: What's best in me is – my hatred.

CAESONIA: Please listen carefully to what I'm going to say. It may sound hard to grasp, but it's as clear as daylight, really. And it's something that would bring about the one real revolution in this world of ours, if people would only take it in.

SCIPIO: Yes? What is it?

CAESONIA: Wait! Try to call up a picture of your father's death, of the agony on his face as they were tearing out his tongue. Think of the blood streaming from his mouth, and recall his screams, like a tortured animal's.

SCIPIO: Yes.

CAESONIA: And now think of Caligula.

SCIPIO [*his voice rough with hatred*]: Yes.

CAESONIA: Now listen. *Try to understand him.* [*She goes out, leaving* SCIPIO *gaping after her in bewilderment.*]
　　　[HELICON *enters.*]

HELICON: Caligula will be here in a moment. Suppose you go for your meal, young poet?

SCIPIO: Helicon, help me.

HELICON: Too dangerous, my lamb. And poetry means nothing to me.

SCIPIO: You can help me. You know . . . so many things.

HELICON: I know that the days go by – and growing boys should have their meals on time . . . I know, too, that you could kill Caligula . . . and he wouldn't greatly mind it. [*Goes out.*]

[CALIGULA *enters.*]

CALIGULA: Ah, it's you, Scipio. [*He pauses. One has the impression that he is somewhat embarrassed.*] It's quite a long time since I saw you last. [*Slowly approaches Scipio.*] What have you been up to? Writing more poems, I suppose. Might I see your latest composition?

SCIPIO [*likewise ill at ease, torn between hatred and some less defined emotion*]: Yes, Caesar, I've written some more poems.

CALIGULA: On what subject?

SCIPIO: Oh, on nothing in particular. Well, on Nature in a way.

CALIGULA: A fine theme. And a vast one. And what has Nature done for you?

SCIPIO [*pulling himself together, in a somewhat truculent tone*]: It consoles me for not being Caesar.

CALIGULA: Really? And do you think Nature could console me for being Caesar?

SCIPIO [*in the same tone*]: Why not? Nature has healed worse wounds than that.

CALIGULA [*in a curiously young, unaffected voice*]: Wounds, you said? There was anger in your voice. Because I put your father to death? . . . That word you used – if you only knew how apt it is! My wounds! [*In a different tone*] Well, well, there's nothing like hatred for developing the intelligence.

SCIPIO [*stiffly*]: I answered your question about Nature.

[CALIGULA *sits down, gazes at Scipio, then brusquely grips his wrists and forces him to stand up. He takes the young man's face between his hands.*]

66

CALIGULA: Recite your poem to me, please.

SCIPIO: No, please, don't ask me that.

CALIGULA: Why not?

SCIPIO: I haven't got it on me.

CALIGULA: Can't you remember it?

SCIPIO: No.

CALIGULA: Anyhow you can tell me what it's about.

SCIPIO [*still hostile; reluctantly*]: I spoke of a . . . a certain harmony . . .

CALIGULA [*breaking in; in a pensive voice*]: . . . between one's feet and the earth.

SCIPIO [*looking surprised*]: Yes, it's almost that . . . and it tells of the wavy outline of the Roman hills and the sudden thrill of peace that twilight brings to them . . .

CALIGULA: And the cries of swifts thridding the green dusk.

SCIPIO [*yielding more and more to his emotion*]: Yes, yes! And that fantastic moment when the sky all flushed with red and gold swings round and shows its other side, spangled with stars.

CALIGULA: And the faint smell of smoke and trees and streams that mingles with the rising mist.

SCIPIO [*in a sort of ecstasy*]: Yes, and the chirr of crickets, the coolness veining the warm air, the rumble of carts and the farmers' shouts, dogs barking . . .

CALIGULA: And the roads drowned in shadow winding through the olive groves . . .

SCIPIO: Yes, yes. That's it, exactly. . . . But how did you know?

CALIGULA [*drawing Scipio to his breast*]: I wonder! Perhaps because the same eternal truths appeal to us both. And perhaps, too, because it's easy to share emotions – provided they are vague enough.

SCIPIO [*quivering with excitement, burying his head on Caligula's breast*]: Anyhow, what matter! All I know is that everything I feel or think of turns to love.

CALIGULA [*stroking his hair*]: That, Scipio, is a privilege of
noble hearts – and how I wish I could share your . . . your
limpidity! But my appetite for life's too keen; Nature can
never sate it. You belong to quite another world, and you
can't understand. You are single-minded for good; and I
am single-minded – for evil.

SCIPIO: I *do* understand.

CALIGULA: No. There's something deep down in me – an
abyss of silence, a pool of stagnant water, rotting weeds.
[*With an abrupt change of manner*] Your poem sounds very
good indeed, but, if you really want my opinion . . .

SCIPIO [*his head on Caligula's breast, murmurs*]: Yes?

CALIGULA: All that's a bit . . . anaemic.

SCIPIO [*recoiling abruptly, as if stung by a serpent, and gazing,
horrified, at Caligula, he cries hoarsely*]: Oh, you brute! You
loathsome brute! You've fooled me again. I know! You
were playing a trick on me, weren't you? And now you're
gloating over your success.

CALIGULA [*with a hint of sadness*]: There's truth in what you
say. I *was* playing a part.

SCIPIO [*in the same indignant tone*]: What a foul, black heart
you have! And how all that wickedness and hatred must
make you suffer!

CALIGULA [*gently*]: That's enough.

SCIPIO: How I loathe you! And how I pity you!

CALIGULA [*angrily*]: Enough, I tell you.

SCIPIO: And how horrible a loneliness like yours must be!

CALIGULA [*in a rush of anger, gripping the boy by the collar, and
shaking him*]: Loneliness! What do *you* know of it? Only the
loneliness of poets and weaklings. You prate of loneliness,
but you don't realize that one is *never* alone. Always we
are attended by the same load of the future and the past.
Those we have killed are always with us. But *they* are no
great trouble. It's those we have loved, those who loved us

68

and whom we did not love; regrets, desires, bitterness and sweetness, whores and gods, the gang celestial! Always, always with us! [*He releases Scipio and moves back to his former place.*] Alone! Ah, if only in this loneliness, this ghoul-haunted wilderness of mine, I could know, but for a moment, real solitude, real silence, the throbbing stillness of a tree! [*Sitting down, in an access of fatigue.*] Solitude? No, Scipio, mine is full of gnashings of teeth, hideous with jarring sounds and voices. And when I am with the women I make mine and darkness falls on us and I think, now my body's had its fill, that I can feel myself my own at last, poised between death and life – ah, then my solitude is fouled by the stale smell of pleasure from the woman sprawling at my side.

[*A long silence.* CALIGULA *seems weary and despondent.* SCIPIO *moves behind him and approaches hesitantly. He slowly stretches out a hand towards him, from behind, and lays it on his shoulder. Without looking round,* CALIGULA *places his hand on Scipio's.*]

SCIPIO: All men have a secret solace. It helps them to endure, and they turn to it when life has wearied them beyond enduring.

CALIGULA: Yes, Scipio.

SCIPIO: Have you nothing of the kind in your life, no refuge, no mood that makes the tears well up, no consolation?

CALIGULA: Yes, I have something of the kind.

SCIPIO: What is it?

CALIGULA [*very quietly*]: Scorn.

CURTAIN

ACT THREE

Before the curtain rises a rhythmic clash of cymbals and the thudding of a drum have been coming from the stage, and when it goes up we see a curtained-off booth, with a small proscenium in front, such as strolling players use at country fairs for an exhibition turn. On the little stage are CAESONIA *and* HELICON, *flanked by cymbal-players. Seated on benches, with their backs to the audience, are some* PATRICIANS *and young* SCIPIO.

HELICON [*in the tone of a showman at a fair*]: Walk up! Walk up! [*A clash of cymbals.*] Once more the gods have come to earth. They have assumed the human form of our heaven-born emperor, known to men as Caligula. Draw near, mortals of common clay; a holy miracle is taking place before your eyes. By a divine dispensation peculiar to Caligula's hallowed reign, the secrets of the gods will be revealed to you. [*Cymbals.*]

CAESONIA: Come, gentlemen. Come and adore him – and don't forget to give your alms. Today heaven and its mysteries are on show, at a price to suit every pocket.

HELICON: For all to see, the secrets of Olympus, revelations in high places, featuring gods in undress, their little plots and pranks. Step this way! The whole truth about your gods! [*Cymbals.*]

CAESONIA: Adore him, and give your alms. Come near, gentlemen. The show's beginning.

[*Cymbals.* SLAVES *are placing various objects on the platform.*]

HELICON: An epoch-making reproduction of the life celestial, warranted authentic in every detail. For the first time the pomp and splendour of the gods are presented to the Roman public. You will relish our novel, breathtaking effects: flashes of lightning [SLAVES *light Greek fires*], peals of thunder [*they roll a barrel filled with stones*], the divine event on its triumphal way. Now watch with all your eyes. [*He draws aside the curtain.*]

[*Grotesquely attired as Venus,* CALIGULA *beams down on them from a pedestal.*]

CALIGULA: I'm Venus today.

CAESONIA: Now for the adoration. Bow down. [*All but* SCIPIO *bend their heads.*] And repeat after me the litany of Venus yclept Caligula.

'Our Lady of pangs and pleasures . . .'

THE PATRICIANS: 'Our Lady of pangs and pleasures . . .'

CAESONIA: 'Born of the waves, bitter and bright with seafoam . . .'

THE PATRICIANS: 'Born of the waves, bitter and bright with seafoam . . .'

CAESONIA: 'O Queen whose gifts are laughter and regrets . . .'

THE PATRICIANS: 'O Queen whose gifts are laughter and regrets . . .'

CAESONIA: 'Rancours and raptures . . .'

THE PATRICIANS: 'Rancours and raptures . . .'

CAESONIA: 'Teach us the indifference that kindles love anew . . .'

THE PATRICIANS: 'Teach us the indifference that kindles love anew . . .'

CAESONIA: 'Make known to us the truth about this world – which is that it has none . . .'

THE PATRICIANS: 'Make known to us the truth about this world – which is that it has none . . .'

CAESONIA: 'And grant us strength to live up to this verity of verities.'

71

THE PATRICIANS: 'And grant us strength to live up to this verity of verities.'

CAESONIA: Now, pause.

THE PATRICIANS: Now pause.

CAESONIA [*after a short silence*]: 'Bestow your gifts on us, and shed on our faces the light of your impartial cruelty, your wanton hatred; unfold above our eyes your arms laden with flowers and murders . . .'

THE PATRICIANS: '. . . your arms laden with flowers and murders.'

CAESONIA: 'Welcome your wandering children home, to the bleak sanctuary of your heartless, thankless love. Give us your passions without object, your griefs devoid of reason, your raptures that lead nowhere . . .'

THE PATRICIANS: '. . . your raptures that lead nowhere . . .'

CAESONIA [*raising her voice*]: 'O Queen, so empty yet so ardent, inhuman yet so earthly, make us drunk with the wine of your equivalence, and surfeit us for ever in the brackish darkness of your heart.'

THE PATRICIANS: 'Make us drunk with the wine of your equivalence, and surfeit us for ever in the brackish darkness of your heart.'

[*When the* PATRICIANS *have said the last response,* CALIGULA, *who until now has been quite motionless, snorts and rises.*]

CALIGULA [*in a stentorian voice*]: Granted, my children. Your prayer is heard. [*He squats cross-legged on the pedestal.*]

[*One by one the* PATRICIANS *make obeisance, deposit their alms, and line up on the right. The last, in his flurry, forgets to make an offering.* CALIGULA *bounds to his feet.*]

CALIGULA: Steady! Steady on! Come here, my lad. Worship's very well, but almsgiving is better. Thank you, We are appeased. Ah, if the gods had no wealth other than the love you mortals give them, they'd be as poor as poor Caligula. Now, gentlemen, you may go, and spread abroad the glad tidings of the miracle you've been allowed to witness. You have seen Venus, seen her godhead with your fleshly eyes, and Venus herself has spoken to you. Go, most favoured gentlemen.

[*The* PATRICIANS *begin to move away.*]

CALIGULA: Just a moment. When you leave, mind you take the exit on your left. I have posted sentries in the others, with orders to kill you.

[*The* PATRICIANS *file out hastily in some disorder. The* SLAVES *and* MUSICIANS *leave the stage.*]

HELICON [*pointing a monitory finger at Scipio*]: Naughty boy, you've been playing the anarchist again.

SCIPIO [*to Caligula*]: You spoke blasphemy, Caius.

CALIGULA: Blasphemy? What's that?

SCIPIO: You're befouling heaven, after bloodying the earth.

CALIGULA: How this youngster loves big words! [*He stretches himself on a couch.*]

CAESONIA [*composedly*]: You should watch your tongue, my lad. At this moment men are dying in Rome for saying much less.

SCIPIO: Maybe – but I've resolved to tell Caligula the truth.

CAESONIA: Hark at him, Caligula! That was the one thing missing in your Empire – a bold young moralist.

CALIGULA [*giving Scipio a curious glance*]: Do you really believe in the gods, Scipio?

SCIPIO: No.

CALIGULA: Then I fail to follow. If you don't believe, why be so keen to scent out blasphemy?

SCIPIO: One may deny something without feeling called on to besmirch it, or deprive others of the right of believing in it.

CALIGULA: But that's humility, the real thing, unless I'm much mistaken. Ah, my dear Scipio, how glad I am on your behalf – and a trifle envious, too. Humility's the one emotion I may never feel.

SCIPIO: It's not I you're envious of; it's the gods.

CALIGULA: If you don't mind, that will remain our secret – the great enigma of our reign. Really, you know, there's only one thing for which I might be blamed today – and that's this small advance I've made upon the path of freedom. For someone who loves power the rivalry of the gods is rather irksome. Well, I've proved to these imaginary gods that any man, without previous training, if he applies his mind to it, can play their absurd parts to perfection.

SCIPIO: That, Caius, is what I meant by blasphemy.

CALIGULA: No, Scipio, it's clear-sightedness. I've merely realized that there's only one way of getting even with the gods. All that's needed is to be as cruel as they.

SCIPIO: All that's needed is to play the tyrant.

CALIGULA: Tell me, my young friend. What exactly *is* a tyrant?

SCIPIO: A blind soul.

CALIGULA: That's a moot point. I should say the real tyrant is a man who sacrifices a whole nation to his ideal or his ambition. But I have no ideal, and there's nothing left for me to covet by way of power or glory. If I use this power of mine, it's to compensate.

SCIPIO: For what?

CALIGULA: For the hatred and stupidity of the gods.

SCIPIO: Hatred does not compensate for hatred. Power is no solution. Personally I know only one way of countering the hostility of the world we live in.

CALIGULA: Yes? And what is it?

SCIPIO: Poverty.

CALIGULA [*bending over his feet and scrutinizing his toes*]: I must try that, too.

SCIPIO: Meanwhile many men round you are dying.

CALIGULA: Oh, come! Not so many as all that. Do you know how many wars I've refused to embark on?

SCIPIO: No.

CALIGULA: Three. And do you know why I refused?

SCIPIO: Because the grandeur of Rome means nothing to you.

CALIGULA: No. Because I respect human life.

SCIPIO: You're joking, Caius.

CALIGUA: Or, anyhow, I respect it more than I respect military triumphs. But it's a fact that I don't respect it more than I respect my own life. And if I find killing easy, it's because dying isn't hard for me. No, the more I think about it, the surer I feel that I'm no tyrant.

SCIPIO: What matter, if it costs us quite as dear as if you were one?

CALIGULA [*with a hint of petulance*]: If you had the least head for figures you'd know that the smallest war a tyrant – however level-headed he might be – indulged in would cost you a thousand times more than all my vagaries (shall we call them?) put together.

SCIPIO: Possibly. But at least there'd be *some* sense behind a war; it would be understandable – and to understand makes up for much.

CALIGULA: There's no understanding Fate; therefore I choose to play the part of Fate. I wear the foolish, unintelligible face of a professional god. And that is what the men who were here with you have learnt to adore.

SCIPIO: That, too, Caius, is blasphemy.

CALIGULA: No, Scipio, it's dramatic art. The great mistake you people make is not to take the drama seriously enough. If you did, you'd know that any man can play

lead in the divine comedy and become a god. All he needs
do is to harden his heart.

SCIPIO: You may be right, Caius. But I rather think you've
done everything that was needed to rouse up against you
a legion of human gods, ruthless as yourself, who will
drown in blood your godhead of a day.

CAESONIA: Really, Scipio!

CALIGULA [*peremptorily*]: No, don't stop him, Caesonia.
Yes, Scipio, you spoke truer than you knew; I've done
everything needed to that end. I find it hard to picture
the event you speak of – but I sometimes dream it. And in
all those faces surging up out of the angry darkness, con-
vulsed with fear and hatred, I see, and I rejoice to see,
the only god I've worshipped on this earth; foul and
craven as the human heart. [*Irritably*] Now go. I've had
enough of you, more than enough. [*In a different tone*] I
really must attend to my toe-nails; they're not nearly red
enough, and I've no time to waste.

[*All go, with the exception of* HELICON. *He hovers round
Caligula, who is busy painting his toe-nails.*]

CALIGULA: Helicon!

HELICON: Yes?

CALIGULA: Getting on with your task?

HELICON: What task?

CALIGULA: You know . . . the moon.

HELICON: Ah yes, the moon. . . . It's a matter of time and
patience. But I'd like to have a word with you.

CALIGULA: I might have patience; only I have not much
time. So you must make haste.

HELICON: I said I'd do my utmost. But, first, I have something to tell you. Very serious news.

CALIGULA [*as if he has not heard*]: Mind you, I've had her
already.

HELICON: Whom?

76

CALIGULA: The moon.

HELICON: Yes, yes ... Now listen please. Do you know there's a plot being hatched against your life?

CALIGULA: What's more, I had her thoroughly. Only two or three times, to be sure. Still, I had her all right.

HELICON: For the last hour I've been trying to tell you about it, only –

CALIGULA: It was last summer. I'd been gazing at her so long, and stroking her so often on the marble pillars in the gardens that evidently she'd come to understand.

HELICON: Please stop trifling, Caius. Even if you refuse to listen, it's my duty to tell you this. And if you shut your ears, it can't be helped.

CALIGULA [*varnishing his toe-nails*]: This varnish is no good at all. But, to come back to the moon – it was a cloudless August night.

[HELICON *looks sulkily away, and keeps silence.*]

CALIGULA: She was coy, to begin with. I'd gone to bed. First she was blood-red, low on the horizon. Then she began rising, quicker and quicker, growing brighter and brighter all the while. And the higher she climbed, the paler she grew, till she was like a milky pool in a dark wood rustling with stars. Slowly, shyly she approached, through the warm night-air, soft, light as gossamer, naked in beauty. She crossed the threshold of my room, glided to my bed, poured herself into it, and flooded me with her smiles and sheen. . . . No, really this new varnish is a failure. . . . So you see, Helicon, I can say, without boasting, that I've had her.

HELICON: Now will you listen, and learn the danger that's threatening you?

CALIGULA [*ceasing to fiddle with his toes, and gazing at him fixedly*]: All I want, Helicon, is – the moon. For the rest, I've always known what will kill me. I haven't yet exhausted all that is to keep me living. That's why I want the moon. And you must not return till you have secured her for me.

HELICON: Very well. . . . Now I'll do my duty and tell you what I've learnt. There's a plot against you. Cherea is the ringleader. I came across this tablet which tells you all you need to know. See, I put it here. [*He places the tablet on one of the seats and moves away.*]

CALIGULA: Where are you off to, Helicon?

HELICON [*from the threshold*]: To get the moon for you.

[*There is a mouse-like scratching at the opposite door.* CALIGULA *swings round and sees the Old Patrician.*]

THE OLD PATRICIAN [*timidly*]: May I, Caius . . .

CALIGULA [*impatiently*]: Come in! Come in! [*Gazes at him.*] So, my pet, you've returned to have another look at Venus.

THE OLD PATRICIAN: Well . . . no. It's not quite that. Ssh! Oh, sorry, Caius! I only wanted to say . . . You know I'm very, very devoted to you – and my one desire is to end my days in peace.

CALIGULA: Be quick, man. Get it out!

THE OLD PATRICIAN: Well, it's . . . it's like this. [*Hurriedly*] It's terribly serious, that's what I meant to say.

CALIGULA: No, it isn't serious.

THE OLD PATRICIAN: But – I don't follow. *What* isn't serious?

CALIGULA: But what are we talking about, my love?

THE OLD PATRICIAN [*glancing nervously round the room*]: I mean to say . . . [*Wriggles, shuffles, then bursts out with it*] There's a plot afoot, against you.

CALIGULA: There! You see. Just as I said; it isn't serious.

THE OLD PATRICIAN: But, Caius, they mean to kill you.

CALIGULA [*approaching him and grasping his shoulders*]: Do you know why I can't believe you?

THE OLD PATRICIAN [*raising an arm, as if to take an oath*]: The gods bear witness, Caius, that . . .

CALIGULA [*gently but firmly pressing him back towards the door*]: Don't swear. I particularly ask you not to swear. Listen, instead. Suppose it were true, what you are telling me – I'd have to assume you were betraying your friends, isn't that so?

THE OLD PATRICIAN [*flustered*]: Well, Caius, considering the deep affection I have for you . . .

CALIGULA [*in the same tone as before*]: And I cannot assume *that*. I've always loathed baseness of that sort so profoundly that I could never restrain myself from having a betrayer put to death. But I know the man you are, my worthy friend. And I'm convinced you neither wish to play the traitor nor to die.

THE OLD PATRICIAN: Certainly not, Caius. Most certainly not.

CALIGULA: So you see I was right in refusing to believe you. You wouldn't stoop to baseness, would you?

THE OLD PATRICIAN: Oh no, indeed!

CALIGULA: Nor betray your friends?

THE OLD PATRICIAN: I need hardly tell you that, Caius.

CALIGULA: Therefore it follows that there isn't any plot. It was just a joke – between ourselves, rather a silly joke – what you've just been telling me, eh?

THE OLD PATRICIAN [*feebly*]: Yes, yes. A joke, merely a joke.

CALIGULA: Good. So now we know where we are. Nobody wants to kill me.

THE OLD PATRICIAN: Nobody. That's it. Nobody at all.

CALIGULA [*drawing a deep breath; in measured tones*]: Then – leave me, sweetheart. A man of honour is an animal so rare in the present-day world that I couldn't bear the sight of one too long. I must be left alone to relish this unique experience.

[*The Old Patrician goes out. For some moments* CALIGULA *gazes, without moving, at the tablet. He picks it up and reads it. Then, again, draws a deep breath. Then summons a palace guard.*]

CALIGULA: Bring Cherea to me.

[*The man starts to leave.*]

CALIGULA: Wait!

[*The man halts.*]

CALIGULA: Treat him politely.

[*The man goes out.* CALIGULA *falls to pacing the room. After a while he approaches the mirror.*]

CALIGULA: You decided to be logical, didn't you, poor simpleton? Logic for ever! The question now is: Where will that take you? [*Ironically*] Suppose the moon were brought here, everything would be different. That was the idea, wasn't it? Then the impossible would become possible, in a flash the Great Change come, and all things be transfigured. After all, why shouldn't Helicon bring it off? One night, perhaps, he'll catch her sleeping in a lake, and carry her here, trapped in a glistening net, all slimy with weeds and water, like a pale bloated fish drawn from the depths. Why not, Caligula? Why not, indeed? [*He casts a glance round the room.*] Fewer and fewer people round me; I wonder why. [*Addressing the mirror, in a muffled voice*] Too many dead, too many dead – that makes an emptiness. . . . No, even if the moon were mine, I could not retrace my way. Even were those dead men thrilling again under the sun's caress, the murders wouldn't go back underground for that. [*Angrily*] Logic, Caligula; follow where logic leads. Power to the uttermost; wilfulness without end. Ah, I'm the only man on earth to know the secret – that power can never be complete without a total self-surrender to the dark impulse of one's destiny. No there's no return. I must go on and on, until the consummation.

[CHEREA *enters.* CALIGULA *is slumped in his chair, the cloak drawn tightly round him.*]

CHEREA: You sent for me, Caius?

CALIGULA [*languidly*]: Yes, Cherea.

[*A short silence.*]

CHEREA: Have you anything particular to tell me?

CALIGULA: No, Cherea.

[*Another silence.*]

CHEREA [*with a hint of petulance*]: Are you sure you really need my presence?

CALIGULA: Absolutely sure, Cherea. [*Another silence. Then, as if suddenly recollecting himself.*] I'm sorry for seeming so inhospitable. I was following up my thoughts, and – Now do sit down, we'll have a friendly little chat. I'm in a mood for some intelligent conversation.

[CHEREA *sits down. For the first time since the play began,* CALIGULA *gives the impression of being his natural self.*]

CALIGULA: Do you think, Cherea, that it's possible for two men of much the same temperament and equal pride to talk to each other with complete frankness – if only once in their lives? Can they strip themselves naked, so to speak, and shed their prejudices, their private interests, the lies by which they live?

CHEREA: Yes, Caius, I think it possible. But I don't think you'd be capable of it.

CALIGULA: You're right. I only wished to know if you agreed with me. So let's wear our masks, and muster up our lies. And we'll talk as fencers fight, padded on all the vital parts. Tell me, Cherea, why don't you like me?

CHEREA: Because there's nothing likeable about you, Caius. Because such feelings can't be had to order. And because

81

I understand you far too well. One cannot like an aspect of oneself which one always tries to keep concealed.

CALIGULA: But why is it you hate me?

CHEREA: There, Caius, you're mistaken. I do not hate you. I regard you as noxious and cruel, vain and selfish. But I cannot hate you, because I don't think you are happy. And I cannot scorn you, because I know you are no coward.

CALIGULA: Then why wish to kill me?

CHEREA: I've told you why; because I regard you as noxious, a constant menace. I like, and need, to feel secure. So do most men. They resent living in a world where the most preposterous fancy may at any moment become a reality, and the absurd transfix their lives, like a dagger in the heart. I feel as they do; I refuse to live in a topsy-turvy world. I want to know where I stand, and to stand secure.

CALIGULA Security and logic don't go together.

CHEREA: Quite true. My plan of life may not be logical, but at least it's sound.

CALIGULA: Go on.

CHEREA: There's no more to say. I'll be no party to your logic. I've a very different notion of my duties as a man. And I know that the majority of your subjects share my view. You outrage their deepest feelings. It's only natural that you should . . . disappear.

CALIGULA: I see your point, and it's legitimate enough. For most men, I grant you, it's obvious. But *you*, I should have thought, would have known better. You're an intelligent man, and given intelligence, one has a choice: either to pay its price or to disown it. Why do you shirk the issue and neither disown it nor consent to pay its price?

CHEREA: Because what I want is to live, and to be happy. Neither, to my mind, is possible if one pushes the absurd

to its logical conclusions. As you see, I'm quite an ordinary
sort of man. True, there are moments when, to feel free
of them, I desire the death of those I love, or I hanker
after women from whom the ties of family or friendship
debar me. Were logic everything, I'd kill or fornicate
on such occasions. But I consider that these passing
fancies have no great ˙importance. If everyone set to
gratifying them, the world would be impossible to live in,
and happiness, too, would go by the board. And these, I
repeat, are the things that count, for me.

CALIGULA: So, I take it, you believe in some higher principle?

CHEREA: Certainly I believe that some actions are – shall I
say? – more praiseworthy than others.

CALIGULA: And *I* believe that all are on an equal footing.

CHEREA: I know it, Caius, and that's why I don't hate you.
I understand and, to a point, agree with you. But you're
pernicious, and you've got to go.

CALIGULA: True enough. But why risk your life by telling
me this?

CHEREA: Because others will take my place, and because I
don't like lying.

[*A short silence.*]

CALIGULA: Cherea!

CHEREA: Yes, Caius?

CALIGULA: Do you think that two men of similar temperament and equal pride can, if only once in their lives, open
their hearts to each other?

CHEREA: That, I believe, is what we've just been doing.

CALIGULA: Yes, Cherea. But you thought I was incapable
of it.

CHEREA: I was wrong, Caius. I admit it, and I thank you.
Now I await your sentence.

CALIGULA: My sentence? Ah, I see. [*Producing the tablet from under his cloak*] You know what this is, Cherea?

CHEREA: I knew you had it.

CALIGULA [*passionately*]: You knew I had it! So your frankness was all a piece of play-acting. The two friends did *not* open their hearts to each other. Well, well! It's no great matter. Now we can stop playing at sincerity, and resume life on the old footing. But first I'll ask you to make just one more effort; to bear with my caprices and my tactlessness a little longer. Listen well, Cherea. This tablet is the one and only piece of evidence against you.

CHEREA: Caius, I'd rather go. I'm sick and tired of all these antics. Only too well I know them, and I've had enough. Let me go, please.

CALIGULA [*in the same tense, passionate voice*]: No, stay. This tablet is the only evidence. Is that clear?

CHEREA: Evidence? I never knew you needed evidence to send a man to his death.

CALIGULA: That's true. Still, for once I wish to contradict myself. Nobody can object to that. It's so pleasant to contradict oneself occasionally; so restful. And I need rest, Cherea.

CHEREA: I don't follow ... and, frankly, I've no taste for these subtleties.

CALIGULA: I know, Cherea, I know. You're not like me; you're an ordinary man, sound in mind and body. And naturally you've no desire for the extraordinary. [*With a burst of laughter*] You want to live and to be happy. That's all!

CHEREA: I think, Caius, we'd better leave it at that.... Can I go?

CALIGULA: Not yet. A little patience, if you don't mind – I shall not keep you long. You see this thing – this piece of evidence? I choose to assume that I can't sentence you to death without it. That's my idea . . . and my repose. Well! See what becomes of evidence in an emperor's hands. [*He holds the tablet to a torch.*]

[CHEREA *approaches. The torch is between them. The tablet begins to melt.*]

CALIGULA: You see, conspirator! The tablet's melting, and as it melts a look of innocence is dawning on your face. What a handsome forehead you have, Cherea! And how rare, how beautiful a sight is an innocent man! Admire my power. Even the gods cannot restore innocence without first punishing the culprit. But your emperor needs only a torch-flame to absolve you and give you a new lease of hope. So carry on, Cherea; follow out the noble precepts we've been hearing, wherever they may take you. Meanwhile your emperor awaits his repose. It's his way of living and being happy.

[CHEREA *stares, dumbfounded, at Caligula. He makes a vague gesture, seems to understand, opens his mouth to speak – and walks abruptly away. Smiling, holding the tablet to the flame,* CALIGULA *follows the receding figure with his gaze.*]

CURTAIN

ACT FOUR

The stage is in semi-darkness. CHEREA *and* SCIPIO *enter.*
CHEREA *crosses right, then comes back left to Scipio.*

SCIPIO [*sulkily*]: What do you want of me?

CHEREA: There's no time to lose. And we must know our minds, we must be resolute.

SCIPIO: Who says I'm not resolute?

CHEREA: You didn't attend our meeting yesterday.

SCIPIO [*looking away*]: That's so, Cherea.

CHEREA: Scipio, I am older than you, and I'm not in the habit of asking others' help. But, I won't deny it, I need you now. This murder needs honourable men to sponsor it. Amongst all these wounded vanities and sordid fears, our motives only, yours and mine, are disinterested. Of course I know that, if you leave us, we can count on your silence. But that is not the point. What I want is – for you to stay with us.

SCIPIO: I understand. But I can't, oh no, I *cannot* do as you wish.

CHEREA: So you are with him?

SCIPIO: No. But I cannot be against him. [*Pauses; then in a muffled voice*] Even if I killed him, my heart would still be with him.

CHEREA: And yet – he killed your father!

SCIPIO: Yes – and that's how it all began. But that, too, is how it ends.

CHEREA: He denies what you believe in. He tramples on all that you hold sacred.

SCIPIO: I know, Cherea. And yet something inside me

86

is akin to him. The same fire burns in both our hearts.

CHEREA: There are times when a man must make his choice. Personally I have silenced in my heart all that might be akin to him.

SCIPIO: But — *I* — I cannot make a choice. I have my own sorrow, but I suffer with him, too; I share his pain. I understand all — that is my trouble.

CHEREA: So that's it. You have chosen to take his side.

SCIPIO [*passionately*]: No, Cherea. I beg you, don't think that. I can never, never again take anybody's side.

CHEREA [*affectionately; approaching Scipio*]: Do you know, I hate him even more for having made of you — what he has made.

SCIPIO: Yes, he has taught me to expect everything of life.

CHEREA: No, he has taught you despair. And to have instilled despair into a young heart is fouler than the foulest of the crimes he has committed up to now. I assure you, *that* alone would justify me in killing him out of hand. [*He goes towards the door.*]

[HELICON *enters.*]

HELICON: I've been hunting for you high and low, Cherea. Caligula's giving a little party here, for his personal friends only. Naturally he expects you to attend it. [*To Scipio*] You, my boy, aren't wanted. Off you go!

SCIPIO [*looking back at Cherea, as he goes out*]: Cherea.

CHEREA [*gently*]: Yes, Scipio?

SCIPIO: Try to understand.

CHEREA [*in the same gentle tone*]: No, Scipio.

[SCIPIO *and* HELICON *go out. A clash of arms in the wings. Two soldiers enter right, escorting the* OLD PATRICIAN *and the* FIRST PATRICIAN, *who show signs of alarm.*]

FIRST PATRICIAN [*to one of the soldiers, in a tone which he*

vainly tries to steady]: But . . . but what *can* he want with us
at this hour of the night?

SOLDIER: Sit there. [*Points to the chairs on the right.*]

FIRST PATRICIAN: If it's only to have us killed – like so
many others – why all these preliminaries?

SOLDIER: Sit down, you old mule.

THE OLD PATRICIAN: Better do as he says. It's clear he
doesn't know anything.

SOLDIER: Yes, darling, quite clear. [*Goes out.*]

FIRST PATRICIAN: We should have acted sooner; I always
said so. Now we're for the torture chamber.

[*The* SOLDIER *comes back with* CHEREA, *then goes out.*]

CHEREA [*seating himself. He shows no sign of apprehension*]: Any
idea what's happening?

FIRST PATRICIAN AND THE OLD PATRICIAN [*speaking
together*]: He's found out about the conspiracy.

CHEREA: Yes? And then?

THE OLD PATRICIAN [*shuddering*]: The torture chamber
for us all.

CHEREA [*still unperturbed*]: I remember that Caligula once
gave 81,000 sesterces to a slave who, though he was tortured nearly to death, wouldn't confess to a theft he had
committed.

FIRST PATRICIAN: A lot of consolation that is – for
us!

CHEREA: Anyhow it shows that he appreciates courage.
What's more, when he was asked, 'Why 81,000 sesterces?'
he answered, 'And why 80,000 or 79,000?' [*To the Old
Patrician*] Would you very much mind not chattering
with your teeth? It's a noise I particularly dislike.

THE OLD PATRICIAN: I'm sorry, but –

FIRST PATRICIAN: Enough trifling! Our lives are at stake.

CHEREA [*coolly*]: Do you know Caligula's favourite remark?

THE OLD PATRICIAN [*on the verge of tears*]: Yes. He says to the executioner, 'Kill him slowly, so that he feels what dying's like!'

CHEREA: No, there's a better one. After an execution he yawns, and says quite seriously: 'What I admire most is my imperturbability.'

FIRST PATRICIAN: Do you hear . . . ?

[*A clanking of weapons is heard off-stage.*]

CHEREA: That remark betrays a weakness in his make-up.

THE OLD PATRICIAN: Would you be kind enough to stop philosophizing? It's something I particularly dislike.

[*A* SLAVE *enters and deposits a sheaf of knives on a seat.*]

CHEREA [*who has not noticed him*]: Philosophizing? I should hardly call it that. Still, there's no denying it's remarkable, the effect this man has on all with whom he comes in contact. He forces one to think. There's nothing like insecurity for stimulating the brain. That, of course, is why he's so much hated.

THE OLD PATRICIAN [*pointing a trembling finger*]: Look!

CHEREA [*noticing the knives, in a slightly altered tone*]: Perhaps you were right.

FIRST PATRICIAN: Yes, waiting was a mistake. We should have acted at once.

CHEREA: I agree. Wisdom's come too late.

THE OLD PATRICIAN: But it's . . . it's crazy. I don't want to die. [*He rises and begins to edge away. Two* SOLDIERS *appear and, after slapping his face, force him back on to his seat.*]

[*The* FIRST PATRICIAN *squirms in his chair.* CHEREA *utters some inaudible words. Suddenly a queer music begins behind the curtain at the back of the stage: a thrumming and tinkling of zithers and cymbals. The* PATRICIANS *gaze at each other in silence. Outlined on the illuminated curtain, in shadow-play,* CALIGULA *appears, makes some grotesque dance movements, and retreats from view. He is wearing ballet-dancer's skirts and his head is garlanded with flowers. A moment later a* SOLDIER *announces gravely,* 'Gentlemen, the performance is over.' *Meanwhile* CAESONIA *has entered soundlessly behind the watching Patricians. She speaks in an ordinary voice, but none the less they give a start on hearing it.*]

CAESONIA: Caligula has instructed me to tell you that, whereas in the past he always summoned you for affairs of state, today he invited you to share with him an artistic emotion. [*A short pause. Then she continues in the same tone*] He added, I may say, that anyone who has not shared in it will be beheaded. [*They keep silent.*] I apologize for insisting; but I must ask you if you found that dance beautiful.

FIRST PATRICIAN [*after a brief hesitation*]: Yes, Caesonia. It was beautiful.

THE OLD PATRICIAN [*effusively*]: Lovely! Lovely!

CAESONIA: And you, Cherea?

CHEREA [*icily*]: It was . . . very high art.

CAESONIA: Good. Now I can describe your artistic emotions to Caligula. [*Goes out.*]

CHEREA: And now we must act quickly. You two stay here. Before the night is out there'll be a hundred of us. [*He goes out.*]

THE OLD PATRICIAN: No, no. *You* stay. Let me go, instead. [*Sniffs the air.*] It smells of death here.

FIRST PATRICIAN: And of lies. [*Sadly*] I said that dance was beautiful!

THE OLD PATRICIAN [*conciliatingly*]: And so it was, in a way. Most original.

[*Some* PATRICIANS *and* KNIGHTS *enter hurriedly.*]

SECOND PATRICIAN: What's on foot? Do you know anything? The Emperor's summoned us here.

THE OLD PATRICIAN [*absentmindedly*]: For a dance, maybe.

SECOND PATRICIAN: What dance?

THE OLD PATRICIAN: Well, I mean ... er ... the artistic emotion.

THIRD PATRICIAN: I've been told Caligula's very ill.

FIRST PATRICIAN: He's a sick man, yes ...

THIRD PATRICIAN: What's he suffering from? [*In a joyful tone*] By God, is he going to die?

FIRST PATRICIAN: I doubt it. His disease is fatal – to others only.

THE OLD PATRICIAN: That's one way of putting it.

SECOND PATRICIAN: Quite so. But hasn't he some other disease less serious, and more to our advantage?

FIRST PATRICIAN: No. That malady of his excludes all others. [*He goes out.*]

[CAESONIA *enters. A short silence.*]

CAESONIA [*in a casual tone*]: If you want to know, Caligula has stomach trouble. Just now he vomited blood.

[*The* PATRICIANS *crowd round her.*]

SECOND PATRICIAN: O mighty gods, I vow, if he recovers, to pay the Treasury two hundred thousand sesterces as a token of my joy.

THIRD PATRICIAN [*with exaggerated eagerness*]: O Jupiter, take my life in place of his!

[CALIGULA *has entered, and is listening.*]

CALIGULA [*going up to the Second Patrician*]: I accept your offer, Lucius. And I thank you. My Treasurer will call on you tomorrow. [*Goes to the Third Patrician and embraces him.*] You can't imagine how touched I am. [*A short silence. Then, tenderly*] So you love me, Cassius, as much as that?

THIRD PATRICIAN [*emotionally*]: Oh Caesar, there's nothing, nothing I wouldn't sacrifice for your sake.

CALIGULA [*embracing him again*]: Ah Cassius, this is really too much; I don't deserve all this love.

[CASSIUS *makes a protesting gesture.*]

CALIGULA: No, no, really I don't! I'm not worthy of it.

[*He beckons to two soldiers.*] Take him away. [*Gently, to Cassius*] Go, dear friend, and remember that Caligula has lost his heart to you.

THIRD PATRICIAN [*vaguely uneasy*]: But – where are they taking me?

CALIGULA: Why, to your death, of course. Your generous offer was accepted, and I feel better already. Even that nasty taste of blood in my mouth has gone. You've cured me, Cassius. It's been miraculous, and how proud you must feel of having worked the miracle of laying your life down for your friend – especially when that friend's none other than Caligula! So now you see me quite myself again, and ready for a festive night.

THIRD PATRICIAN [*shrieking, as he is dragged away*]: No! No! I don't want to die. You can't be serious!

CALIGULA [*in a thoughtful voice, between the shrieks*]: Soon the sea-roads will be golden with mimosas. The women will wear their lightest dresses. And the sky! Ah Cassius, what a blaze of clean, swift sunshine! The smiles of life. [*Cassius is near the door.* CALIGULA *gives him a gentle push. Suddenly his tone grows serious.*] Life, my friend, is something to be cherished. Had you cherished it enough, you wouldn't have gambled it away so rashly. [*Cassius is led off.* CALIGULA *returns to the table.*] The loser must pay. There's no alternative. [*A short silence.*] Come, Caesonia. [*He turns to the others.*] By the bye, an idea has just waylaid me, and it's such an apt one that I want to share it with you. Until now my reign has been too happy. There's been no world-wide plague, no religious persecution, not even a rebellion – nothing in fact to make us memorable. And that, I'd have you know, is why I try to remedy the stinginess of Fate. I mean – I don't know if you've followed me – that, well [*he gives a little laugh*], it's I who replace the epidemics that we've missed. [*In a different tone*] That's enough. I see Cherea's coming. Your turn, Caesonia. [*Goes out.*]

[CHEREA *and the* FIRST PATRICIAN *enter.* CAESONIA *hurries towards Cherea.*]

CAESONIA: Caligula is dead. [*She turns her head, as if to hide her tears; her eyes are fixed on the others, who keep silence. Everyone looks horrified, but for different reasons.*]

FIRST PATRICIAN: You . . . you're *sure* this dreadful thing has happened? It seems incredible. Only a short while ago he was dancing.

CAESONIA: Quite so – and the effort was too much for him. [CHEREA *moves hastily from one man to the other. No one speaks.*]

CAESONIA: You've nothing to say, Cherea?

CHEREA [*in a low voice*]: It's a great misfortune for us all, Caesonia.

[CALIGULA *bursts in violently and goes up to Cherea.*]

CALIGULA: Well played, Cherea. [*He spins round and stares at the others. Petulantly*] Too bad! It didn't come off. [*To Caesonia*] Don't forget what I told you. [*Goes out.*]

[CAESONIA *stares after him without speaking.*]

THE OLD PATRICIAN [*hoping against hope*]: Is he ill, Caesonia?

CAESONIA [*with a hostile look*]: No, my pet. But what you don't know is that the man never has more than two hours' sleep and spends the best part of the night roaming about the corridors in his Palace. Another thing you don't know – and you've never given a thought to – is what may pass in this man's mind in those deadly hours between midnight and sunrise. Is he ill? No, not ill – unless you invent a name and medicine for the black ulcers that fester in his soul.

CHEREA [*seemingly affected by her words*]: You're right, Caesonia. We all know that Caius . . .

CAESONIA [*breaking in, emotionally*]: Yes, you know it – in your fashion. But, like all those who have none, you can't abide anyone who has too much soul. Healthy people loathe invalids. Happy people hate the sad. Too much soul! That's what bites you, isn't it? You prefer to label it a disease; that way all the dolts are justified and pleased. [*In a changed tone*] Tell me, Cherea. Has love ever meant anything to you?

CHEREA [*himself again*]: I'm afraid we're too old now, Caesonia, to learn the art of love-making. And anyhow it's highly doubtful if Caligula will give us time to do so.

CAESONIA [*who has recovered her composure*]: True enough. [*She sits down.*] Oh, I was forgetting . . . Caligula asked me to impart some news to you. You know, perhaps, that it's a red-letter day today, consecrated to art.

THE OLD PATRICIAN: According to the calendar?

CAESONIA: No, according to Caligula. He's convoked some poets. He will ask them to improvise a poem on a set theme. And he particularly wants those of you who are poets to take part in the competition. He specially mentioned young Scipio and Metellus.

METELLUS: But we're not ready.

CAESONIA [*in a level tone, as if she has not heard him*]: Needless to say there are prizes. There will be penalties, too. [*Looks of consternation.*] Between ourselves, the penalties won't be so very terrible.

[CALIGULA *enters, looking gloomier than ever.*]

CALIGULA: All ready?

CAESONIA: Yes. [*To a soldier*] Bring in the poets.

[*Enter, two by two, a dozen* POETS, *keeping step; they line up on the right of the stage.*]

CALIGULA: And the others?

CAESONIA: Metellus! Scipio!

[*They cross the stage and take their stand beside the poets.*

CALIGULA *seats himself, back stage on the left, with Caesonia and the Patricians. A short silence.*]

CALIGULA: Subject: Death. Time-limit: one minute.

[*The* POETS *scribble feverishly on their tablets.*]

THE OLD PATRICIAN: Who will compose the jury?

CALIGULA: I. Isn't that enough?

THE OLD PATRICIAN: Oh yes, indeed. Quite enough.

CHEREA: Won't you take part in the competition, Caius?

CALIGULA: Unnecessary. I made my poem on that theme long ago.

THE OLD PATRICIAN [*eagerly*]: Where can one get a copy of it?

CALIGULA: No need to get a copy. I recite it every day, after my fashion.

[CAESONIA *eyes him nervously.* CALIGULA *rounds on her almost savagely.*]

CALIGULA: Is there anything in my appearance that displeases you?

CAESONIA [*gently*]: I'm sorry . . .

CALIGULA: No meekness, please. For heaven's sake, no meekness. You're exasperating enough as it is, but if you start being humble . . .

[CAESONIA *slowly moves away.* CALIGULA *turns to Cherea.*]

CALIGULA: I continue. It's the only poem I have made. And it's proof that I'm the only true artist Rome has known – the only one, believe me – to match his inspiration with his deeds.

CHEREA: That's only a matter of having the power.

CALIGULA: Quite true. Other artists create to compensate for their lack of power. I don't need to make a work of art; I *live* it. [*Roughly*] Well, poets, are you ready?

METELLUS: I think so.

THE OTHERS: Yes.

CALIGULA: Good. Now listen carefully. You are to fall out

95

of line and come forward one by one. I'll whistle. Number One will start reading his poem. When I whistle, he must stop, and the next begin. And so on. The winner, naturally, will be the one whose poem hasn't been cut short by the whistle. Get ready. [*Turning to Cherea, he whispers*] You see, organization's needed for everything, even for art. [*Blows his whistle.*]

FIRST POET: Death, when beyond thy darkling shore . . .
[*A blast of the whistle. The* POET *steps briskly to the left.* THE OTHERS *will follow the same procedure. These movements should be made with mechanical precision.*]

SECOND POET: In their dim cave, the Fatal Sisters Three . . .
[*Whistle.*]

THIRD POET: Come to me death, beloved . . .
[*A shrill blast of the whistle. The* FOURTH POET *steps forward and strikes a dramatic posture. The whistle goes before he has opened his mouth.*]

FIFTH POET: When I was in my happy infancy . . .

CALIGULA [*yelling*]: Stop that! What earthly connexion has a blockhead's happy infancy with the theme I set? The connexion! Tell me the connexion!

FIFTH POET: But, Caius, I've only just begun, and . . .
[*Shrill blast.*]

SIXTH POET [*in a high-pitched voice*]: Ruthless, he goes his hidden ways . . .
[*Whistle.* SCIPIO *comes forward without a tablet.*]

CALIGULA: You haven't a tablet?

SCIPIO: I do not need one.

CALIGULA: Well, let's hear you. [*He chews at his whistle.*]

SCIPIO [*standing very near Caligula, he recites listlessly, without looking at him*]:
Pursuit of happiness that purifies the heart,
Skies rippling with light,
O wild, sweet, festal joys, frenzy without hope!

CALIGULA [*gently*]: Stop, please. The others needn't compete. [*To Scipio*] You're very young to understand so well the lessons we can learn from Death.

SCIPIO [*gazing straight at Caligula*]: I was very young to lose my father.

CALIGULA [*turning hastily*]: Fall in, the rest of you. No, really a sham poet is too dreadful an infliction. Until now I'd thought of enrolling you as my allies; I sometimes pictured a gallant band of poets defending me in the last ditch. Another illusion gone! I shall have to relegate you to my enemies. So now the poets are against me – and that looks much like the end of all. March out in good order. As you go past you are to lick your tablets so as to efface the atrocities you scrawled on them. Attention! Forward! [*He blows his whistle in short rhythmic jerks.*]

[*Keeping step, the* POETS *file out by the right, tonguing their immortal tablets.*]

CALIGULA [*adds in a lower tone*]: Now leave me, everyone.

[*In the doorway, as they are going out,* CHEREA *touches the First Patrician's shoulder, and speaks in his ear.*]

CHEREA: Now's our opportunity.

[SCIPIO, *who has overheard, halts on the threshold and walks back to Caligula.*]

CALIGULA [*acidly*]: Can't you leave me in peace – as your father's doing?

SCIPIO: No, Caius, all that serves no purpose now. For now I know, I *know* that you have made your choice.

CALIGULA: Won't you leave me in peace!

SCIPIO: Yes, you shall have your wish; I am going to leave you, for I think I've come to understand you. There's no way out left to us, neither to you nor to me – who am like you in so many ways. I shall go away, far away, and try to discover the meaning of it all. [*He gazes at Caligula for some moments. Then, with a rush of emotion*] Good-bye, dear

Caius. When all is ended, remember that I loved you. [*He turns away.*]

    [CALIGULA *makes a vague gesture. Then, almost savagely, he pulls himself together and takes some steps towards Caesonia.*]

SCIPIO: You have chosen, Caligula. [*Goes out.*]

CAESONIA: What did he say?

CALIGULA: Nothing you'd understand . . . But come beside me.

    [*A short silence.*]

CAESONIA [*nestling against him*]: What are you thinking about?

CALIGULA: I was wondering why I'd kept you with me so long.

CAESONIA: Why, because you're fond of me.

CALIGULA: No. But I think I'd understand – if I had you killed.

CAESONIA: Yes, that would be a solution. Do so, then. . . . But why, oh why can't you relax, if only for a moment, and live freely, without constraint?

CALIGULA: I have been doing that for several years; in fact I've made a practice of it.

CAESONIA: I don't mean that sort of freedom. I mean – Oh, don't you realize what it can be to live and love quite simply, naturally, in . . . in purity of heart?

CALIGULA: This purity of heart you talk of – every man acquires it, in his own way. Mine has been to follow the essential to the end. . . . Still all that needn't prevent me from putting you to death. [*Laughs.*] It would round off my career so well, the perfect climax. [*He rises and swings the mirror round towards himself. Then he walks in a circle, letting his arms hang limp, almost without gestures; there is something feral in his gait, as he continues speaking.*] How strange! When I don't kill, I feel alone. The living don't suffice to people my world and dispel my boredom. I have an impression of an enormous void when you and the others are here, and my eyes see nothing but empty air. No, I'm at ease only in the company of my dead. [*He takes his stand facing the audience, leaning a little forward. He has forgotten Caesonia's presence.*] Only the dead are real. They are of my kind. I see them waiting for me, straining towards me. And I have long talks with this man or that, who screamed to me for mercy and whose tongue I had cut out.

CAESONIA: Come. Lie down beside me. Put your head on my knees.

[CALIGULA *does so.*]

CAESONIA: That's better, isn't it? Now rest. How quiet it is here!

CALIGULA: Quiet? You exaggerate, my dear. Listen! [*Distant metallic tinklings, as of swords or armour.*] Do you hear those thousands of small sounds all around us, hatred stalking its prey? [*Murmuring voices, footsteps.*]

CAESONIA: Nobody would dare . . .

CALIGULA: Yes, stupidity.

CAESONIA: Stupidity doesn't kill. It makes men slow to act.

CALIGULA: It can be murderous, Caesonia. A fool stops at nothing when he thinks his dignity offended. No, it's not the men whose sons or fathers I have killed who'll murder me. *They*, anyhow, have understood. They're with me, they have the same taste in their mouths. But the others – those I made a laughing-stock of – I've no defence against their wounded vanity.

CAESONIA [*passionately*]: We will defend you. There are many of us left who love you.

CALIGULA: Fewer every day. It's not surprising. I've done all that was needed to that end. And then – let's be fair – it's not only stupidity that's against me. There's the courage and the simple faith of men who ask to be happy.

CAESONIA [*in the same tone*]: No, *they* will not kill you. Or, if they tried, fire would come down from heaven and blast them, before they laid a hand on you.

CALIGULA: From heaven! There is no heaven, my poor dear woman! [*He sits down.*] But why this sudden access of devotion? It wasn't catered for in our agreement, if I remember rightly.

CAESONIA [*who has risen from the couch and is pacing the room*]: Don't you understand? Hasn't it been enough to see you killing others, without my also knowing you'll be killed as well? Isn't it enough to feel you hard and cruel, seething with bitterness, when I hold you in my arms; to breathe a reek of murder when you lie on me? Day after day I see all that's human in you dying out, little by little. [*She turns towards him.*] Oh I know. I know I'm getting old, my beauty's on the wane. But it's you only I'm concerned for now; so much so that I've ceased troubling whether you love me. I only want you to get well, quite well again. You're still a boy, really; you've a whole life ahead of you. And, tell me, what greater thing can you want than a whole life?

CALIGULA [*rising, looks at her fixedly*]: You've been with me a long time now, a very long time.

CAESONIA: Yes . . . But you'll keep me, won't you?

CALIGULA: I don't know. I only know that, if you're with me still, it's because of all those nights we've had together, nights of fierce, joyless pleasure; it's because you alone know me as I am. [*He takes her in his arms, bending her head back a little with his right hand.*] I'm twenty-nine. Not a great age really. But today when none the less my life seems so long, so crowded with scraps and shreds of my past selves, so complete in fact, you remain the last witness. And I can't avoid a sort of shameful tenderness for the old woman that you soon will be.

CAESONIA: Tell me that you mean to keep me with you.

CALIGULA: I don't know. All I know – and it's the most terrible thing of all – is that this shameful tenderness is the one sincere emotion that my life has given up to now.

[CAESONIA *frees herself from his arms.* CALIGULA *follows her. She presses her back to his chest and he puts his arms round her.*]

CALIGULA: Wouldn't it be better that the last witness should disappear?

CAESONIA: That has no importance. All I know is: I'm happy. What you've just said has made me very happy. But why can't I share my happiness with you?

CALIGULA: Who says I'm unhappy?

CAESONIA: Happiness is kind. It doesn't thrive on bloodshed.

CALIGULA: Then there must be two kinds of happiness, and I've chosen the murderous kind. For I *am* happy. There was a time when I thought I'd reached the extremity of pain. But, no, one can go farther yet. Beyond the frontier of pain lies a splendid, sterile happiness. Look at me. [*She turns towards him.*] It makes me laugh, Caesonia, when I think how for years and years all Rome carefully avoided uttering Drusilla's name. Well, all Rome was mistaken. Love isn't enough for me; I realized it then. And I realize it again today, when I look at you. To love someone means that one's willing to grow old beside that person. That sort of love is right outside my range. Drusilla old would have been far worse than Drusilla dead. Most people imagine that a man suffers because out of the blue Death snatches away the woman he loves. But his real suffering is less futile; it comes from the discovery that grief, too, cannot last. Even grief is vanity.

You see, I had no excuses, not the shadow of a real love, neither bitterness nor profound regret. Nothing to plead

in my defence! But today – you see me still freer than I
have been for years; freed as I am from memories and
illusion. [*He laughs bitterly.*] I know now that nothing,
nothing lasts. Think what that knowledge means! There
have been just two or three of us in history who really
achieved this freedom, this crazy happiness. Well, Caesonia, you have seen out a most unusual drama. It's time
the curtain fell, for you. [*He stands behind her, linking his
forearm round Caesonia's neck.*]

CAESONIA [*terrified*]: No, it's impossible! How can you call
it happiness, this terrifying freedom?

CALIGULA [*gradually tightening his grip on Caesonia's throat*]:
Happiness it is, Caesonia; I know what I'm saying. But for
this freedom I'd have been a contented man. Thanks to
it, I have won the godlike enlightenment of the solitary.
[*His exaltation grows as little by little he strangles Caesonia, who
puts up no resistance, but holds her hands half-opened, like a
suppliant's, before her. Bending his head, he goes on speaking,
into her ear.*] I live, I kill, I exercise the rapturous power of
a destroyer, compared with which the power of a creator
is merest child's-play. And this, *this* is happiness; this and
nothing else – this intolerable release, devastating scorn,
blood, hatred all around me; the glorious isolation of a
man who all his life long nurses and gloats over the joy
ineffable of the unpunished murderer; the ruthless logic
that crushes out human lives [*he laughs*], that's crushing
yours out, Caesonia, so as to perfect at last the utter
loneliness that is my heart's desire.

CAESONIA [*struggling feebly*]: Oh, Caius . . .

CALIGULA [*more and more excitedly*]: No. No sentiment. I
must have done with it, for the time is short. My time is
very short, dear Caesonia. [CAESONIA *is gasping, dying.*
CALIGULA *drags her to the bed and lets her fall on it. He stares
wildly at her; his voice grows harsh and grating.*] You, too,

were guilty. But killing is not the solution. [*He spins round and gazes crazily at the mirror.*] Caligula! You, too; you, too, are guilty. Then what of it – a little more, a little less? Yet who can condemn me in this world where there is no judge, where nobody is innocent? [*He brings his eyes close to his reflected face. He sounds genuinely distressed.*] You see, my poor friend. Helicon has failed you. I shan't have the moon. Never, never, never! But how bitter it is to know all, and to have to go through to the consummation! Listen! That was a sound of weapons. Innocence arming for the fray – and innocence will triumph. Why am I not in their place, amongst them? And I'm afraid. That's cruellest of all, after despising others, to find oneself as cowardly as they. Still, no matter. Fear, too, has an end. Soon I shall attain that emptiness beyond all understanding, in which the heart has rest. [*He steps back a few paces, then returns to the mirror. He seems calmer. When he speaks again his voice is steadier, less shrill.*]

Yet, really, it's quite simple. If I'd had the moon, if love were enough, all might have been different. But where could I quench this thirst? What human heart, what god, would have for me the depth of a great lake? [*Kneeling, weeping*] There's nothing in this world, or in the other, made to my stature. And yet I know, and you too know [*still weeping, he stretches out his arms towards the mirror*] that all I need is for the impossible to be. The impossible! I've searched for it at the confines of the world, in the secret places of my heart. I've stretched out my hands; [*his voice rises to a scream*] see, I stretch out my hands, but it's always you I find, you only, confronting me, and I've come to hate you. I have chosen a wrong path, a path that leads to nothing. My freedom isn't the right one . . . Nothing, nothing yet. Oh, how oppressive is this darkness! Helicon has not come; we shall be for ever guilty.

The air tonight is heavy as the sum of human sorrows. [*A clash of arms and whisperings are heard in the wings.* CALIGULA *rises, picks up a stool and returns to the mirror, breathing heavily. He contemplates himself, makes a slight leap forward and, watching the symmetrical movement of his reflected self, hurls the stool at it, screaming*] To history, Caligula! Go down to history! [*The mirror breaks and at the same moment armed conspirators rush in.* CALIGULA *swings round to face them, with a mad laugh.* SCIPIO *and* CHEREA, *who are in front, fling themselves at him and stab his face with their daggers.* CALIGULA's *laughter turns to gasps. All strike him, hurriedly, confusedly. In a last gasp, laughing and choking,* CALIGULA *shrieks*] I'm still alive!

CURTAIN

CROSS PURPOSE

Characters

THE OLD MANSERVANT, *no determinate age*
MARTHA, *the sister, aged thirty*
THE MOTHER, *aged sixty*
JAN, *the son, aged thirty-eight*
MARIA, *his wife, aged thirty*

ACT ONE

Noon. The inn-parlour; a clean, brightly lit room. Everything is very spick and span.

THE MOTHER: He'll come back.

MARTHA: Did he tell you so?

THE MOTHER: Yes.

MARTHA: Alone?

THE MOTHER: That I can't say.

MARTHA: He doesn't look like a poor man.

THE MOTHER: No, and he never asked what our charges were.

MARTHA: A good sign, that. But usually rich men don't travel alone. Really it's *that* makes things so difficult. You may have to wait ages when you're looking out for a man who is not only rich but quite alone.

THE MOTHER: Yes, we don't get so many opportunities.

MARTHA: It means, of course, that we've had many slack times these last few years. This place is often empty. Poor folks who stop here never stay long, and it's mighty seldom rich ones come.

THE MOTHER: Don't grumble about that, Martha. Rich people give a lot of extra work.

MARTHA [*looking hard at her*]: But they pay well. [*A short silence.*] Tell me, mother; what's come over you? For some time I've noticed that you weren't quite . . . quite your usual self.

THE MOTHER: I'm tired, my dear, that's all. What I need is a long rest.

MARTHA: Listen, mother. I can take over the household

work you're doing now. Then you'll have your days free.

THE MOTHER: That wasn't quite the sort of rest I meant. Oh, I suppose it's just an old woman's fancy. All I'm longing for is peace – to be able to relax a little. [*She gives a little laugh.*] I know it sounds silly, Martha, but some evenings I feel almost like taking to religion.

MARTHA: You're not so very old, mother; you haven't come to that yet. And, anyhow, I should say *you* could do better.

THE MOTHER: Of course I was only joking, my dear. All the same . . . at the end of one's life, it's not a bad idea to take things easy. One can't be always on the stretch, as you are, Martha. And it isn't natural for a woman of your age, either. I know plenty of girls who were born the same year as you, and they think only of pleasure and excitements.

MARTHA: Their pleasures and excitements are nothing compared to ours, don't you agree, mother?

THE MOTHER: I'd rather you didn't speak of that.

MARTHA [*thoughtfully*]: Really one would think that nowadays some words burn your tongue.

THE MOTHER: What can it matter to you – provided I don't shrink from acts? But that has no great importance. What I really meant was that I'd like to see you smile now and again.

MARTHA: I do smile sometimes, I assure you.

THE MOTHER: Really? I've never seen you.

MARTHA: That's because I smile when I'm by myself, in my bedroom.

THE MOTHER [*looking closely at her*]: What a hard face you have, Martha!

MARTHA [*coming closer; calmly*]: Ah, so you don't approve of my face?

THE MOTHER [*after a short silence, still looking at her*]: I wonder . . . Yes, I think I do.

MARTHA [*emotionally*]: Oh, mother, can't you understand? Once we have enough money in hand, and I can escape from this shut-in valley; once we can say good-bye to this inn and this dreary town where it's always raining; once we've forgotten this land of shadows – ah then, when my dream has come true, and we're living beside the sea, *then* you will see me smile. Unhappily one needs a great deal of money to be able to live in freedom by the sea. That is why we mustn't be afraid of words; that is why we must take trouble over this man who's come to stay here. If he is rich enough, perhaps my freedom will begin with him.

THE MOTHER: If he's rich enough, and if he's by himself.

MARTHA: That's so. He has to be by himself as well. Did he talk much to you, mother?

THE MOTHER: No, he said very little.

MARTHA: When he asked for his room, did you notice how he looked?

THE MOTHER: No. My sight's none too good, as you know, and I didn't really look at his face. I've learnt from experience that it's better not to look at them too closely. It's easier to kill what one doesn't know. [*A short silence.*] There! That should please you. You can't say now that I'm afraid of words.

MARTHA: Yes, and I prefer it so. I've no use for hints and evasions. Crime is crime, and one should know what one is about. And, from what you've just said, it looks as if you had it in mind when you were talking to that traveller.

THE MOTHER: No, I wouldn't say I had it in mind – it was more from force of habit.

MARTHA: Habit? But you said yourself that these opportunities seldom come our way.

THE MOTHER: Certainly. But habit begins with the second crime. With the first nothing starts, but something ends. Then, too, while we have had few opportunities, they have been spread out over many years, and memory helps to build up habits. Yes, it was force of habit that made me keep my eyes off that man when I was talking to him and, all the same, convinced me he had the look of a victim.

MARTHA: Mother, we must kill him.

THE MOTHER [*in a low tone*]: Eh, yes, I suppose we'll have to.

MARTHA: You said that in a curious way.

THE MOTHER: I'm tired, that's a fact. Anyhow, I'd like this one to be the last. It's terribly tiring to kill. And, though really I care little where I die – beside the sea or here, far inland – I do hope we will get away together, the moment it's over.

MARTHA: Indeed we shall – and what a glorious moment that will be! So, cheer up, mother, there won't be much to do. You know quite well there's no question of killing. He'll drink his tea, he'll go to sleep, and he'll be still alive when we carry him to the river. Some day, long after, he will be found jammed against the weir, along with others who didn't have his luck and threw themselves into the water with their eyes open. Do you remember last year when we were watching them repair the sluices, how you said that our ones suffered least, and life was crueller than we? So don't lose heart, you'll be having your rest quite soon and I'll be seeing what I've never seen.

THE MOTHER: Yes, Martha, I won't lose heart. And it was quite true, what you said about 'our ones'. I'm always glad to think they never suffered. Really, it's hardly a crime, only a sort of intervention, a flick of the finger given to unknown lives. And it's also quite true that, by the look of it, life is crueller than we. Perhaps that is why I can't manage to feel guilty. I can only just manage to feel tired.

[*The old* MANSERVANT *comes in. He seats himself behind the bar counter and remains there, neither moving nor speaking, until* JAN'S *entrance.*]

MARTHA: Which room shall we put him in?

THE MOTHER: Any room, provided it's on the first floor.

MARTHA: Yes, we had a lot of needless trouble last time, with the two flights of stairs. [*For the first time she sits down.*] Tell me, mother, is it true that down on the coast the sand's so hot it scorches one's feet?

THE MOTHER: As you know, Martha, I've never been there. But I've been told the sun burns everything up.

MARTHA: I read in a book that it even burns out people's souls and gives them bodies that shine like gold but are quite hollow, there's nothing left inside.

THE MOTHER: Is that what makes you want to go there so much?

MARTHA: Yes, my soul's a burden to me, I've had enough of it. I'm eager to be in that country, where the sun kills every question. I don't belong here.

THE MOTHER: Unfortunately we have much to do beforehand. Of course, when it's over, I'll go there with you. But I am not like you; I shall not have the feeling of going to a place where I belong. After a certain age one knows there is no resting-place anywhere. Indeed there's something to be said for this ugly brick house we've made our home and stocked with memories; there are times when one can fall asleep in it. But, naturally it would mean something, too, if I could have sleep and forgetfulness together. [*She rises and walks towards the door.*] Well, Martha, get everything ready. [*Pauses.*] If it's really worth the effort.

[MARTHA *watches her go out. Then she, too, leaves by another door. For some moments only the old* MANSERVANT *is on the stage.* JAN *enters, stops, glances round the room and sees the old man sitting behind the counter.*]

JAN: Nobody about? [*The old man gazes at him, rises, crosses the stage and goes out.* MARIA *enters.* JAN *swings round on her.*] So you followed me!

MARIA: Forgive me – I couldn't help it. I may not stay long. Only please let me look at the place where I'm leaving you.

JAN: Somebody may come, and your being here will upset all my plans.

MARIA: Do please let us take the chance of someone's coming and my telling who you are. I know you don't want it, but – [*He turns away fretfully. A short silence.* MARIA *is examining the room.*] So this is the place?

JAN: Yes. That's the door I went out by, twenty years ago. My sister was a little girl. She was playing in that corner. My mother didn't come to kiss me. At the time I thought I didn't care.

MARIA: Jan, I can't believe they failed to recognize you just now. A mother's bound to recognize her son; it's the least she can do.

JAN: Perhaps. Still, twenty years' separation makes a difference. Life has been going on since I left. My mother's grown old, her sight is failing. I hardly recognized her myself.

MARIA [*impatiently*]: I know. You came in; you said 'Good day'; you sat down. This room wasn't like the one you remembered.

JAN: Yes, my memory had played me false. They received me without a word. I was given the glass of beer I asked for. I was looked at, but I wasn't *seen*. Everything was more difficult than I'd expected.

MARIA: You know quite well it needn't have been difficult; you had only to speak. On such occasions one says 'It's I' and then it's all plain sailing.

JAN: True. But I'd been imagining – all sorts of things. I'd expected a welcome like the prodigal son's. Actually I was given a glass of beer, against payment. It took the words out of my mouth, and I thought I'd better let things take their course.

MARIA: There was nothing to take its course. It was another of those ideas of yours – and a word would have been enough.

JAN: It wasn't an idea of mine, Maria; it was the force of things. What's more, I'm not in such a hurry. I have come here to bring them my money and, if I can, some happiness. When I learnt about my father's death I realized I had duties towards these two women and now, as a result, I'm doing what it's right for me to do. But evidently it is not so easy as people think, coming back to one's old home, and it takes time to change a stranger into a son.

MARIA: But why not let them know the truth at once? There are situations in which the normal way of acting is obviously the best. If one wants to be recognized, one starts by telling one's name; that's common sense. Otherwise, by pretending to be what one is not, one simply muddles everything. How could you expect not to be treated as a stranger in a house you entered under false colours? No, dear, there's something . . . something morbid about the way you're going on.

JAN: Oh come, Maria! It's not so serious as that. And, mind you, it suits my plan. I shall take this opportunity of seeing them from the outside. Then I'll have a better notion of what to do to make them happy. Afterwards, I'll find some way of getting them to recognize me. It's just a matter of choosing one's words.

MARIA: No, there's only one way, and it's to do what any ordinary mortal would do – to say, 'It's I,' and to let one's heart speak for itself.

JAN: The heart isn't so simple as all that.

MARIA: But it uses simple words. Surely there was no difficulty in saying, 'I'm your son. This is my wife. I've been living with her in a country we both love, a land of endless sunshine beside the sea. But something was lacking there, to complete my happiness, and now I feel I need you.'

JAN: Don't be unfair, Maria. I don't need them; but I realized they may need me, and a man doesn't live only for himself.

[*A short silence.* MARIA *looks away from him.*]

MARIA: Perhaps you are right. I'm sorry for what I said. But I have grown terribly suspicious since coming to this country where I've looked in vain for a single happy face. This Europe of yours is so sad. Since we've been here, I haven't once heard you laugh and, personally, I feel my nerves on edge all the time. Oh, why did you make me leave my country? Let's go away, Jan; we shall not find happiness here.

JAN: It's not happiness we've come for. We had happiness already.

MARIA [*passionately*]: Then why not have been satisfied with it?

JAN: Happiness isn't everything; there is duty, too. Mine was to come back to my mother and my own country. [MARIA *makes a protesting gesture and is about to answer.* JAN *checks her. Footsteps can be heard.*] Someone's coming. Do please go, Maria.

MARIA: No, I can't, I can't! Not yet, anyhow!

JAN [*as the footsteps approach*]: Go there. [*He gently pushes her towards the door at the back. The old* MANSERVANT *crosses*

the room without seeing Maria, and goes out by the other door.]
Now, leave at once. You see, luck is on my side.

MARIA: Do, please, let me stay. I promise not to speak a
word, only to stay beside you till you're recognized.

JAN: No. You'd give me away.

[*She turns away, then comes back and looks him in the eyes.*]

MARIA: Jan, we've been married for five years.

JAN: Yes, almost five years.

MARIA [*lowering her eyes*]: And this will be the first night we
spend apart. [*He says nothing and she looks up, gazing
earnestly at him.*] I've always loved everything about you,
even what I didn't understand, and I know that really
I wouldn't wish you to be other than you are. I'm not
a very troublesome wife, am I? But here I'm scared of
the empty bed you are sending me to, and I'm afraid,
too, of your forsaking me.

JAN: Surely you can trust my love better than that?

MARIA: I do trust it. But besides your love there are your
dreams – or your duties; they're the same thing. They take
you away from me so often, and at those moments it's
as if you were having a holiday from me. But I can't
take a holiday from you, and tonight [*she presses herself to
him, weeping*], this night without you – oh, I shall never
be able to bear it!

JAN [*clasping her tightly*]: But this is childishness, my dear!

MARIA: Of course it's childish. But ... but we were so
happy over there, and it's not my fault if the nights in
this country terrify me. I don't want to be alone tonight.

JAN: But do try to understand, my dear; I've a promise to
keep, and it's most important.

MARIA: What promise?

JAN: The one I made to myself on the day I understood
my mother needed me.

MARIA: You've another promise to keep.

JAN: Yes?

MARIA: The promise you made me on the day you joined your life to mine.

JAN: But surely I can keep both promises. What I'm asking of you is nothing very terrible. Nor is it a mere caprice. Only one evening and one night in which to take my bearings here, get to know better these two women who are dear to me, and to secure their happiness.

MARIA [*shaking her head*]: A separation always means a lot to people who love each other – with the right kind of love.

JAN: But, you romantic little creature, you know quite well I love you with the right kind of love.

MARIA: No, Jan. Men do not know how real love should be. Nothing they have can ever satisfy them. They're always dreaming dreams, building up new duties, going to new countries and new homes. Women are different; they know that life is short and one must make haste to love, to share the same bed, embrace the man one loves, and dread every separation. When one loves one has no time for dreams.

JAN: But, really, dear, aren't you exaggerating? It's such a simple thing I'm doing; trying to get in touch again with my mother, to help her and bring her happiness. As for my dreams and duties, you'll have to take them as they are. Without them I'd be a mere shadow of myself; indeed you'd love me less, were I without them.

MARIA [*turning her back to him abruptly*]: Oh, I know you can talk me round, you can always find good reasons for anything you want to do. But I refuse to listen, I stop my ears when you start speaking in that special voice I know so well. It's the voice of your loneliness, not of love.

JAN [*standing behind her*]: Don't let's talk of that now, Maria.

All I'm asking is to be left here by myself, so that I can clear up certain things in my mind. Really it's nothing so very terrible, or extraordinary, my sleeping under the same roof as my mother. God will see to the rest and He knows, too, that in acting thus I'm not forgetting you. Only – no one can be happy in exile or estrangement. One can't remain a stranger all one's life. It is quite true that a man needs happiness, but he also needs to find his true place in the world. And I believe that coming back to my country, making the happiness of those I love, will help me to do this. I don't look any farther.

MARIA: Surely you could do it without all these . . . these complications? No, Jan, I'm afraid you are going the wrong way about it.

JAN: It's the right way, because it's the only way of finding out whether or not I did well to have those 'dreams'.

MARIA: I hope you'll find that you did well. Personally, I have only one dream – of that country where we were happy together; and only one duty – towards you.

JAN [embracing her]: Let me have my way, dear. I'll find the things to say that will put everything right.

MARIA [in an access of emotion]: Then follow your dream, dear. Nothing matters, if only I keep your love. Usually I can't be unhappy when you hold me in your arms. I bide my time, I wait till you come down from the clouds; and then my hour begins. What makes me so unhappy today is that, though I'm quite sure of your love, I'm no less sure you will not let me stay with you. That's why men's love is so cruel, so heart-rending. They can't prevent themselves from leaving what they value most.

JAN [holding her face between his hands, and smiling]: Quite true, my dear. But come now! Look at me! I'm not in any danger, as you seem to fear. I'm carrying out my plan, and I know all will be well. You're entrusting me for just

one night to my mother and my sister; there's nothing so
alarming about that, is there?

MARIA [*freeing herself*]: Then – good-bye! And may my love
shield you from harm. [*She goes to the door, and holds out her
hands.*] See how poor I am; they're empty! You – you're
going forward to adventure. I can only wait. [*After a
momentary hesitation she goes out.*]

   [JAN *sits down.* MARTHA *enters.*]

JAN: Good afternoon. I've come about the room.

MARTHA: I know. It's being got ready. But, first, I must
enter you in our Visitors' Book. [*She goes out and comes
back with the register.*]

JAN: I must say, your servant is a very queer fellow.

MARTHA: This is the first time we've had any complaint
about him. He always carries out his duties quite satis-
factorily.

JAN: Oh, I wasn't complaining. I only meant that he
seemed a bit of a character. Is he dumb?

MARTHA: It's not that.

JAN: Ah! then he does speak.

MARTHA: As little as possible and only when really necessary.

JAN: Anyhow, he doesn't seem to hear what one says.

MARTHA: It's not so much that he doesn't hear; only he
hears badly. Now I must ask you for your name and Christian names.

JAN: Hasek, Karl.

MARTHA: Only Karl?

JAN: Yes.

MARTHA: Date and place of birth?

JAN: I'm thirty-eight.

MARTHA: Yes, but where were you born?

JAN [*after a brief hesitation*]: Oh, in . . . in Bohemia.

MARTHA: Profession?

JAN: None.

MARTHA: One has to be very rich, or very poor, to travel, when one does no work.

JAN [*smiling*]: I'm not very poor and, for several reasons, I'm glad it's so.

MARTHA [*in a different tone*]: You're a Czech, I suppose?

JAN: Certainly.

MARTHA: Your usual residence?

JAN: In Bohemia.

MARTHA: Have you come from there?

JAN: No, I've come from the south. [*She looks at him questioningly.*] From across the sea.

MARTHA: Ah, yes. [*A short silence.*] Do you go there often?

JAN: Fairly often.

MARTHA [*she seems lost in thought for some moments before continuing*]: And where are you going?

JAN: I've not decided. It will depend on a lot of things.

MARTHA: Then do you propose to stay here?

JAN: I don't know. It depends on what I find here.

MARTHA: That doesn't matter. Is no one here expecting you?

JAN: No, I couldn't say anyone's expecting me.

MARTHA: You have your identity papers, I suppose?

JAN: Yes, I can show you them.

MARTHA: Don't trouble. I've only got to write down whether you have an identity card or a passport.

JAN [*producing a passport from his pocket*]: I've a passport. Here it is. Will you have a look at it?

[*She takes it, but her thoughts are obviously elsewhere. She seems to be weighing it in her palm; then she hands it back.*]

MARTHA: No, keep it. When you're over there, do you live near the sea?

JAN: Yes.

[*She gets up, seems about to put the book away; then, changing her mind, holds it open in front of her.*]

MARTHA [*with sudden harshness*]: Ah, I was forgetting. Have you a family?

JAN: Well, I had one once. But I left them many years ago.

MARTHA: No, I meant, are you married?

JAN: Why do you ask that? I've never had the question put to me in any other hotel.

MARTHA: It's one of the questions on the list given us by the police.

JAN: You surprise me ... Yes, I'm married. Didn't you notice my wedding ring?

MARTHA: No, I didn't. It's none of my business to look at your hands; I'm here to fill in your registration form. Your wife's address, please.

JAN: Well, she ... as a matter of fact, she's stayed behind, in her country.

MARTHA: Ah! Very good. [*Closes the book.*] Shall I bring you a drink now, while your room's being got ready?

JAN: No, thanks. But, if you don't mind, I'll stay here. I hope I shan't be in your way.

MARTHA: Why should you be in my way? This is a public room, for the use of our customers.

JAN: Quite so. But someone by himself can be more of a nuisance than a crowd of people.

MARTHA: Why? I presume you don't intend to waste my time with idle chatter. I've no use for folks who come here and try to play the fool – and you should have guessed that. The people hereabouts have learnt it, anyhow, and you'll very soon see for yourself that this is a quiet inn, and you'll have all the calm you want. Hardly anybody comes here.

JAN: That can't be very good for business.

MARTHA: We may lose some takings, but we make up for them in peace, and peace is something for which you can't pay too high a price. And don't forget that one good customer is better than a roaring trade; so that's what we are out for – the right kind of visitor.

JAN: But . . . [*He hesitates.*] Isn't your life here a bit dull at times? Don't you and your mother find it very lonely?

MARTHA [*rounding on him angrily*]: I decline to answer such questions. You had no business to ask them, and you should have known it. I can see I'll have to warn you how things stand. As a guest at this inn you have the rights and privileges of a guest, but nothing more. Still, don't be afraid, you will have every attention you're entitled to. You will be very well looked after and I shall be greatly surprised if ever you complain of your reception here. But I fail to see why we should go out of our way to give you special reasons for satisfaction. That's why your questions are out of place. It has nothing to do with you whether or not we feel lonely; just as you need not trouble yourself whether you cause us inconvenience or ask too much of us. By all means stand upon your rights as a guest. But do not go beyond them.

JAN: I beg your pardon. Nothing was further from my intention than to offend you; I only wanted to show my good will. I had a feeling that perhaps we weren't quite so remote from each other as you seem to think; no more than that.

MARTHA: I can see I must repeat what I was saying. There can be no question of offending me or not offending me. Since you seem determined to adopt an attitude which you have no right to adopt, I prefer to make things clear. I can assure you I'm not in the least vexed. Only it is in our interest, yours and mine, that we should keep our distance. If you persist in talking in a manner unbecoming a guest, there's no alternative; we must refuse to have you here. But if you will understand, as I cannot doubt you will, that two women who let you a room in their hotel are under no obligation to treat you as a friend into the bargain, all will go smoothly.

JAN: I quite agree; and it was inexcusable, my giving you an impression that I failed to understand this.

MARTHA: Oh, there's no great harm done. You are not the first who's tried to take that line. But I always made it pretty clear how we felt about such matters, and that settled it.

JAN: Yes, you certainly have made it clear, and I suppose I'd better say no more – for the present.

MARTHA: Not at all. There's nothing to prevent your talking as a guest should talk.

JAN: And how should a guest talk?

MARTHA: Most of our guests talk about all sorts of things: politics, their travels, and so forth. Never about my mother or myself – and that is as it should be. Some of them even talk about their private lives or their jobs. And that, too, is within their rights. After all, one of the services for which we're paid is listening to our customers. But it goes without saying that the charges made for board and lodging don't oblige hotel keepers to answer personal questions. My mother may do so sometimes, out of indifference; but I make a principle of refusing. Once you've grasped this, we shall not only be on excellent terms, but you'll discover you have many things to tell us, and that sometimes it's quite pleasant to be listened to when one's talking about oneself.

JAN: I'm afraid you won't find me much good at talking about myself. But, really, that won't be necessary. If I stay here only a short time, there will be no point in your getting to know me. And if I make a long stay, you'll have plenty of opportunity of knowing who I am, without my speaking.

MARTHA: I hope that you will not bear me any malice for

what I've told you. There'd be no reason for it, anyhow. I've always found it better to be quite frank, and I had to stop your talking in a tone that was bound to lead to strained relations. Really I'm asking nothing out-of-the-way. Until today there was nothing in common between us, and some very special reasons would be needed for our suddenly becoming intimate. And you must forgive me if I fail to see, so far, anything in the least resembling a reason of that kind.

JAN: I'd forgiven you already. Indeed, I quite agree that intimacy isn't come by at a moment's notice; one has to earn it. So if you now consider that everything's been cleared up between us, I can only say I'm very glad of it.

[THE MOTHER *enters*.]

THE MOTHER: Good afternoon, sir. Your room is ready now.

JAN: Thanks very much, madame.

[THE MOTHER *sits down*.]

THE MOTHER [*to Martha*]: Have you filled in the form?

MARTHA: Yes, I've done that.

THE MOTHER: May I have a look? You must excuse me, sir, but the police here are very strict. . . . Yes, I see my daughter's not put down whether you've come here on business, or for reasons of health, or as a tourist.

JAN: Well, let's say as a tourist.

THE MOTHER: To see the Monastery, no doubt? It's thought very highly of, I'm told.

JAN: Yes, indeed; I've heard a lot about it. Also I wanted to see this place again. It has very pleasant memories for me.

THE MOTHER: Did you ever live here?

JAN: No, but a long time ago I happened to come this way, and I've never forgotten that visit.

THE MOTHER: Still, this is just an ordinary little country town.

JAN: That's so. But I'm much attached to it. Indeed, ever since I came here I've been feeling almost at home.

THE MOTHER: Will you be staying long?

JAN: Really I don't know. I dare say that surprises you, but it's the truth. I don't know. To stay in a place you need to have reasons – friendships, the presence of people you are fond of. Otherwise there'd be no point in staying there rather than elsewhere. And since it's hard to know if one will be made welcome, it's natural for me to be uncertain about my plans.

THE MOTHER: That sounds a little vague, if I may say so.

JAN: I know, but I can't express myself better, I'm afraid.

THE MOTHER: Anyhow, I expect you'll soon have had enough of this place.

JAN: No, I've a faithful heart, and I soon build up memories and attachments, if I'm given a chance.

MARTHA [*impatiently*]: A faithful heart, indeed! Hearts count for mighty little here!

JAN [*seeming not to have heard her; to the Mother*]: You seem terribly disillusioned. Have you been living long in this hotel?

THE MOTHER: For years and years. So many years that I have quite forgotten when it began and the woman I was then. This girl is my daughter. She's kept beside me all through those years, and probably that's why I know she is my daughter. Otherwise I might have forgotten her, too.

MARTHA: Really, mother! You've no reason to tell him all that.

THE MOTHER: You're right, Martha.

JAN [*hastily*]: Please don't say any more. But how well I understand your feelings, madame; they're what one comes to at the end of a long, hard-working life. Yet perhaps it might have been quite different if you'd been helped, as every woman should be helped, and given the support of a man's arm.

THE MOTHER: Oh, once upon a time I had it – but there was too much work to do. My husband and I, together, could hardly cope with it. We hadn't even time to think of each other; I believe I had forgotten him even before he died.

JAN: That, too, I can understand. But [*he hesitates for a moment*] – perhaps if a son had been here to give you a helping hand, you wouldn't have forgotten *him*?

MARTHA: Mother, you know we've a lot of work to do.

THE MOTHER: A son? Oh, I'm too old, too old! Old women forget to love even their sons. Hearts wear out, sir.

JAN: That's so. But he, I'm sure, doesn't forget.

MARTHA [*standing between them; peremptorily*]: If a son came here, he'd find exactly what an ordinary guest can count on: amiable indifference, no more and no less. All the men we have had here received that, and it satisfied them. They paid for their rooms and were given a key. They didn't talk about their hearts. [*A short silence.*] That simplified our work.

THE MOTHER: Don't talk about that.

JAN [*reflectively*]: Did they stay here long?

MARTHA: Some of them, a very long time. We did all that was needed for them to stay. Those who weren't so well off left after the first night. We didn't do anything for them.

JAN: I've plenty of money and I propose to stay some little time in this hotel – if you're willing to keep me. I forgot to mention that I can pay you in advance.

THE MOTHER: Oh, we never ask people to do that.

MARTHA: If you are rich, so much the better. But no more talk about your heart, please. We can do nothing about that. In fact your way of speaking got so much on my

125

nerves that I very nearly asked you to go. Take your key and make yourself comfortable in your room. But remember you are in a house where the heart isn't catered for. Too many bleak years have passed over this little spot of Central Europe, and they've drained all the warmth out of this house. They have killed any desire for friendliness and, let me repeat it, you won't find anything in the least like intimacy here. You will get what the few travellers who lodge with us are used to get, and it has nothing to do with sentiment. So take your key and bear this well in mind: we're accepting you as a guest, in our quiet way, for interested motives, and if we keep you it will be in our quiet way, for interested motives.

[JAN *takes the key and watches her go out.*]

THE MOTHER: Don't pay too much attention to what she says. But it's a fact there's some things she never could bear talking about. [*She starts to rise. He comes forward to help her.*] Don't trouble, my son; I'm not a cripple yet. Look at my hands; they're still quite strong. Strong enough to hold up a man's legs. [*A short silence. He is gazing at the key.*] Is it what I just said that you're thinking about?

JAN: No. I'm sorry, I hardly heard it. But, tell me, why did you say 'my son' just now?

THE MOTHER: Oh, I shouldn't have done that, sir. I didn't mean to take liberties. It was just . . . a manner of speaking.

JAN: I quite understand. Now I'll have a look at my room.

THE MOTHER: Certainly, sir. Our old manservant is waiting for you in the passage. [*He gazes at her, on the brink of speaking.*] Is there anything you want?

JAN [*hesitantly*]: Well . . . no, madame. Except that I'd like to thank you for your welcome. [*He goes out.*]

[*Left to herself,* THE MOTHER *sits down again, lays her hands on the table, and contemplates them.*]

THE MOTHER: That was a queer thing I did just now, talking about my hands. Still, if he had really looked at them, perhaps he'd have guessed what he refused to understand in Martha's words. But why must this man be so much bent on dying, and I so little on killing? If only he'd leave – then I could have another long night's rest! I'm too old. Too old to lock my hands again on a man's ankles and feel the body swaying, swaying, all the way down to the river. Too old for that last effort when we launch him into the water. It will leave me gasping for breath, and every muscle aching, with my arms hanging limp, without even the strength to wipe off the drops that splash up when the sleeping body plunges into the eddies. Too old, too old! ... Well, well, since I must, I must! He is the perfect victim and it's for me to give him the sleep I wanted for my own night. And so ...

[MARTHA *enters abruptly.*]

MARTHA: There you are, day-dreaming again! And yet – we've much to do.

THE MOTHER: I was thinking of that man. No, really I was thinking of myself.

MARTHA: You'd do better to think about tomorrow. What good was it, not looking at that man, if you can't keep your thoughts off him? You said yourself, it's easier to kill what one doesn't know. Do be *sensible.*

THE MOTHER: That was one of your father's favourite words, I remember. But I'd like to feel sure this is the last time we'll have to be ... sensible. It's odd. When your father used that word it was to drive away the fear of being found out, but when you tell me to be sensible it's only to quench the little spark of goodness that was kindling in my heart.

MARTHA: What you call a spark of goodness is merely sleepiness. But, only postpone your languor till tomorrow, and then you'll be able to take things easy for the rest of your days.

THE MOTHER: You're right, I know. But why should chance have sent us a victim who is so . . . so unsuitable?

MARTHA: Chance doesn't enter into it. But I admit this traveller is really too confiding, his innocence is too much of a good thing. What would the world come to if condemned men started unbosoming their sentimental troubles to the hangman? It's unsound in principle. But it aggravates me too, and when I'm dealing with him, I'll bring to bear some of the anger I always feel at the stupidity of men.

THE MOTHER: That, too, is unsound. In the past we brought neither anger nor pity to our task; only the indifference it needed. But tonight I am tired, and you, I see, are angered. Are we really obliged to go through with it under these conditions, and to override everything for the sake of a little more money?

MARTHA: Not for money, but for a home beside the sea, and forgetfulness of this hateful country. You may be tired of living, but I, too, am tired, tired to death of these narrow horizons. I feel I couldn't endure another month here. Both of us are sick of this inn and everything to do with it. You, who are old, want no more than to shut your eyes and to forget. But I can still feel in my heart some of the absurd desires I had when I was twenty, and I want to act in such a way as to have done with them for ever – even if, for that, we must go a little further with the life we want to leave. And really it's your duty to help me; it was you who brought me into the world in a land of clouds and mist, instead of a land of sunshine.

THE MOTHER: Martha, I almost wonder if it wouldn't be better for me to be forgotten, as I've been forgotten by your brother, than to hear you speaking to me in that tone, the tone of an accuser.

MARTHA: You know well I did not mean to wound you. [*A short silence; then passionately*] What could I do without you? What would become of me if you were far away? I, anyhow, could never, never forget you, and if at times the strain of this life we lead makes me fail in the respect I owe you, I beg you, mother, to forgive me.

THE MOTHER: You are a good daughter, Martha, and I can well believe that an old woman is sometimes hard to understand. But, I feel this is the moment to tell you what I've been trying all this time to say: 'Not tonight.'

MARTHA: What! Are we to wait till tomorrow? You know quite well you've never had such an idea before; and it would never do for him to have time to meet people here. No, we must act while we have him to ourselves.

THE MOTHER: Perhaps. I don't know. But not tonight. Let him be for this one night. It will give us a reprieve; we shall breathe freely for a while and enjoy the little lull of peace that comes, they say, at the heart of the worst crimes. Yes, let us have this respite. And perhaps it's through him we shall save ourselves.

MARTHA: Save ourselves? Why should we want to do that, and what an absurd thing to say! All you can hope for is to gain by what you do tonight the right to sleep your fill, once it's over.

THE MOTHER: That's what I meant by 'saving ourselves'. To retain the hope of sleep.

MARTHA: Good! Then I swear it's in our hands to work out our salvation. Mother, we must have done with indecision. Tonight it shall be; or not at all.

CURTAIN

ACT TWO

A bedroom at the inn. Dusk is falling. JAN *is gazing out of the window.*

JAN: Maria was right. This evening hour tells on the nerves. [*A short pause.*] I wonder what her thoughts are, what she is up to, in that other hotel bedroom. I picture her huddled up in a chair; she's not crying, but her heart's like ice. Over there the nightfall brought a promise of happiness. But here . . . [*Looks round the room.*] Nonsense! I've no reason for feeling this uneasiness. When a man starts something, he has no business to look back. It's in this room everything will be settled.

[*A sharp rap on the door.* MARTHA *comes in.*]

MARTHA: I hope I'm not disturbing you. I only wanted to change the towels and fill your jug.

JAN: Oh, I thought it had been done.

MARTHA: No. The old man who works for us sometimes forgets things like that.

JAN: They're only details, anyhow. . . . But I hardly dare to tell you that you're not disturbing me.

MARTHA: Why?

JAN: I'm not sure that's allowed for in our . . . our agreement.

MARTHA: You see! You can't answer like any ordinary person, even when you want to make things easy.

JAN [*smiling*]: Sorry. I shall have to train myself. Only you must give me a little time.

MARTHA [*busy with the room*]: Yes, that's the whole point. [*He turns and looks out of the window. She studies him. His back*

130

is to her. She continues speaking as she works.] I'm sorry, sir, that this room is not as comfortable as you might wish.

JAN: It's spotlessly clean, and that is something one appreciates. Unless I'm much mistaken, you had it done up not very long ago.

MARTHA: Quite true. But how can you tell that?

JAN: Oh, by some details.

MARTHA: Anyhow, many of our guests grumble because there isn't running water, and I can hardly blame them. Also, there should be a lamp above the bed; for some time we've been meaning to have one installed. It must be rather a nuisance for people who're used to reading in bed to have to get up to switch the light off.

JAN [*turning towards her*]: That's so. I hadn't noticed. Still it's not a very serious drawback.

MARTHA: It's kind of you to take it like that. I am glad the defects of our hotel don't trouble you; in fact you seem to notice them less than we do. I've known people whom they'd have been enough to drive away.

JAN: I hope you'll let me make a remark that goes beyond our pact – and say that you're a very surprising person. One certainly doesn't expect hotel-keepers to go out of their way to point out defects in the accommodation. Really it almost looks as if you wanted to make me leave.

MARTHA: That wasn't quite what I had in mind. [*Coming to a sudden decision*] But it's a fact that mother and I are rather reluctant to have you here.

JAN: I must say I noticed that you weren't doing much to keep me. Still, I can't imagine why. You have no reason to doubt my solvency, and I hardly think I give the impression of someone with a crime on his conscience.

MARTHA: Certainly not. If you must know, not only don't you look in the least like a criminal, but you produce the opposite effect – of complete innocence. Our reasons were quite different from what you think. We intend to leave this hotel shortly and we've been meaning every day to close down, so as to start preparing for the move. That had no difficulties, as we get so few visitors. But we could never quite make up our minds. It's your coming that has made us realize how thoroughly we'd abandoned any idea of going on with the business.

JAN: Am I to understand you definitely want to see me go?

MARTHA: As I said, we can't decide; I, especially, can't decide. Actually everything depends on me and I haven't made up my mind yet, one way or the other.

JAN: Please remember this; I don't want to be a burden on you and I shall behave exactly as you wish. However, I'd like to say that it will suit me if I can stay here for one or two days. I have some problems to thrash out before moving on, and I counted on finding here the peace and quietness I need.

MARTHA: I quite understand your desire, I assure you, and, if you like, I'll reconsider the matter. [*A short silence. She takes some steps hesitantly towards the door.*] Am I right in thinking you'll go back to the country from which you've come?

JAN: Yes – if necessary.

MARTHA: It's a pretty country, isn't it?

JAN [*looking out of the window*]: Yes, a very pretty country.

MARTHA: Is it true that there are long stretches of the coast where you never meet a soul?

JAN: Quite true. There's nothing to remind you that men exist. Sometimes at dawn you find the traces of birds' feet on the sand. Those are the only signs of life. And in the evenings . . .

MARTHA [*softly*]: Yes? What are the evenings like?

JAN: Marvellous, indescribable! Yes, it's a lovely country.

MARTHA [*in a tone she has not used before*]: I've thought of it,

132

often and often. Travellers have told me things, and I've read what I could. And often, in the harsh, bleak spring we have here, I dream of the sea and the flowers over there. [*After a short silence, in a low, pensive voice*] And what I picture makes me blind to everything around me.

[*After gazing at her thoughtfully for some moments,* JAN *sits down facing her.*]

JAN: I can understand that. Spring over there grips you by the throat and flowers burst into bloom by thousands, above the white walls. If you roamed the hills that overlook my town for only an hour or so, you'd bring back in your clothes a sweet, honeyed smell of yellow roses.

[MARTHA, *too, sits down.*]

MARTHA: How wonderful that must be! What we call spring here is one rose and a couple of buds struggling to keep alive in the monastery garden. [*Scornfully*] And that's enough to stir the hearts of the men in this part of the world. Their hearts are as stingy as that rose-tree. A breath of richer air would wilt them; they have the spring-time they deserve.

JAN: You're not quite fair; you have the autumn, too.

MARTHA: What's the autumn?

JAN: A second spring when every leaf's a flower. [*He looks at her keenly.*] Perhaps it's the same thing with some hearts; perhaps they'd blossom if you helped them with your patience.

MARTHA: I've no patience for this dreary Europe, where autumn has the face of spring and the spring smells of poverty. No, I prefer to picture those other lands over which summer breaks in flame, where the winter rains flood the cities, and where . . . things are what they are.

[*A short silence.* JAN *gazes at her with growing interest. She notices this and rises abruptly from the chair.*]

MARTHA: Why are you looking at me like that?

JAN: Sorry. But since we seem to have dropped our convention for the present, I don't see why I shouldn't tell you. It strikes me that, for the first time, you've been talking to me with – shall I say? – some human feeling.

MARTHA [*violently*]: Don't be too sure of that. And even if I have been, you've no cause for rejoicing. What you call human feeling is not the nicest part of me. What is human in me is what I desire, and to get what I desire, I'd stick at nothing, I'd sweep away every obstacle on my path.

JAN: I can understand that sort of violence. And I have no cause to let it frighten me, as I'm not an obstacle on your path, and I've no motive for opposing your desires.

MARTHA: Certainly you have no reason to oppose them. But it's equally true you have no reason for furthering them and, in some cases, that might bring things to a head.

JAN: Why be so sure I have no reason for furthering them?

MARTHA: Common sense tells me that; also my wish to keep you outside my plans.

JAN: Ah! That means, I take it, that we've returned to our conventions?

MARTHA: Yes, and we did wrong to depart from them – you can see that for yourself. Now it remains for me to thank you for having spoken of that country where you lived, and I must excuse myself for having, perhaps, wasted your time. [*She is on her way to the door.*] Still, let me tell you, the time was not wholly wasted. Our talk roused desires in me that were beginning to fall asleep. If you're really bent on staying here you've won your case without knowing it. When I entered this room I had almost decided to ask you to leave, but, as you see, you've played on my human feelings; now I hope you'll stay. And so my longing for the sea and sunshine will be the gainer by it.

[*He gazes at her without speaking for a moment.*]

JAN [*thoughtfully*]: You have a very strange way of talking.
Still, if I may, and if your mother, too, has no objection,
I'll stay on.

MARTHA: My mother's desires are weaker than mine; that's
only natural. She doesn't think enough about the sea and
those lonely beaches to make her realize you have got to
stay. So she hasn't the same motives for wanting to keep
you. But, at the same time, she hasn't any really strong
motive for opposing me; and that will settle it.

JAN: So, if I've not misunderstood, one of you will let me
stay for the sake of money, and the other through indifference.

MARTHA: What more can a traveller expect? But there's
truth in what you said. [*She opens the door.*]

JAN: Well, I suppose I should be glad of that. Still perhaps
you'll let me say that everything here strikes me as very
strange; the people and their way of speaking. Really this
is a queer house.

MARTHA: Perhaps that's only because you are behaving
queerly in it. [*She goes out.*]

JAN [*looking towards the door*]: Maybe she's right. I wonder,
though. [*Goes to the bed and sits down.*] Really the one wish
that girl has given me is the wish to leave at once, to
return to Maria and our happiness together. I've been
behaving stupidly. What business have I to be here? . . .
No, I have a reason, a good reason; I owe a duty to my
mother and sister. I've neglected them too long. It's up to
me to do something for them, to atone for my neglect. It's
not enough in such cases to declare oneself, 'It's I.' One
has to make oneself loved, as well. [*He rises.*] Yes, this is
the room in which all will be decided. A wretchedly cold
room, by the way. I can't recognize anything in it. Everything's been changed, and now it might be a bedroom in
any one of those commercial hotels where men by them-

selves stay a night in passing. I've had experience of them, and I always used to think there was something they had to say – something like an answer or a message. Perhaps I shall get the answer here, tonight. [*He looks out of the window.*] Clouding up, I see. It's always like this in an hotel bedroom; the evenings are depressing for a lonely man. I can feel it again, that vague uneasiness I used to feel in the old days – here, in the hollow of my chest – like a raw place which the least movement irritates . . . And I know what it is. It's fear, fear of the eternal loneliness, fear that there is no answer. And who could there be to answer in an hotel bedroom?

[*He has moved to the bell; after some hesitation he puts his finger on the bell-push. For a while there is silence; then one hears approaching footsteps, a knock. The door opens. The old* MANSERVANT *is standing on the threshold. He neither moves nor speaks.*]

JAN: It's nothing. Sorry to have disturbed you. I only wanted to see if the bell was working and anyone would answer.

[*The old man stares at him, then closes the door. Receding footsteps.*]

JAN: The bell works, but *he* doesn't speak. That's no answer. [*He looks at the sky.*] The clouds are banking up still. A solid mass of darkness that will burst and fall upon the earth. What should I do? Which is right: Maria or my dreams?

[*Two knocks on the door.* MARTHA *enters with a tray.*]

JAN: What's this?

MARTHA: The tea you ordered.

JAN: But – I didn't order anything.

MARTHA: Oh? The old man must have heard wrong. He often understands badly. Still, as the tea is here, I suppose you'll have it? [*She puts the tray on the table.* JAN *makes a vague gesture.*] Don't trouble; it won't go down on the bill.

JAN: No, it isn't that. But I'm glad you brought me some tea. Most kind of you.

MARTHA: Please don't mention it. What we do is in our interests.

JAN: I can see you're determined not to leave me any illusions! But frankly I don't see where your interest comes in, in this case.

MARTHA: It does, I assure you. Sometimes a cup of tea's enough to keep our guests here. [*She goes out.*]

[JAN *picks up the cup, stares at it, puts it down again.*]

JAN: So the prodigal son's feast is continuing. First, a glass of beer – but in exchange for my money; then a cup of tea – because it encourages the visitor to stay on. But I'm to blame, too; I cannot strike the right note. When I'm confronted by that girl's almost brutal frankness, I search in vain for the words that would put things right between us. Of course, her part is simpler; it's easier to find words for a rebuff than those which reconcile. [*He picks up the cup, is silent for some moments, then continues in a low, tense voice.*] Oh God, give me the power to find my words aright, or else make me abandon this vain attempt, and return to Maria's love. And then give me the strength, once I have chosen, to abide by my choice. [*He raises the cup to his lips.*] The feast of the returning prodigal. The least I can do is to do it honour; and so I shall have played my part until I leave this place. [*He drinks. Loud knocking at the door.*] Who's there?

[*The door opens.* THE MOTHER *enters.*]

THE MOTHER: I'm sorry to disturb you, sir, but my daughter tells me she brought you some tea.

JAN: There it is.

THE MOTHER: Have you drunk it?

JAN: Yes. Why do you ask?

THE MOTHER: Excuse me, I've come to fetch the tray.

JAN [*smiling*]: I'm sorry this cup of tea is causing so much trouble.

THE MOTHER: It isn't quite that. But, as a matter of fact, that tea was not meant for you.

JAN: Ah, there's the explanation. It was brought without my having ordered it.

THE MOTHER [*wearily*]: Yes, that's it. It would have been better if . . . Anyhow that hasn't any great importance, whether you've drunk it or not.

JAN [*in a puzzled tone*]: I'm exceedingly sorry, I assure you, but your daughter insisted on leaving it, and I never imagined . . .

THE MOTHER: I'm sorry, too. But please don't excuse yourself. It was just a mistake. [*She puts the cup and saucer on the tray and moves towards the door.*]

JAN: Madame!

THE MOTHER: Yes?

JAN: I must apologize again. I've just come to a decision. I think I'll leave this evening, after dinner. Naturally I'll pay for the room, for the night. [*She gazes at him, in silence.*] I quite understand your looking surprised. But please don't imagine you are in any way responsible for my sudden change of plan. I have a great regard for you, a very great regard. But, to be candid, I don't feel at ease here, and I'd rather not stay the night.

THE MOTHER: That's quite all right, sir. Of course you can do exactly as you wish. Still, perhaps you may change your mind between now and dinner-time. Sometimes one yields to a passing impression, but, later on, things settle themselves and one gets used to new conditions.

JAN: I doubt it, madame. However, I would not like you to believe I am leaving because I'm dissatisfied with you.

On the contrary, I am very grateful to you for welcoming me as you have done. For, I must say, I seemed to notice you had a certain . . . friendliness towards me.

THE MOTHER: That was only natural, sir, and I'm sure you understand I had no personal reasons for showing any ill-will.

JAN [*with restrained emotion*]: That may be so – I hope so. But, if I told you that, it is because I want us to part on good terms. Later on, perhaps, I'll come back. In fact I'm sure I shall. And then things will certainly go better, and I've no doubt we shall find pleasure in meeting again. But just now I feel that I have made a mistake, I have no business to be here. In a word – though this may strike you as an odd way of putting it – I have a feeling that this house isn't for me.

THE MOTHER: I know what you mean, sir. But usually one feels that sort of thing immediately; you have been rather slow, it seems to me, to discover it.

JAN: I agree. But just now I'm rather at sea. I've come to Europe on some urgent business, and it's always a bit disconcerting, returning to a country after years and years of absence. I trust you understand what I mean.

THE MOTHER: Yes, I do understand, and I'd have liked things to turn out as you wished. But I think that, as far as we're concerned, there's nothing more we can do about it.

JAN: So it seems, I admit. Still, really, one never can be sure.

THE MOTHER: Anyhow, I think we have done everything needed to have you stay with us.

JAN: Indeed you have, and I've nothing to complain of. The truth is that you are the first people I have met since my return, so it's natural my first taste of the difficulties ahead should come when I'm with you. Obviously I alone am to blame for this; I haven't found my feet yet.

THE MOTHER: It's often like that in life; one makes a bad start, and nobody can do anything about it. In a way it's quite true that what has happened vexes me as well. But I tell myself that, after all, I've no reason to attach importance to it.

JAN: Well, it's something that you share my discomfort and that you try to understand me. I can hardly tell you how touched I am by your attitude, and how much I appreciate it. [*He stretches his hand towards her.*] Really I . . .

THE MOTHER: Oh, what you call my attitude's quite natural, really. It's our duty to make ourselves agreeable to our guests.

JAN [*in a disappointed tone*]: That's so. [*A short silence.*] So it comes to this: all I owe you is an apology and, if you think fit, some compensation. [*He draws his hand over his forehead. He seems exhausted and is speaking less easily.*] You may have made preparations, gone to some expense; so it's only fair . . .

THE MOTHER: The only preparations we've made are those we always make in such cases. And I can assure you that you owe us no compensation. It was not on our account that I was regretting your indecision, but on yours.

JAN [*leaning against the table*]: Oh, that doesn't matter. The great thing is that we understand each other and I shan't leave you with too bad an impression of myself. Personally I shall not forget this house – be sure of that – and I hope that when I return I'll be in a better mood to appreciate it. [*She goes to the door without speaking.*] Madame! [*She turns. He speaks with some difficulty, but ends more easily than he began.*] I'd like . . . Excuse me, but my journey's tired me. [*Sits on the bed.*] I'd like anyhow to thank you for the tea, and for the welcome you have given me. And I'd also like you to know that when I leave this house I shan't feel quite a stranger.

THE MOTHER: Really, sir, we have done very little for you. And please don't think I meant to be disagreeable about the tea; only it's a fact it wasn't meant for you. Being thanked for something due to a mistake is always embarrassing. [*She goes out.*]

[JAN *watches her, makes as if to move, but one can see he is feeling limp. Then, leaning his elbow on the pillow, he seems to abandon himself to his growing lethargy.*]

JAN: Yes, I must handle it quite simply, quite straightforwardly. Tomorrow I'll come here with Maria and I shall say 'It's I.' There's nothing to prevent my making them happy. Maria was right; I can see that now. [*He sighs, and leans back on the pillow.*] I don't like the feel of this evening; everything seems so far away. [*He stretches himself full-length on the bed, murmuring almost inaudibly*] Yes, or no?

[*After tossing about a little,* JAN *falls asleep. The room is in almost complete darkness. A long silence. The door opens. The two women enter, with a lamp.*]

MARTHA [*after holding the lamp above the sleeping man; in a whisper*]: All's well.

THE MOTHER [*in a low voice at first, but gradually raising it*]: No, Martha! I dislike having my hand forced like this. I'm being dragged into this act; you began it so that I'd have no chance of drawing back. I don't like your way of riding roughshod over my reluctance.

MARTHA: It is a way that simplifies everything. If you had given me any clear reason for your reluctance, I'd have been bound to consider it. But as you couldn't make up your mind, it was right for me to help you by taking the first step.

THE MOTHER: I know, of course, that it does not greatly matter; this man or some other, today or some later day, tonight or tomorrow – it had to come to that. None the less, I don't feel pleased about it.

MARTHA: Come, mother! Think of tomorrow, instead, and let's get busy. Our freedom will begin when this night ends. [*She unbuttons Jan's coat, extracts his wallet, and counts the notes.*]

THE MOTHER: How soundly he's sleeping!

MARTHA: He's sleeping as they all slept . . . Now let's start.

THE MOTHER: Wait a little, please. Isn't it strange how helpless and defenceless men look when they're asleep?

MARTHA: It's a rest they take before becoming again the savage brutes or silly apes they all are.

THE MOTHER [*meditatively*]: No, men aren't quite so remarkable as you seem to think, and really they don't change when they're asleep. It's we who look at them with different eyes, and the sudden nakedness of their faces, without any glow of passion or frown of discontent, takes us aback. But of course you, Martha, don't know what I mean.

MARTHA: No, mother, I don't. But I do know that we are wasting time.

THE MOTHER [*with a sort of weary irony*]: Oh, there's no such hurry. On the contrary, this is the moment we can relax, now that the main thing's done. It's not the act itself that counts, but the embarking on it. Once a start is made, one's peace of mind returns. Why work yourself up like this? Is it really worth while?

MARTHA: Nothing's worth while, the moment one talks about it. It's better to get on with the work in hand and ask no questions of oneself.

THE MOTHER [*calmly*]: Let's sit down, Martha.

MARTHA: Here? Beside him?

THE MOTHER: Certainly. Why not? He has entered on a sleep that will take him far, and it's not likely he will wake up and inquire what we're doing here. As for the rest of the world – it stops short at that closed door. Why shouldn't we enjoy this little breathing space in peace?

MARTHA: You're joking, and it's my turn to tell you I don't appreciate your way of talking.

THE MOTHER: You're wrong. I don't feel in the least like joking. I'm merely showing calmness while you are letting your nerves run wild. No, Martha, sit down [*she gives a curious laugh*] and look at that man who's even more innocent in sleep than in his talk. He, anyhow, is through with the world. From now on, everything will be easy for him. He will pass from a dreamful sleep into dreamless sleep. And what for others is a cruel wrench will be for him no more than a protracted rest.

MARTHA: Innocence has the sleep that innocence deserves. And this man, anyhow, I had no reason for hating. So I'm glad he is being spared any pain. But I've no reason, either, for looking at him, and I think it a bad idea of yours, staring like that at a man whom presently you'll have to carry.

THE MOTHER [*shaking her head; in a low voice*]: When the hour comes we shall carry him. But we still have time in hand and perhaps it won't be such a bad idea – for him at any rate – if we look at him attentively. For it's not too late yet; sleep isn't death. Yes, Martha, look at him. He is living through a moment when he has no say in his fate; when his hopes of life are made over to indifferent hands. Let these hands stay as they are, folded in my lap, until the dawn and, without his knowing anything, he'll have entered on a new lease of life. But if they move towards him and form a hard ring round his ankles, he will lie in an unremembered grave for ever.

MARTHA [*rising brusquely*]: Mother, you're forgetting that all nights end, and we have much to do. First, we must look through the papers in his pockets and carry him downstairs. Then we'll have to put out all the lights and keep watch in the doorway as long as needs be.

THE MOTHER: Yes, there is much for us to do, and that is where we are in a different case from his; he, at least, is free now of the burden of his life. He has done with the anxiety of making decisions, with thoughts of work that must be done, with strain and stress. A cross is lifted from his shoulders; the cross of that inner life which allows of no repose, no weakness, no relaxing. At this moment he exacts nothing of himself and, old and tired as I am, I almost think that there lies happiness.

MARTHA: We've no time for wondering where happiness lies. When I have kept watch as long as needs be, there will still be much to do. We shall have to go down to the river and make sure some drunk man isn't sleeping on the bank. Then we'll have to carry him down there as quickly as we can – and you know the effort that means. We shall have to do it in several stages and, once we are on the bank, swing him out as far as possible into mid stream. And let me remind you again that nights don't last for ever.

THE MOTHER: Yes, all that lies before us, and the mere thought of it makes me tired, with a tiredness that has lasted so long that my old blood can't cope with it. And, meanwhile, this man has no suspicion; he is enjoying his repose. If we let him wake he'll have to start life again and, from what I've seen of him, I know he is much like other men and cannot live in peace. Perhaps that is why we must take him there and make him over to the mercy of the dark water. [*She sighs.*] But it's a sad thing so much effort should be needed to rid a man of his follies and put him in the way of peace.

MARTHA: I can only think, mother, that your wits are wandering. I repeat, we have much to do. Once he's thrown in, we shall have to efface the marks on the river bank, blur our footsteps on the path, destroy his clothes and baggage – make him vanish from the face of the earth, in fact. Time's passing and soon it will be too late to carry all this out with the composure that it needs. Really I cannot understand what has come over you, to be sitting at that man's bedside and staring at him, though you can hardly see him, and persisting in this absurd, useless talk.

THE MOTHER: Tell me, Martha. Did you know that he meant to leave this evening?

MARTHA: No, I didn't. But if I'd known, it wouldn't have changed anything, once I had made up my mind.

THE MOTHER: He told me that just now, and I didn't know how to answer him.

MARTHA: Ah! So you had a talk with him?

THE MOTHER: Yes, when you said you'd brought his tea, I came here. I'd have stopped him from drinking it, if I had been in time. As it was, once I knew the beginning had been made, I felt we'd better let things take their course; really it hadn't much importance.

MARTHA: If you still feel like that, there's no reason for dawdling here. So please get up from that chair and help me finish off this business – which is getting on my nerves.

THE MOTHER [*rising*]: Yes, I suppose I'll end by helping you. Only you might allow a few minutes more to an old woman whose blood doesn't flow as fast as yours. You've been on the rush ever since this morning, and you expect me to keep pace with you! Even that man there couldn't manage it; before he had framed the thought of leaving, he'd drunk the tea you gave him.

MARTHA: If you must know, it was he who made up my mind for me. You talked me into sharing your reluctance. But then he started telling me about those countries where I've always longed to go, and by working on my feelings hardened my heart against him. Thus innocence is rewarded.

THE MOTHER: And yet he'd come to understand. He said he felt that this house was not his home.

MARTHA [*violently and impatiently*]: Of course it is not his home. For that matter it is nobody's home. No one will ever find warmth or comfort or contentment in this house. Had he realized that sooner, he'd have been spared, and spared us, too. He would have spared our having to teach him that this room is made for sleeping in, and this world for dying in. Come, mother, and for the sake of the God you sometimes call on, let's have done with it.

[THE MOTHER *takes a step towards the bed.*]

THE MOTHER: Very well, Martha, we'll begin. But I have a feeling that tomorrow's dawn will never come.

CURTAIN

ACT THREE

The inn-parlour. THE MOTHER, MARTHA, *and the* MANSERVANT *are on the stage. The old man is sweeping and tidying up the room;* MARTHA, *standing behind the bar counter, drawing back her hair.* THE MOTHER *is walking towards the door.*

MARTHA: Well, you see that dawn has come and we've got through the night without mishap.

THE MOTHER: Yes. And tomorrow I'll be thinking it's a good thing to have done with it. But, just now, all I feel is that I'm dead tired and my heart's dried up within me. Ah, it was a hard night indeed!

MARTHA: But this morning is the first for years when I breathe freely. Never did a killing cost me less. I almost seem to hear the waves already, and I feel like crying out for joy.

THE MOTHER: So much the better, Martha. So much the better. As for me, I feel so old this morning that I can't share anything with you. But perhaps tomorrow I'll be in a better way.

MARTHA: Yes, and everything will, I hope, be better. But do please stop complaining and give me a chance of relishing my new-found happiness. I'm like a young girl again this morning; I feel my blood flowing warm, and I want to run about and sing! . . . Oh, mother, may I ask you something . . . [*Pauses.*]

THE MOTHER: What's come over you, Martha? You're like a different person.

MARTHA: Mother . . . [*Hesitates; then in a rush*] Tell me, am I still pretty?

THE MOTHER: Yes, I think you're looking really pretty this morning. Some acts seem to have a good effect on you.

MARTHA: Oh, no! Those acts you mean lie on me so lightly. But this morning I feel as if I'd been born again, to a new life; at last I'm going to a country where I shall be happy.

THE MOTHER: No doubt, no doubt. And, once I've got over my tiredness, I, too, shall breathe freely. Even now, it makes up for all those sleepless nights of ours, to know they'll have brought you happiness. But this morning I must rest; all I'm conscious of is that the night has been a hard one.

MARTHA: What does last night matter? Today is a great day. [*To the servant*] Keep your eyes open when you're sweeping; we dropped some of his papers on the way out and I couldn't stop to pick them up. They're on the floor somewhere. [THE MOTHER *leaves the room. Sweeping under a table, the old man comes on Jan's passport, opens it, runs his eyes over it, and hands it, open, to Martha.*] I don't need to see it. Put it with the other things; we'll burn them all together. [*The old man goes on holding the passport to Martha. She takes it.*] What is it? [*The old man goes out.* MARTHA *reads the passport slowly, without showing any emotion; then calls in a voice that sounds completely calm*] Mother!

THE MOTHER [*from the next room*]: What do you want now?

MARTHA: Come here.

[THE MOTHER *returns.* MARTHA *gives her the passport.*]

MARTHA: Read!

THE MOTHER: You know quite well my eyes are tired.

MARTHA: Read!

[THE MOTHER *takes the passport, sits at the table, spreads it open, and reads. For a long while she stares at the page in front of her.*]

THE MOTHER [*in a toneless voice*]: Yes, I always knew it would turn out like this one day – and that would be the end. The end of all!

MARTHA [*coming from behind the bar counter, and standing in front of it*]: Mother!

THE MOTHER: No, Martha, let me have my way; I've lived quite long enough. I have lived many years more than my son. That isn't as it should be. Now I can go and join him at the bottom of the river, where already the weeds have covered up his face.

MARTHA: Mother! Surely you won't leave me alone?

THE MOTHER: You have been a great help to me, Martha, and I am sorry to leave you. If such words have any meaning left for us, I can honestly say you were a good daughter, in your fashion. You have always shown me the respect you owed me. But now I am very weary; my old heart, which seemed indifferent to everything, has learnt again today what grief means, and I'm not young enough to come to terms with it. In any case, when a mother is no longer capable of recognizing her own son, it's clear her role on earth is ended.

MARTHA: No. Not if her daughter's happiness remains to be ensured. And, no less than my heart, my hopes are shattered when I hear you speaking in this new, amazing way – you who had taught me to respect nothing.

THE MOTHER [*in the same listless tone*]: It only proves that in a world where everything can be denied, there are forces undeniable; and on this earth where nothing's sure we have our certainties. [*Bitterly*] And a mother's love for her son is now my certainty.

MARTHA: So you are not sure that a mother can love her daughter?

THE MOTHER: It's not now I'd want to wound you, Martha, but love for a daughter can never be the same thing. It strikes less deep. And how could I now live without my son's love?

MARTHA: A wonderful love – that forgot you utterly for twenty years!

THE MOTHER: Yes, it was a wonderful love that outlasted twenty years of silence and brought back to his home a son who seemed forgetful as he was forgotten. Say what you will, that love is wonderful enough for me – since I can't live without it. [*She rises from her chair.*]

MARTHA: It's not possible you can talk like that, without any thought for your daughter, without the least stirring of revolt!

THE MOTHER: Hard as it is on you, it *is* possible. I have no thought for anything; still less any feeling of revolt. No doubt this is my punishment, and for all murderers a time comes when, like me, they are dried up within, sterile, with nothing left to live for. That's why society gets rid of them; they're good for nothing.

MARTHA: I can't bear to hear you talking like that, about crime and punishment; it's . . . despicable!

THE MOTHER: I'm not troubling to pick my words; I've ceased to have any preference. But it's true that by one act I have ruined everything. I have lost my freedom and my hell has begun.

MARTHA [*going up to her mother; fiercely*]: You never spoke like that before. During all these years you've stood beside me, and your hands never flinched from gripping the legs of those who were to die. A lot you thought of hell or freedom in those days! It never occurred to you that you had no right to live, and you went on – doing as you did. What change can your son have brought to that?

THE MOTHER: I went on with it; that's true. But what I lived through then, I lived through by dint of habit, which is not so very different from death. An experience of grief was enough to change all that, and my son's coming has brought that change. [MARTHA *makes a gesture and seems about to speak*.] Oh I know, Martha, that doesn't make sense. What has a criminal to do with grief? But I'd have you notice that my grief is not the wild grief that mothers feel; I haven't raised my voice as yet. It's no more than the pain of feeling love rekindle in my heart; and yet it's too much for me. I know that this pain, too, doesn't make sense. [*In a changed tone*] But then this world we live in doesn't make sense, and I have a right to judge it, since I've tested all it has to offer, from creation to destruction. [*She walks resolutely towards the door*.]

    [MARTHA *slips in front of her and bars the way*.]

MARTHA: No, mother, you shall not leave me. Don't forget that it was I who stayed beside you, and *he* went away. For a whole lifetime I have been with you, and he left you in silence. That must come into the reckoning. That must be paid for. And it's your duty to come back to me.

THE MOTHER [*gently*]: That's true enough, Martha. But he, my son, was killed by me.

    [MARTHA *has half-turned away and seems to be gazing at the door*.]

MARTHA [*after a short silence, with rising emotion*]: All that life can give a man was given him. He left this country. He came to know far horizons, the sea, free beings. But I stayed here, eating my heart out in the shadows, small and insignificant, buried alive in a gloomy valley in the heart of Europe. Buried alive! No one has ever kissed my mouth and no one, not even you, has seen me naked. Mother, I swear to you, that *must* be paid for. And now, when at last I am to get what's due to me, you cannot, *must* not desert me on the vain pretext that a man is dead. Do try to understand that for a man who has lived his life death is a little thing. We can forget my brother and your son. What has happened to him has no importance; he had nothing more to get from life. But for me it's different, and you are spoiling me of everything, cheating me of the pleasures he enjoyed. Why must that man deprive me of my mother's love as well and drag you down with him into the icy darkness of the river? [*They gaze silently at each other;* MARTHA *lowers her eyes. She speaks now in a very low voice.*] I ask so little, so very little of life. Mother, there are words I never could bring myself to use, but – don't you think it would be soothing if we started our life again just as it used to be, you and I together?

THE MOTHER: Did you recognize him?

MARTHA: No, I didn't. I had not the slightest recollection of what he looked like, and everything happened as it was bound to happen. You said it yourself; this world doesn't make sense. But you weren't altogether wrong in asking me that question. For I know now that if I'd recognized him, it would have made no difference.

THE MOTHER: I prefer to think that isn't true. No soul is wholly criminal, and the wickedest murderers have moments when they lay down their arms.

MARTHA: I have such moments, too. But I would not have lowered my head to a brother whom I did not know and who meant nothing to me.

THE MOTHER: To whom then would you lower your head?

[MARTHA *lowers her head.*]

MARTHA: To you.

[*A short silence.*]

THE MOTHER [*quietly*]: Too late, Martha. I can do nothing more for you. [*Half-averting her eyes*] Oh, why did he keep silence? Silence is fatal. But speaking is as dangerous; the little he said hurried it on. [*Turns towards her daughter.*] Are you crying, Martha? No, you wouldn't know how to cry. Can you remember the time when I used to kiss you?

MARTHA: No, mother.

THE MOTHER: I understand. It was so long ago, and I forgot so soon to hold out my arms to you. But I never ceased loving you. [*She gently thrusts aside Martha, who gradually makes way for her.*] I know it now; now that your brother's coming has brought to life again that intolerable love which I now must kill – together with myself.

[*The doorway is free for her to pass.*]

MARTHA [*burying her face in her hands*]: But what, oh what can mean more to you than your daughter's grief?

THE MOTHER: Weariness, perhaps . . . and my longing for rest. [*She goes out.*]

[MARTHA *makes no effort to detain her. Once her mother has left she runs to the door, slams it to, and presses herself against it. She breaks into loud, fierce cries.*]

MARTHA: No, no! What concern of mine was it to look after my brother? None whatever! And yet now I'm an outcast in my own home, there is no place for me to lay my head, my own mother will have none of me. No, it wasn't my duty to look after him – oh the unfairness of it all, the injustice done to innocence! For he – he now has what he wanted, while I am left lonely, far from the sea I longed for. Oh, how I hate him! All my life was spent waiting for this great wave that was to lift me up and sweep me far away, and now I know it will never come again. I am doomed to stay here with all those other countries, other nations, on my left hand and my right, before me and behind; all those plains and mountains that are barriers to the salt winds blowing from the sea, and the rumour of whose voices drowns its low, unceasing summons. [*In a lower tone*] There are places to which, far as they may be from the sea, the evening wind brings sometimes a smell of seaweed. It tells of moist sea beaches, loud with the cries of seagulls, or of golden sands bathed in a sunset glow that has no limit. But the sea winds fail long before they reach this place. Never, never shall I have what's due to me. I may press my ear to the earth but I shall not hear the crash of icy breakers, or the measured breathing of a happy sea. I am too far from all I love, and my exile is beyond remedy. I hate him, yes, I hate him for having got what he wanted! My only home is in this gloomy, shut-in country where the sky has no horizons; for my hunger I have nothing but the sour Moravian sloes, for my thirst only the blood that I have shed. That is the price one must pay for a mother's love!

There is no love for me, so let her die. Let every door be shut against me; all I wish is to be left in peace with my anger, my very rightful anger. For I have no intention of rolling my eyes heavenwards or pleading for forgiveness before I die. In that southern land, guarded by the sea, to which one can escape, where one can breathe freely, press one's body to another's body, roll in the waves – to that sea-guarded land the gods have no access. But here one's gaze is cramped on every side, everything is planned to make one look up in humble supplication. I hate this narrow world in which we are reduced to gazing up at God.

But I have not been given my rights and I am smarting from the injustice done me; I will not bend my knee. I have been cheated of my place on earth, cast away by my mother, left alone with my crimes, and I shall leave this world without being reconciled. [*A knock at the door.*] Who's there?

MARIA: A traveller.

MARTHA: We're not taking any guests now.

MARIA: But my husband's here. I have come to see him. [*Enters.*]

MARTHA [*staring at her*]: Your husband. Who's that?

MARIA: He came here yesterday evening and he promised

to call for me this morning. I can't understand why he didn't come.

MARTHA: He said his wife was abroad.

MARIA: He had special reasons for that. But we'd arranged to meet this morning.

MARTHA [*who has kept her eyes fixed on Maria*]: That may be difficult. Your husband's gone.

MARIA: Gone? I don't follow. Didn't he book a room here?

MARTHA: Yes, but he left it during the night.

MARIA: Really I can't believe that. I know his reasons for wanting to stay in this house. But the way you speak alarms me. Please tell me frankly whatever you have to tell.

MARTHA: I have nothing to tell you, except that your husband is no longer here.

MARIA: I simply cannot understand; he would not have gone away without me. Did he say that he was going for good, or that he'd come back?

MARTHA: He has left us for good.

MARIA: Please listen. I can't bear to be kept in suspense any longer. Since yesterday I've been waiting, waiting, in this strange land, and now my anxiety has brought me to this house. I will not go away before I have seen my husband or been told where I can find him.

MARTHA: Your husband's whereabouts is your concern, not mine.

MARIA: You are wrong. You, too, are concerned in this, and closely. I don't know if my husband will approve of my telling you this, but I'm sick and tired of this futile game of make-believe. The man who came here yesterday is the brother you'd heard nothing of for years and years.

MARTHA: That's no news to me.

MARIA [*violently*]: Then – what can have happened? If everything has been cleared up, how is it Jan's not here?

Did you not welcome him home, you and your mother, and weren't you full of joy at his return?

MARTHA: My brother is no longer here – because he is dead.
[MARIA *gives a start and stares at Martha for some moments without speaking. Then she takes a step towards her, smiling.*]

MARIA: Ah, you're joking, of course. Jan's often told me that when you were little you loved mystifying people. You and I are almost sisters and –

MARTHA: Don't touch me. Stay where you are. There is nothing in common between us. [*Pauses.*] I can assure you I'm not joking; your husband died last night. So there's no reason for you to stay here any longer.

MARIA: But you're mad, stark staring mad! People don't die like that – when one's arranged to meet them, from one moment to the other, all of a sudden. I can't believe you. Let me see him and then I may believe what I can't even imagine.

MARTHA: That's impossible. He's at the bottom of the river. [MARIA *stretches her hand towards her.*] Don't touch me! Stay there. I repeat; he is at the bottom of the river. My mother and I carried him to the river last night, after putting him to sleep. He didn't suffer, but he is dead sure enough, and it was we, his mother and I, who killed him.

MARIA [*shrinking away*]: It must be I who am mad. I'm hearing words that have never before been said on this earth. I knew that no good would come to me here, but this is sheer craziness and I will not share in it. At the very moment when your words strike death into my heart, it seems to me that you are talking of some other man, not of the man who shared my nights, and all this is a tale of long ago, in which my love never had a part.

MARTHA: It's not for me to convince you; only to tell you the truth. A truth which you will have to recognize before long.

MARIA [*in a sort of reverie*]: But why, *why* did you do it?

MARTHA: What right have you to question me?

MARIA [*passionately*]: What right? . . . My love for him.

MARTHA: What does that word mean?

MARIA: It means – it means all that at this moment is tearing, gnawing at my heart; it means this rush of frenzy that makes my fingers itch for murder. It means all my past joys, and this wild, sudden grief you have brought me. Yes, you crazy woman, if it wasn't that I've steeled my heart against believing, you'd learn the meaning of that word, when you felt my nails scoring your cheeks.

MARTHA: Again, you are using language I cannot understand. Words like love and joy and grief are meaningless to me.

MARIA [*making a great effort to speak calmly*]: Listen, Martha – that's your name, isn't it? Let's stop this game, if game it is, of cross-purposes. Let's have done with useless words. Tell me quite clearly what I want to know quite clearly, before I let myself break down.

MARTHA: Surely I made it clear enough. We did to your husband last night what we had done to other travellers, before; we killed him and took his money.

MARIA: So his mother and sister were criminals?

MARTHA: Yes. But that's their business, and no one else's.

MARIA [*still controlling herself with an effort*]: Had you learnt he was your brother when you did it?

MARTHA: If you *must* know, there was a misunderstanding. And if you have any experience at all of the world, that won't surprise you.

MARIA [*going towards the table, her hands clenched on her breast; in a low, sad voice*]: Oh, my God, I knew it! I knew this play-acting was bound to end in tragedy and we'd be punished, he and I, for having lent ourselves to it. I felt danger in the very air one breathes in this country. [*She *stops in front of the table and goes on speaking, without looking at Martha.*] He wanted to make his homecoming a surprise, to get you to recognize him and to bring you happiness. Only at first he couldn't find the words that were needed. And then, while he was groping for the words, he was killed. [*Weeping*] And you, like two madwomen, blind to the marvellous son who had returned to you – for marvellous he was, and you will never know the greatheartedness, the noble soul, of the man you killed last night. . . . He might have been your pride, as he was mine. But, no, you were his enemy – oh, the pity of it! – for else how could you bring yourself to speak so calmly of what should make you rush into the street, screaming out your heart, like a wounded animal?

MARTHA: You have no right to sit in judgement without knowing all. By now my mother's lying with her son, pressed to the sluice-gate, and the current is beginning to gnaw their faces, and buffeting them against the rotting piles. Soon their bodies will be drawn up and buried together in the same earth. But I cannot see what there is even in this to set me screaming with pain. I have a very different idea of the human heart, and, to be frank, your tears revolt me.

MARIA [*swinging round on her fiercely*]: My tears are for the joys I've lost for ever; for a life's happiness stolen from me. And this is better for you than the tearless grief I shall have presently, which could kill you without the flutter of an eyelid.

MARTHA: Do not imagine talk like that affects me; really it would make little difference. For I, too, have seen and heard enough; I, too, have resolved to die. But I shall not join them; why, indeed, would I want their company? I shall leave them to their new-found love, to their dark embraces. Neither you nor I have any part in these; all

that is ended and they are unfaithful to us – for ever.
Luckily I have my bedroom and the roof-tree's strong.

MARIA: What does it matter to me that you die or the whole
world falls in ruins, if through you I have lost the man I
love, and henceforth I am doomed to live in a dark night
of loneliness, where every memory is torture?

[MARTHA *comes behind her and speaks over her head.*]

MARTHA: Don't let's exaggerate. You have lost your husband and I have lost my mother. We are quits. But you
have only lost him once, after enjoying his love for years
and without his having cast you off. My lot is worse. First
my mother cast me off, and now she is dead. I have lost
her twice.

MARIA: Yes, perhaps I might be tempted to pity you and
share my grief with you, did I not know what was awaiting
him, alone in his room, last night, when you were plotting
his death.

MARTHA [*her voice has a sudden accent of despair*]: I'm quits
with your husband, too, for I have suffered as he suffered.
Like him, I thought I had made sure my home for always;
I thought that crime had forged a bond between me and
my mother that nothing could ever break. And on whom
in all the world should I rely, if not on the woman who
had killed beside me? I was mistaken. Crime, too, means
solitude, even if a thousand people join together to commit it. And it is fitting that I should die alone, after having
lived and killed alone.

[MARIA *turns towards her, tears streaming down her cheeks.*
MARTHA *moves back; her voice grows hard again.*]

MARTHA: Stop! I told you not to touch me. At the mere
thought that a human hand could lay its warmth on me
before I die; at the mere thought that anything at all
resembling the foul love of men is dogging me still, I feel
the blood pulsing in my temples in a fury of disgust.

[MARIA *has risen to her feet. The two women now are face to face, standing very near each other.*]

MARIA: Have no fear. I shall do nothing to prevent your dying as you wish. For with this hideous pain that grips my body like a vice, I feel a sort of blindness falling on my eyes and everything around me is growing dim. Neither you nor your mother will ever be more to me than vague, fleeting faces that came and went in the course of a tragedy which can never end. For you, Martha, I have no hatred and no pity. I have lost the power of loving or hating anybody. [*Suddenly she buries her face in her hands.*] But then – I have hardly had time to suffer or to rebel. My calamity was . . . too big for me.

MARTHA [*who has taken some steps towards the door, comes back towards Maria*]: But still not big enough; it has left you eyes to weep with. And I see that something remains for me to do before leaving you for ever. I have yet to drive you to despair.

MARIA [*gazing at her, horror-stricken*]: Oh, please leave me alone! Go away, and let me be!

MARTHA: Yes, I am going, and it will be a relief for me, as well. Your love and your tears are odious to me. But before I go to die, I must rid you of the illusion that you are right, that love isn't futile, and that what has happened was an accident. On the contrary, it's now that we are in the normal order of things, and I must convince you of it.

MARIA: What do you mean by that?

MARTHA: That in the normal order of things no one is ever recognized.

MARIA [*distractedly*]: Oh, what do I care? I only know that my heart is torn to shreds, and nothing, nothing matters to it except the man you killed.

MARTHA [*savagely*]: Be silent! I will not have you speak of that man; I loathe him. And he is nothing to you now. He has gone down into the bitter house of eternal exile. The fool! Well, he has got what he wanted; he is with the woman he crossed the sea to find. So all of us are served now, as we should be, in the order of things. But fix this in your mind; neither for him nor for us, neither in life nor in death, is there any peace or homeland. [*With a scornful laugh*] For you'll agree one can hardly call it a home, that place of clotted darkness underground, to which we go from here, to feed blind animals.

MARIA [*weeping*]: I can't, oh no, I can't bear to hear you talk like that. And I know he, too, wouldn't have borne it. It was to find another homeland that he crossed the sea.

MARTHA [*who has walked to the door, swings round on her*]: His folly has received its wages. And soon you will receive yours. [*Laughing as before*] We're cheated, I tell you. Cheated! What do they serve, those blind impulses that surge up in us, the yearnings that rack our souls? Why cry out for the sea, or for love? What futility! Your husband knows now what the answer is: that charnel house where in the end we shall lie huddled together, side by side. [*Vindictively*] A time will come when you, too, know it, and then, could you remember anything, you would recall as a delightful memory this day which seems to you the beginning of the cruellest of exiles. Try to realize that no grief of yours can ever equal the injustice done to man.

And now – before I go, let me give a word of advice; I owe it to you, since I killed your husband. Pray your God to harden you to stone. It's the happiness He has assigned Himself, and the one true happiness. Do as He does, be deaf to all appeals, and turn your heart to stone while there still is time. But if you feel you lack the courage to enter into this hard, blind peace – then come and join us in our common house. Good-bye, my sister. As you see, it's all quite simple. You have a choice between the mindless happiness of stones and the slimy bed in which we are awaiting you. [*She goes out.*]

[MARIA, *who has been listening in horrified amazement, sways, stretching out her arms in front of her.*]

MARIA [*her voice rising to a scream*]: Oh God, I cannot live in this desert! It is on You that I must call, and I shall find the words to say. [*She sinks on her knees.*] I place myself in your hands. Have pity, turn towards me. Hear me and raise me from the dust, oh Heavenly Father! Have pity on those who love each other and are parted.

[*The door opens. The old* MANSERVANT *is standing on the threshold.*]

THE OLD MANSERVANT [*in a clear, firm tone*]: What's all this noise? Did you call me?

MARIA [*gazing at him*]: Oh! . . . I don't know. But help me, help me, for I need help. Be kind and say that you will help me.

THE OLD MANSERVANT [*in the same tone*]: No.

CURTAIN

THE JUST

Characters

DORA DOULEBOV
BORIS ANNENKOV *(Boria)*
STEPAN FEDOROV
ALEXIS VOINOV
IVAN KALIAYEV *(Yanek)*
GUARD
FOKA
SKOURATOV, *Chief of Police*
GRAND-DUCHESS

action takes place in Moscow. The year – 1906.

ACT ONE

Scene: The terrorists' flat. The morning sun is shining through a window. When the curtain rises, DORA DOULEBOV *and* BORIS ANNENKOV *are standing in the middle of the room. Silence. Then the front-door bell rings once.* DORA *seems about to say something, but* ANNENKOV *signals to her to keep quiet. Two more rings in quick succession . . .*

ANNENKOV: It's him! [*Exits . . .* DORA *waits motionless; . . .* ANNENKOV *returns with* STEPAN FEDOROV, *whom he clasps affectionately by the shoulders.*] Here he is! It's Stepan, he's back!

DORA [*going up to* STEPAN *and clasping his hand*]: Welcome home, Stepan!

STEPAN: Hello, Dora.

DORA: Three years – just think. [*She is gazing at him.*]

STEPAN: Yes . . . three long years. The day they arrested me I was coming to join you.

DORA: Yes, we were expecting you all the time. I shall never forget how my heart sank as the minutes ticked away. We didn't dare look at each other.

ANNENKOV: Of course we had to move to another flat immediately.

STEPAN: I know.

DORA: How was it inside, Stepan?

STEPAN: Inside?

DORA: I mean in prison.

STEPAN: You can sometimes escape.

ANNENKOV: You know how we felt when we heard you'd got through to Switzerland.

STEPAN: Switzerland's a prison too.

ANNENKOV: Well, at least they're free there.

STEPAN: 'Freedom' will remain a prison until every man on earth is free! I was free of course, but all I could think about were Russia and ... her slaves. [*Short pause.*]

ANNENKOV: I'm glad they've sent you here.

STEPAN: I had to come. I was suffocating. At least I can do something. [*Looks at* ANNENKOV.] We *are* going to kill him, aren't we?

ANNENKOV: Yes we are.

STEPAN: We'll kill the murderer....You're the one who gives the orders, Boria, and I will always obey you.

ANNENKOV: I don't need any promises, Stepan. We are all brothers.

STEPAN: We must have discipline. That's one thing I did learn in prison. The Socialist Revolution must have discipline. Then we will kill the Grand Duke and crush tyranny for ever.

DORA [*going towards him*]: Sit down, Stepan. You must be tired after your long journey.

STEPAN: I'm never tired. [*A pause* ... DORA *sits.*] Is everything ready, Boria?

ANNENKOV [*changing tone*]: For the last month, two of our men have been studying the Duke's movements. Dora has got together all the materials we need.

STEPAN: Has the proclamation been drafted yet?

ANNENKOV: Yes. All Russia shall know that the Socialist Revolutionary party has killed the Grand Duke Sergei to hasten the liberation of the Russian people. The Imperial Court will learn that we are determined to continue our reign of terror until the land is returned to the people.

Yes, Stepan, everything is ready! We haven't long to wait.

STEPAN: What's my job?

ANNENKOV: To begin with, you will help Dora. You'll replace Schweitzer, who used to work with her.

STEPAN: He was killed, was he?

ANNENKOV: Yes.

STEPAN: How?

DORA: An accident. [STEPAN *looks at* DORA, *who lowers her gaze.*]

STEPAN: What do I do after that?

ANNENKOV: We'll see about that later. You must be ready as a replacement, if necessary, and you must make sure that we keep in contact with Headquarters.

STEPAN: Who are our friends here?

ANNENKOV: You met Voinov in Switzerland. He's young but thoroughly reliable. Then there's Yanek... you don't know him, do you?

STEPAN: Yanek?

ANNENKOV: His real name is Kaliayev. We also called him the 'Poet'.

STEPAN: That's no name for a terrorist.

ANNENKOV [*laughing*]: Well, Yanek thinks it is. He says that all poetry is revolutionary.

STEPAN: Only bombs are revolutionary ... [*A pause.*]. ... Do you think I'll be able to help you, Dora?

DORA: Oh yes! You'll have to be careful when you're handling the fuse though.

STEPAN: What if it breaks?

DORA: That's how Schweitzer was killed. [*A pause.*] What are you smiling at, Stepan?

STEPAN: Was I smiling?

DORA: Yes, you were.

STEPAN: I do ... sometimes. [*A pause.*] Tell me, Dora, would one bomb be enough to blow up this house?

DORA: Not one by itself, but it would do a lot of damage.

STEPAN: How many bombs would it take to blow up Moscow?

ANNENKOV: Are you out of your mind? What do you mean?

STEFAN: Oh, nothing ... [*Slight pause, the bell rings once ... they wait, listening ... the bell rings twice ...* ANNENKOV *goes through into the hall and returns with* ALEXIS VOINOV.]

VOINOV: Stepan!

STEPAN: Hello, Alexis. [*They shake hands ...* VOINOV *then goes to* DORA *and embraces her.*]

ANNENKOV: Everything all right, Alexis?

VOINOV: Yes.

ANNENKOV: Have you studied the route from the palace to the theatre?

VOINOV: I can map it out for you now. [*He takes out a sheet of paper from his jacket and draws.*] Look. Turnings, narrow streets, crossroads ... the carriage will go by under our window.

ANNENKOV: What do those two crosses mean?

VOINOV: One is a little square where the horses will have to slow down; the other is the theatre, where they'll stop. Those are the best places, I think.

ANNENKOV: Right – give it to me.

STEPAN: What about police spies?

VOINOV [*hesitantly*]: They're all over the place.

STEPAN: They worry you, do they?

VOINOV: Well, I'm not very happy about them.

ANNENKOV: Nobody is. Don't worry, Alexis.

VOINOV: It's not that I'm afraid; I'm just not used to lying, that's all.

STEPAN: Everybody lies. The important thing is to lie well.

VOINOV: It's not so easy. When I was at University, the other students always laughed at me, because I could never hide my feelings. I always blurted everything out. I was expelled in the end.

STEPAN: Why?

VOINOV: In my history course, my tutor asked me how Peter the Great founded Petrograd ...

STEPAN: Good question.

VOINOV: I said that he founded it on murder and brutality. In the end I was expelled.

STEPAN: And what then?

VOINOV: Then I realized that it wasn't enough just to denounce injustice. One must give one's life to fighting it. So, now I'm happy.

STEPAN: And yet you have to lie.

VOINOV: I do *now*, yes. But I'll have finished lying on the day I throw the bomb ... [*The bell rings – twice and then once* ... DORA *gets up with a start.*]

ANNENKOV: It's Yanek. [DORA *rushes out.*]

STEPAN: It was a different signal.

ANNENKOV: Oh, it's just one of Yanek's whims. He has his private signal ... [STEPAN *shrugs his shoulders* ... DORA's *voice is heard in the hall* ... DORA *and* IVAN KALIAYEV *come in, arm in arm* ... KALIAYEV *is laughing.*]

DORA: Yanek, this is Stepan – he's replacing Schweitzer.

KALIAYEV: Welcome, Stepan!

STEPAN: Thank you. [DORA *and* KALIAYEV *both sit down, facing the others.*]

ANNENKOV: You'll recognize the carriage, Yanek?

KALIAYEV: Yes. I've had two long looks at it and I'd recognize it a mile off! I've noted every detail – one of the panes of the left-hand lamp is chipped, for instance.

VOINOV: What about police spies?

KALIAYEV [*laughing*]: Oh, they're all over the place, but we're old friends – I sell them cigarettes!!

ANNENKOV: Has Pavel confirmed our information?

KALIAYEV: The Grand Duke is due to go to the theatre this week. Pavel will soon know the exact day ... he'll leave a message at the door ... [*Turning to* DORA *and laughing.*] Oh, Dora, we're in luck.

DORA [*looking at him*]: I see you've taken off your peddlar's outfit. You're a proper gentleman now! You look quite handsome! Don't you miss your fluffy coat?

KALIAYEV [*laughing*]: I certainly do ... I was very proud of it. [*To* STEPAN *and* ANNENKOV.] First I spent two months watching the peddlars at work, then another month or so practising in my room. They never suspected a thing. 'He's amazing,' they used to say. 'He'd sell the Tsar's horses and get away with it!' In fact, they tried to pick up a few hints!

DORA: And of course you laughed.

KALIAYEV: You know I can't help laughing. The disguise, the new life ... everything amused me.

DORA: I can't bear fancy-dress. [*Pointing to her dress.*] And then, this luxurious get-up! Boria might have found something else. Me! An actress? No, I'm *simple*-hearted.

KALIAYEV [*laughing*]: But you look so pretty in it.

DORA: Pretty? I'd like to be pretty, but I mustn't think about that ...

KALIAYEV: Oh, Dora! Why not? There is always such a sad look in your eyes. You should be full of joy and pride. ... There *is* beauty and happiness in the world! 'In those quiet places where my heart once longed for you ...'

DORA [*smiling*]: ' ... I breathed eternal summer.'

KALIAYEV: Oh, Dora! You remember those lines ... and you're smiling. Oh, I'm so happy!

STEPAN [*cutting in*]: We're wasting our time. Boria, hadn't we better go down and see the porter? [KALIAYEV *looks at* STEPAN *with bewilderment.*]

ANNENKOV: Yes. Would you go down, Dora? ... and don't forget the tip. Then Alexis will help you get the stuff together in the other room. [DORA *and* VOINOV *exit ...* STEPAN *walks quickly up to* ANNENKOV.]

STEPAN: I want to throw the bomb.

ANNENKOV: No, Stepan. It's already been decided.

STEPAN: I beg you to let me throw the bomb. You know how much it means to me.

ANNENKOV: No, orders are orders. [*A pause.*] I'm not throwing the bomb either ... I'll be waiting here too; it's hard, but those are the rules.

STEPAN: Who *is* going to throw the first bomb?

KALIAYEV: I am ... and Voinov's throwing the second one.

STEPAN: You!

KALIAYEV: Yes. Does it surprise you? Don't you trust me?

STEPAN: It's a matter of experience.

KALIAYEV: Experience? You know you can only throw the bomb once ... and then ... no one's ever had a second chance.

STEPAN: You need a steady hand.

KALIAYEV [*holding out his hand*]: Look! Do you think that hand will tremble? [STEPAN *turns round.*] No, it won't tremble. Do you think that I shall hesitate when the Grand Duke's there in front of me? Surely you cannot think that! [STEPAN *turns his back on* KALIAYEV.] And even if my arm did begin to tremble ... I know a sure way of killing him.

STEPAN: What's that?

KALIAYEV: I'd throw myself under the horses' feet.

[STEPAN *shrugs his shoulders, walks to the back of the room and sits.*]

ANNENKOV: There won't be any need for that. Your orders are to try to get away. The Organization needs you – you save yourself if you can.

KALIAYEV: All right, Boria, but what an honour for me and I shall live up to it!

ANNENKOV: Stepan ... you will be in the street while Yanek and Alexis are waiting for the carriage. I want you to walk up and down in front of our window at regular intervals – we'll settle on a signal later. Dora and I will wait here and issue the proclamation when the time comes. With a bit of luck the Grand Duke will be dead.

KALIAYEV [*triumphantly*]: Yes, I shall kill him ... and how glorious it will be if it is successful! But, of course, the Grand Duke is nothing ... we must strike higher.

ANNENKOV: But we must start with the Grand Duke.

KALIAYEV: And suppose we fail, Boria ... then we must do what the Japanese did.

ANNENKOV: What do you mean?

KALIAYEV: During the war, the Japanese never surrendered ... they killed themselves!

ANNENKOV: No, Yanek, don't think of suicide.

KALIAYEV: What should I think of then?

ANNENKOV: Of carrying on our work of terrorism.

STEPAN [*still facing the back of the room*]: To commit suicide, a man must have a great love for himself. A true revolutionary cannot love himself.

KALIAYEV [*turning on* STEPAN ... *sharply*]: A true revolutionary? Why are you treating me like this ... what have you got against me?

STEPAN: I don't like people who dabble with revolution because they're bored.

ANNENKOV: Stepan!

STEPAN [*gets up and walks down towards them*]: Yes, I'm brutal
... but for me hatred is not just a game. We aren't here
to admire each other ... we are here to succeed.

KALIAYEV [*in a soft voice*]: Why are you taking it out on me?
Who told you that I was bored?

STEPAN: There was no need to tell me. You change the
signals. You like dressing up as a peddlar. You recite
poems and now you want to throw yourself under the
horses' feet. [*A pause* ... STEPAN *looks at* KALIAYEV.]
No, I can't say you inspire me with confidence.

KALIAYEV [*louder*]: You don't know me, brother. I love life
and I'm never bored. I joined the revolution *because*
I love life!

STEPAN: I don't love life ... I love something higher than
mere life ... I love justice.

KALIAYEV [*with visible restraint*]: Each of us serves justice in
his own way – you in yours and I in mine. Why not agree
to be different? Let's love one another if we can.

STEPAN: We cannot.

KALIAYEV [*shouting*]: What are you doing with us then?

STEPAN: I have come to kill a man, not to love him or agree
to differ from him.

KALIAYEV [*passionately*]: You will not kill him by yourself... for no cause! You will kill him with us ... on
behalf of the Russian people! That is your only justification.

STEPAN [*furiously*]: I don't need any justification! I got all
the justification I'll ever want three years ago, one night
in prison ... and I won't put up with ...

ANNENKOV: That's enough! Are you both out of your
minds? Have you forgotten who we are? We are all
brothers working hand in hand to put an end to tyranny
and set our people free! *Together*, we will kill, and nothing
can divide us! [*Silence* ... *he looks at them.*] Come along,

Stepan ... we must settle the signals. [*Exit* STEPAN.]
Don't take it to heart, Yanek. Stepan has been through a
lot ... I'll have a word with him.

KALIAYEV [*he is very pale*]: He insulted me, Boria. [*Enter*
DORA.]

DORA [*seeing* KALIAYEV]: What's wrong?

ANNENKOV: Nothing. [*He exits.*]

DORA [*to* KALIAYEV]: What's wrong, Yanek?

KALIAYEV: We've had a row already. He doesn't like me.
[DORA *sits in silence ... a pause.*]

DORA: I don't think he likes anyone, but he'll be happier
when it's all over. Don't worry, Yanek.

KALIAYEV: But I *do* worry. I want you all to love me. I've
sacrificed everything for the Organization and I couldn't
bear it if my brothers turned away from me. Sometimes
I feel they don't understand me. Perhaps it's my fault ...
I know I often don't say the right things and I ...

DORA: They *do* love you ... they *do* understand you; only
Stepan is different.

KALIAYEV: No, Dora. I know what he thinks. Schweitzer
used to say the same sort of thing: 'Yanek! Yanek's too
eccentric to be a revolutionary ...' If only I could convince them I'm not eccentric. They think I'm a bit mad,
too impulsive, but I believe in our cause just as they do.
I am ready to lay down my life for it like them! *I* can be
cunning and cool, secretive and efficient ... only I am still
convinced that life is a glorious thing – love ... beauty ...
and happiness. That's why I hate tyranny! But how can
I explain it to them? Revolution – yes! ... but revolution
for the sake of life – to give life a chance ... do *you*
understand?

DORA: Yes, I understand! ... [*Pause ... more softly*] ... but
what we're giving is not life ... but death.

KALIAYEV: We? ... Oh, I see what you mean. No, that's
not the same thing at all. We are killing to build a world
where there'll be no killing at all. We must accept our
role as criminals, until finally everyone on earth is
innocent ...

DORA: Suppose it doesn't work out like that?

KALIAYEV: No, Dora! You know that's impossible. Stepan
would be right then ... and we'd have to spit in the face of
beauty.

DORA: I've been in the Organization longer than you have
and I know that nothing is as simple as you think. But
you have faith ... and faith is what we all need.

KALIAYEV: Faith? [*Long pause.*] No ... no, only one man
had that ...

DORA: You have conviction in your soul. You will push
aside everything to fulfil your ideal. Why did you ask to
throw the first bomb?

KALIAYEV: Can you just talk about revolution without
actually taking part in it? [*He begins to pace about.*]

DORA: No ...

KALIAYEV: No, you must be right at the heart of it all.

DORA [*thoughtfully*]: Yes ... there you are, right out in front
... and then the final moment – that's what we must
think of. That's when we need courage and inspiration.

KALIAYEV: I've thought of nothing else for a year. This is
the moment I've been waiting for all my life, and I now
know that I would die right there beside the Grand Duke
... I would shed my blood to the very last drop or shrivel
up in the heat of the explosion. Do you understand why
I asked to throw the first bomb? To die for our ideal – it's
the only way to prove myself worthy of it ... it's the only
justification.

DORA: I would like to die like that too.

KALIAYEV: It's the greatest happiness one could wish for
... and yet ... sometimes, at night, when I'm lying awake
on a thin straw mattress – that's all a peddlar can afford –
sometimes it worries me to think that they have forced us
to be murderers ... but then I remember that I am going
to die too ... and everything's all right. I smile to myself
... like a child, and go back to sleep again.

DORA: That's how it should be, Yanek – to kill and to die
... but I think there is an even greater happiness ...
[a pause] ... [lowering her gaze as KALIAYEV looks at her]
... the scaffold.

KALIAYEV [fervently]: I have thought about that too....
Yes, there's something incomplete about dying on the
spot ... but between that moment and the scaffold, there
is an eternity ... perhaps the only eternity man can ever
know.

DORA [she is intense and eager ... she takes his hands in hers]:
That's the thought that will help you through: we are
giving more than we take.

KALIAYEV: What do you mean?

DORA: We are forced to kill, aren't we? We deliberately
sacrifice a life, don't we? A single life?

KALIAYEV: Yes.

DORA: But throwing a bomb and then climbing the scaffold
... that's giving one's life twice ... so we give more than
we take.

KALIAYEV: Yes ... that's dying twice. Thank you, Dora.
No one can reproach us for anything now ... now I am
sure of myself! [A pause.] What is it, Dora?

DORA: I'd like to help you more ... only ...

KALIAYEV: Only what?

DORA: No, I mustn't.

KALIAYEV: Don't you trust me?

DORA: Darling, it's myself I don't trust. Since Schweitzer died, some strange thoughts have occurred to me ... but it's not for me to tell you what will be difficult.

KALIAYEV: I like things that are difficult. If you *respect* me at all, you will tell me.

DORA [*looking at him*]: I know. You are very brave. That's what worries me. You laugh, you work yourself up, you go forward eagerly to the sacrifice ... but in a few hours, you will have to come out of your dream and face reality. Perhaps it's best to talk about this before, so that there is no surprise, no possibility of flinching.

KALIAYEV: I shall not falter! ... but please ... carry on.

DORA: Throwing the bomb, the scaffold, dying twice over – that's the easy part. Your heart will see you through ... but you'll be standing right out in front ... [*she looks at him and seems to hesitate*] ... and you'll see him.

KALIAYEV: See who?

DORA: The Grand Duke.

KALIAYEV: Yes, but only for a moment.

DORA: In that moment, you'll look at him. ... Oh, Yanek, it's best for you to know, to be warned. A man is a man – the Grand Duke may have gentle eyes. Perhaps you'll see him smiling to himself or scratching his ear. Perhaps, who knows, you'll see a little scar on his cheek where he cut himself shaving ... and if he looks at you at the moment ...

KALIAYEV: It's not him I'm destroying ... I'm destroying tyranny!

DORA: Yes, I know; tyranny must be destroyed. ... I'll get the bomb ready, and when I'm screwing in the tube – that's the moment when it's touch and go, when one's nerves are all on edge ... and yet I'll feel strangely happy ... but then I don't know the Grand Duke. It wouldn't be nearly so easy, if he was sitting in front of me while I was screwing in the tube, looking at me ... but *you will* see him ... he'll be quite near you, just a yard or two away.

KALIAYEV [*passionately*]: I shall not see him!

DORA: Why? ... are you going to shut your eyes?

KALIAYEV: No ... but with God's help, my ... hatred will surge up just in time and blind me! [*The bell rings once ... they do not move ...* STEPAN *and* VOINOV *enter ... voices are heard in the hall ... enter* ANNENKOV.]

ANNENKOV [*a pause*]: It's the porter. The Grand Duke is going to the theatre ... tomorrow! [*He looks at them all.*] Everything must be ready, Dora.

DORA [*in a low voice*]: Right. [*Exit* DORA.]

KALIAYEV [*watches her go ... then, turning to* STEPAN, *in a quiet voice*]: I shall kill him ... with joy!

CURTAIN

ACT TWO

Scene: The same . . . the following evening. ANNENKOV *is looking out of the window.* DORA *is standing by the table.*

ANNENKOV: Yanek and Alexis are ready. Stepan has just lit a cigarette.

DORA: When is the Grand Duke due to go by?

ANNENKOV: Any minute now. Listen! . . . isn't that a carriage? No . . .

DORA: Be patient, Boria. Sit down.

ANNENKOV: What about the bombs?

DORA: Do sit down – there's nothing more we can do.

ANNENKOV: Yes, there is – we can envy them . . .

DORA: You belong here: you're in charge.

ANNENKOV: Yes, I'm in charge, but Yanek's a better man; perhaps he's the one . . .

DORA: The risk is the same for everyone – for the man who throws the bomb and the man who doesn't.

ANNENKOV: In the long run, yes, the risk is the same, but today it is Yanek and Alexis who are in the firing line. Oh, I know I haven't the right to be with them, but sometimes I can't help thinking that perhaps I'm a little too ready to play my part. After all, it's much easier not to have to throw the bomb yourself.

DORA: What if it is? The only thing that really matters is that you do your duty to the end.

ANNENKOV: Oh, you're so calm, Dora!

DORA: I'm not calm: I'm frightened! I've been with the Group for three years, and for two years I've been making

179

the bombs. I have done everything I was told to do, and I don't think I've ever let you down....

ANNENKOV: Of course you haven't, Dora...

DORA: Well ... all those three years ... I've been afraid. I've been haunted by that creeping fear that leaves you only when you go to sleep; but when you wake up, there it is waiting at your bedside ... so I just had to get used to it. I've trained myself to keep calm just when I'm most afraid. But it's nothing to be proud of.

ANNENKOV: You should be proud. Look at me ... I've never really mastered anything. You know ... I sometimes find myself regretting the old days ... the gay life, pretty women ... yes, I used to enjoy the drinking ... and the women, and those nights that went on for ever....

DORA: I always thought so, Boria! That's why I'm so fond of you; you still have a heart, even if it still longs for pleasure.... Surely that is better than the awful coldness that sometimes stifles all emotion.

ANNENKOV: Dora, what are you saying? Is it possible? Hearing that from you!

DORA [*standing up abruptly as the sound of a carriage passing by is heard*]: Ssh! Listen! [*Silence.*] No, it isn't him; my heart is pounding. You see ... I've still a lot to learn.

ANNENKOV [*going to the window*]: Hold it! Stepan's signalling ... It's him! He's coming!... [*They listen to the distant rumbling of a carriage, which draws nearer and nearer and then goes by the window ... a long silence ...*] In a few seconds ... [*a pause*] ... oh, how time drags. What can have happened? [DORA *flinches ... long silence ... church bells are heard in the distance.*] Oh, no! Yanek should have thrown the bomb by now. The carriage must have reached the theatre. What about Alexis? Look! Stepan's running back towards the theatre.

DORA [*flinging herself against* ANNENKOV]: Yanek's been arrested! They've arrested him ... they have, they have! Oh, Boria, we must do something!

ANNENKOV: Wait ... [*He listens.*] No... well, that's it then.

DORA: How did it happen? How can Yanek have been arrested when he hasn't done anything? He was ready for it, I know he was: he wanted the prison and the trial ... but after he had killed the Grand Duke ... not like this ... oh, no, not like this! [ANNENKOV *glances outside.*]

ANNENKOV: It's Alexis ... quickly ... [DORA *rushes to the door and opens it to reveal* VOINOV *looking distraught.*] What's happened, Alexis? What's happened?

VOINOV: I don't know ... I was waiting for the first bomb ... I ... I saw the carriage rounding the corner ... and nothing happened ... I panicked ... I thought you'd changed the plans at the last minute ... and I hesitated ... and ... and then I ran back here.

ANNENKOV: What about Yanek?

VOINOV: I haven't seen him.

DORA: He *has* been arrested!

ANNENKOV [*looking out of the window*]: No ... there he is! [KALIAYEV *comes in, tears streaming down his face.*]

KALIAYEV [*distraught*]: Forgive me ... I ... I couldn't do it. ... [DORA *goes to him and takes his hand.*]

DORA: It's all right, Yanek ... it's all right ...

ANNENKOV: What happened?

DORA: Don't worry, Yanek – it's like that sometimes; at the last minute everything goes wrong.

ANNENKOV: No, I can't believe it!

DORA: Leave him alone. You're not the only one, Yanek – Schweitzer couldn't pull it off the first time either.

ANNENKOV: Were you afraid?

KALIAYEV [*with a start*]: Afraid! No! ... you've got no right to.... [*The bell rings once and then twice ... they all stand quite still ... at a signal from* ANNENKOV, VOINOV *goes out* ... KALIAYEV *is crushed ... silence ... enter* STEPAN.]

ANNENKOV: Well?

STEPAN: There were children in the Grand Duke's carriage.

ANNENKOV: Children!

STEPAN: Yes... his nephew and niece.

ANNENKOV: Orlov said the Grand Duke would be alone.

STEPAN: The Grand Duchess was there as well: too many people for our poet, I suppose! Luckily, the police-spies didn't notice anything. [ANNENKOV *speaks quietly to* STEPAN ... *they all watch* KALIAYEV, *who stares at* STEPAN.]

KALIAYEV [*dazed*]: I never thought it would be like that ... children ... oh no, not children! Have you ever looked at a child and seen those grave, intent eyes?... somehow I can never face them ... and to think that only a moment before I was so gloriously happy ... standing on the corner of that little side-street ... in a patch of shadow.... The moment I saw the carriage lights shining in the distance, my heart began to race, with joy ... yes, with joy.... It beat faster and faster as the rumbling of the wheels drew nearer ... I wanted to leap in the air ... I really believe ... I was laughing and I kept on saying, 'Yes ... Yes!' ... do you understand? [*He looks away from* STEPAN *and sinks again into depression.*] I ran forward!... it was then that I saw the children. [*A pause.*] *They* weren't laughing ... just staring in front of them, holding themselves ... very straight. How sad they looked!... swamped in their best clothes, their hands resting on their thighs, like two little statues framed in the windows on each side of the door ... I didn't see the Grand Duchess ... I only saw them. If they had looked at me then I think I would have thrown the bomb, if only to shut out the sad look in their eyes!... But they just kept staring ... staring straight ahead. [*He looks at each of them in turn ... silence ... then in a low, broken voice.*] I cannot explain what happened to me then.... My arms ... went limp ... my legs began to tremble ... and a moment later ... it was too late! [*Silence ... he looks at the ground.*] Dora! Was I dreaming ... or did I hear bells ringing?

DORA: No, Yanek, you weren't dreaming. [*She takes his arm.*]

KALIAYEV [*seeing them all looking at him, he raises his head and stands up*]: Yes, look at me ... go on, look at me!... but I'm no coward! I didn't falter, Boria ... I just didn't expect them ... everything happened so quickly ... those two serious little faces and that hideous weight in my hand ... I was going to have to throw it at them ... just like that ... straight at them.... Oh, no!... I just couldn't do it! [*He looks at each of them in turn ... they are all quite still and silent.*] In the old days, when I used to go driving on our estate in the Ukraine, I always drove like a madman, because I wasn't afraid of anything ... except of running down a child. That was my only fear. I used to imagine the shock, the small head hitting the ground.... [*He breaks down*] ... oh, help me ... help me ... [*silence*]. I meant to kill myself just now. I only came back because I thought I owed it to you ... you are the only people who can judge me ... say if I was right or wrong ... but you don't say anything! [*He is desperate ...* DORA *goes to him and touches him.... he looks at them all and then dejectedly ...*] If you decide that those children must die, I shall go to the theatre and wait for them to come out ... I shall throw the bomb and I can promise not to miss ... just make up your minds ... I'll do what you decide.

STEPAN: The Organization ordered you to kill the Grand Duke!

KALIAYEV: Yes, but I wasn't ordered to murder children!

ANNENKOV: Yanek's right – we weren't expecting that.

STEPAN: It was his duty to obey orders.

ANNENKOV: I'm in charge, and I should have foreseen everything so that no one could have hesitated to carry out orders. It was my fault. Now we have to decide if we are to let this chance go by or tell Yanek to wait outside the theatre for them. Alexis?

VOINOV: I don't know what to say. . . . I think I would have done what Yanek did . . . but I'm not sure of myself . . . [more quietly] It's my hands . . . they are trembling.

ANNENKOV: Dora?

DORA [passionately]: I would have held back like Yanek. How can I ask others to do what I couldn't do myself?

STEPAN: Do you people realize what this decision means? Two months of shadowing, of hair's-breadth escapes – two wasted months! Egor arrested . . . for nothing! Rikov hanged . . . for nothing! Have we got to start all over again? Weeks and weeks of endless suspense, of sleepless nights . . . plotting and scheming, before we get another opportunity like this. Are you all out of your minds?

ANNENKOV: You know very well that in two days' time the Grand Duke will be going to the theatre again.

STEPAN: Two days . . . in which we risk being caught at any moment – you've said so yourself.

KALIAYEV: I'm going . . .

DORA: No, wait. Stepan, could you fire point blank at a child with your eyes open?

STEPAN: I could if the Organization ordered it.

DORA: Then why did you shut your eyes?

STEPAN: What? I shut my eyes?

DORA: Yes.

STEPAN: Then it was because I wanted to picture the scene more vividly so that my answer could be truthful.

DORA: Open your eyes, Stepan, and try to realize that the Organization would lose its power and its influence, if it tolerated for a moment the idea of children being blown to pieces by our bombs.

STEPAN: I'm sorry, but I don't suffer from a tender heart! Not until the day comes when we stop being sentimental about children, will the revolution triumph and we be masters of the world.

DORA: When that day comes, the revolution will be loathed by the entire human race.

STEPAN: What does that matter if we love it enough to force our revolution on it, to rescue humanity from itself...

DORA: Suppose the whole human race rejects the revolution? Suppose the masses you're fighting for won't put up with their children being killed? Would you strike at *them* too?

STEPAN: Yes, if it was necessary, and I'd go on striking at them until they understood ... I too love the people.

DORA: That's not what love is.

STEPAN: Who says it isn't.

DORA: I do.

STEPAN: You are a woman!... and your idea of love is a poor one.

DORA [*violently*]: At least I have a very good idea of what shame is.

STEPAN: Shame? Once and only once in my life have I felt ashamed ... when I was flogged ... yes! *I* was flogged! Do you know what it's like to be flogged. Vera was there beside me ... and she killed herself as a protest;

but *I* lived on ... so why should I be ashamed of anything now?

ANNENKOV: All of us love and respect you, Stepan; but whatever your reasons are for feeling this way, you must not say that anything is justifiable ... thousands of us have died to prove that everything is *not* justifiable.

STEPAN: Nothing that can serve our cause should be ruled out.

ANNENKOV [*angrily*]: Is it justifiable to go over to the police and play a double game, as Evno suggested?

STEPAN: Yes, if it was necessary.

ANNENKOV [*getting up*]: We will forget what you've said, Stepan, because of all that you have done for us and with us. The point is this: are we or are we not going to throw the bombs at these children?

STEPAN: Children! There you go again, always talking about children! Don't you see what this means? Because Yanek didn't kill those *two, thousands* of Russian children will go on dying of starvation for years to come! Have you ever seen children dying of starvation ... I have, and to be killed by a bomb is pleasant compared to that ... but Yanek! ... Yanek has never seen children starving to death. He only saw the Grand Duke's little pair of lapdogs! Can't you see what will happen, or do you just live for the present? In that case, go on! ... indulge in charity ... and cure each petty little suffering that comes along, but don't meddle with the revolution, which exists to cure all suffering ... now and in the future.

DORA: Yanek will kill the Grand Duke because his death may help to bring nearer the day when Russian children no longer die of starvation. That by itself is no easy task for him, but killing the Grand Duke's niece and nephew won't prevent a single child from starving. Even destruction has a right and a wrong way, and there *are* limits ...

STEPAN [*violently*]: There are *no* limits! What it really means is that you don't believe in the revolution! [*They all get up except* KALIAYEV.] No, you don't believe in it – any of you! If you had your whole heart in it, if you were sure that our sacrifices and our triumphs will be the foundation of a new Russia, freed from tyranny ... a land of freedom that will gradually spread over the entire world and if you were convinced that then and only then will man, freed from tyrants and superstitions, at last look up to the sky – a god in his own right, how could the death of two children be weighed in the balance against such a faith? Surely you'd feel justified in doing anything and everything that might bring that day nearer ... so, if you won't kill those two children, it simply means that you're not sure you are justified ... so you don't believe in the revolution! [*Silence.*]

KALIAYEV [*gets up*]: I am ashamed of myself, Stepan, but I can't let you go on ... I am ready to kill to overthrow the tyranny, but behind your words I can see the threat of another kind of tyranny ... and if it ever comes into power, it will make me a murderer! It's justice that I try to fight for!

STEPAN: What does it matter if you're fighting for justice or you're murderers, as long as justice is done? You and I, we don't count!

KALIAYEV: Yes, we do and you know it. It's only pride that makes you say that.

STEPAN: My pride is my own business, but man's pride, his rebellions, the injustice that is done to him ... that concerns us all!

KALIAYEV: Man does not live only by justice ...

STEPAN: When his bread is stolen, what else has he to live by?

KALIAYEV: By justice ... and innocence ...

STEPAN: Innocence? ... I'm sure I'm aware of it, but I prefer to shut my eyes to it and to shut other men's eyes to it, so that one day it will have a universal meaning.

KALIAYEV: One must be very sure that that day will come, if one denies everything that makes a man willing to live.

STEPAN: I *am* sure it will come.

KALIAYEV: No, you can't be as sure as that! Perhaps as many as three generations will have to be sacrificed before it can be known which of us ... you or I ... is right. There will have been many wars and bloody revolutions, and by the time all this blood has seeped into the earth, you and I will long ago have turned to dust!

STEPAN: Then others will come and I will hail them as my brothers.

KALIAYEV [*shouting*]: Others, yes! ... but I love the men who are alive today ... who walk on the same earth as I do! It is for *them* that I am fighting, and it is for *them* that I am ready to lay down my life! I shall not strike my brothers in the face for the sake of some unknown ... distant city! I refuse to add to the living injustice around me for the sake of a ... dead ... justice ... [*more quietly, but firmly*] I want to tell you something that the simplest peasant knows: killing children is a crime against a man's honour, and if the revolution should ever break with honour ... then I should break with the revolution. If you decide that I must do it, I will go and wait for them to leave the theatre ... but I will throw myself under the horses' feet.

STEPAN: Honour is a luxury reserved for those who have carriages.

KALIAYEV: No! It is the one wealth left for the poor man. *You* know that, and you know too that the revolution has its honour. It's what we're all prepared to die for!... and it's what made you hold up your head, Stepan, when they flogged you and it's behind what you've been saying today.

STEPAN [*with a shout*]: I forbid you to speak of that.

KALIAYEV [*incensed*]: No!... I let you tell me that I didn't believe in the revolution, which was as good as telling me that I was prepared to kill the Grand Duke ... for nothing!... that I was nothing but a common murderer! ... I let you say that and I managed to keep my hands off you ...

ANNENKOV: Yanek!

STEPAN: Not to kill enough is killing for nothing sometimes.

ANNENKOV: None of us agrees with you, Stepan. We've made up our minds.

STEPAN: Then I accept your ... decision, but let me tell you again that squeamishness has no place in terrorism. We are murderers and that's what we've chosen to be.

KALIAYEV [*beside himself with rage*]: No! I have chosen death to prevent murder from triumphing in the world ... I have chosen to be innocent!

ANNENKOV: Yanek! Stepan! That's enough. We've decided that slaughtering these children would serve no purpose. We must start again from the beginning and be ready to try again in two days' time.

STEPAN: And suppose the children are there again?

KALIAYEV: We'll wait for another opportunity.

STEPAN: And if the Grand Duchess is with the Grand Duke?

KALIAYEV: I will not spare her.

ANNENKOV: Listen! [*The sound of a carriage is heard ...*
KALIAYEV *goes irresistibly to the window ... the others wait*

189

... *the carriage comes nearer, passes by the window and disappears* ...]

VOINOV [*looking at* DORA, *who goes towards him*]: Yes, Dora, we will have to start again.

STEPAN [*scornfully*]: Yes, Alexis ... start again; but of course, we must do something for our precious honour ...

CURTAIN

ACT THREE

Scene: The same ... two days later ... it is evening.

STEPAN: What's Voinov up to? He should be here by now.

ANNENKOV: He can do with some sleep, and we've got another half hour yet.

STEPAN: I could go down and see if there's any news.

ANNENKOV: No. We mustn't take unnecessary risks. [*Silence.*] Why are you so silent, Yanek?

KALIAYEV: I've got nothing to say, but don't worry about me ... [*The bell rings once and then twice.*] Here he is! [*Enter* VOINOV.]

ANNENKOV: Get some sleep?

VOINOV: A bit.

ANNENKOV: Did you sleep all night?

VOINOV: No.

ANNENKOV: You ought to have done. There are ways of making yourself sleep.

VOINOV: I tried ... but ... I'm too tired.

ANNENKOV: Your hands are shaking.

VOINOV: No, they're not! [*They are all looking at him.*] Why are you all staring at me? What's wrong with being tired?

ANNENKOV: That's not the point ... we're concerned about you.

VOINOV [*suddenly violent*]: You should have thought about that two days ago! If the bomb had been thrown then, we wouldn't be tired now.

KALIAYEV: I'm sorry, Alexis. I've made things harder for everyone.

VOINOV [*more quietly*]: What do you mean, harder? I'm tired, that's all.

DORA: Well, it won't be long now ... in an hour it will all be over.

VOINOV: Yes ... it will all be over, in an hour's time ... [*He looks around ... DORA gets up and takes his hand ... he leaves his hand in hers, then pulls it away.*] Boria, I want to talk to you.

ANNENKOV: In private?

VOINOV: Yes ... in private. [*They all glance at one another ... KALIAYEV, DORA and STEPAN exit.*]

ANNENKOV: What is it? ... [*Silence.*] Go on ... tell me, Alexis.

VOINOV: I'm ashamed, Boria ... [*Silence.*] I'm ashamed, but I must tell you the truth.

ANNENKOV: You don't want to throw the bomb ... is that it?

VOINOV: I can't bring myself to do it.

ANNENKOV: Do you mean you're scared? Is that it? Is that all? That's nothing to be ashamed of.

VOINOV: Yes, I am scared ... and I *am* ashamed of it.

ANNENKOV: But the day before yesterday you were so happy, so calm. When you went out, there was a gleam in your eye.

VOINOV: I've always been scared. The day before yesterday, I'd summoned up my courage, and when I heard the carriage rumbling in the distance, I said to myself: 'Only a minute to go!' I gritted my teeth ... and every muscle in my body was tense: if I'd thrown the bomb at that moment, I think the force of the throw alone would have killed the Grand Duke. I waited ... waited for the first explosion, which would set everything going ... and then ... nothing! It never came! The carriage rumbled past me ... how fast it went ... it passed me in a flash ... and then I realized that Yanek hadn't thrown his bomb. I went cold all over, and suddenly I felt as weak as a child ...

ANNENKOV: Don't worry, Alexis ... your strength will return to you.

VOINOV: Two days have gone by, but it hasn't come back. I lied to you just now ... I could sleep last night.... My heart was pounding. Oh, Boria! I give up ...

ANNENKOV: You mustn't give up, Alexis! We've all been through it as well. You won't be asked to throw the bomb.... A month's rest in Finland, and then you can come back to us.

VOINOV: No ... it's not as simple as that. If I don't throw the bomb today, I'll never throw it.

ANNENKOV: What are you going to do then?

VOINOV: I'll carry on with propaganda and committees, but I wasn't made for terrorism – I realize that now.... The best thing is for me to leave you.

ANNENKOV: The risk is the same.

VOINOV: Yes, but you can keep your eyes shut.... You don't know ... and that makes all the difference.

ANNENKOV: What do you mean?

VOINOV [*passionately*]: You don't see what happens; it's easy to go to meetings, to work out plans and then pass on orders to be carried out. You risk your life, I know ... but there's a sort of veil between you and the real thing: but it's different going down into the street when it's getting dark and standing among the crowds of people hurrying home to their evening meals, their children and their wives waiting on the doorstep ... and having to stand there ... grim and silent, with the weight of the bomb tugging at your arm ... and knowing that in three minutes, in two minutes, in a few seconds ... you will dash out towards a glistening carriage, the bomb in your hand.... That's what terrorist action is, and I know now that I couldn't start it all over again, without feeling the blood drained from my veins. Yes, I'm ashamed ... I aimed too high. I must be given the job I'm fit for – a humble job ... the only one I'm worthy of.

ANNENKOV: There are no humble jobs. All our paths lead to prison and the gallows.

VOINOV: Yes, but they're not staring you in the face. The man you're going to kill ... he's right there in front of you. You have to imagine ... prison and the gallows, and luckily I have no imagination ... [*He laughs nervously.*] I never really did believe in the secret police, you know ... funny, isn't it? ... for a terrorist? I'll believe they exist when I get my first kick in the stomach ... not before.

ANNENKOV: And when you're in prison? You can't help knowing and seeing.... There you have to face facts.

VOINOV: You don't have to make any more decisions in prison! That's what it is ... no more decisions ... no more saying to yourself: 'Now it's up to you, up to *you* to decide when to strike.' One thing I'm sure of now is that I shall not try to escape, if I'm arrested.... You have to make decisions to escape, you have to take the initiative. If you don't try to escape, *they* take the initiative ... they do all the work ...

ANNENKOV: Yes ... they hang you ...

VOINOV: ... but dying will be easier than ... [*desperately*] ... than carrying my life and another's in my hand and having to decide when to plunge those lives into oblivion.... No, Boria, the only way I can redeem myself is to accept myself for what I am ... [*silence*] ... even cowards can help the revolution – they've just got to find out how they can be useful.

ANNENKOV: We are all cowards really, but we aren't always forced to show it. ... Well, that's settled then ... it's up to you.

VOINOV: I shall leave at once. I don't think I could face the others. You'll tell them, won't you?

ANNENKOV: Yes ... I'll tell them. [*He goes towards* VOINOV.]

VOINOV: Tell Yanek it's not his fault ... and tell him I love him ... as I love you all ... [*Silence.* ANNENKOV *embraces him.*]

ANNENKOV: Good-bye, Alexis. ... It'll work out all right. ... *One* day Russia will be happy!

VOINOV: Oh yes, Boria ... happy! ... happy ... [*They go to the door. Exit* VOINOV.]

ANNENKOV: You can come in now. [*Enter* DORA, STEPAN *and* KALIAYEV.]

STEPAN: What was that about?

ANNENKOV: Voinov isn't going to throw the bomb. He's exhausted and he might bungle it.

KALIAYEV: It's my fault, isn't it, Boria?

ANNENKOV: He asked me to tell you that he loves you.

KALIAYEV: Will we see him again?

ANNENKOV: Maybe. ... He's leaving us for the time being.

STEPAN: Why?

ANNENKOV: He'll be more useful on the committees.

STEPAN: Did he ask to go? Has he lost his nerve?

ANNENKOV: No. ... It was my decision entirely.

STEPAN: So you're making us one short at the last minute.

ANNENKOV: I had to decide by myself. It was too late to talk it over with you. I shall take Voinov's place...

[STEPAN *makes a gesture of protest and starts to say something.*] No, Stepan.

KALIAYEV: You are our leader, Boria. It's your duty to stay here.

ANNENKOV: Sometimes it is the leader's duty to be a coward, provided that he proves his courage when the time comes. I've made up my mind. Stepan, you will replace me for as long as it is necessary.... Now come and listen to your instructions ... come along. [STEPAN *and* ANNENKOV *exit.... * KALIAYEV *sits ...* DORA *goes towards him, her hand outstretched ... but she withdraws it.*]

DORA: It's not your fault, Yanek.

KALIAYEV: I've hurt him ... I've hurt him deeply. Do you know what he said to me the other day?

DORA: He never stopped saying how happy he was.

KALIAYEV: Yes, but he told me that there was no happiness for him, except when he's with us. The Organization is everything in the world today ... and we are the Organization – we are the new spirit of truth. Oh, Dora, why did this have to happen?

DORA: He'll come back.

KALIAYEV: No ... I know what I'd feel like, if I were he, I'd be desperate.

DORA: *Aren't* you desperate?

KALIAYEV [*sadly*]: Now? ... now I'm with you, and I'm happy ... as *he* was.

DORA [*slowly*]: Yes, it's a wonderful happiness. [*A pause.*]

KALIAYEV: Yes ... it *is* a wonderful happiness ...

DORA: Then why are you so depressed? Two days ago, your face was shining. You looked as if you were inspired, but today ...

KALIAYEV [*getting up and pacing up and down*]: Today ... today I know something I didn't know then. You were right, Dora – it's not so simple after all. I thought it was easy to kill ... I thought that courage and the ideal would be enough; but I'm not so different, and I now know that there is no happiness in hatred ... I can see the vileness in myself and in the others – murder, cowardice, injustice. ... I've got to kill him ... I've *got* to, but I shall see it through to the end! I shall go beyond hatred!

DORA: Beyond? There is nothing beyond.

KALIAYEV: Yes, there is ... there's love!

DORA: Love? No, that's not what's needed.

KALIAYEV: Dora! How can you say that? ...

DORA: There's too much blood, too much brutality. Those who really have their hearts set on justice have no right to love. They stand upright like me, their heads held high, their eyes fastened on their goal. What room is there for love? Love pulls these proud heads down. ... Our heads must stay high, Yanek.

KALIAYEV: But we love our fellow men!

DORA: Yes, of course we love them, but with a vast, ungrounded love, with an unhappy love. We are so cut off from them, shut in our little rooms, lost in our thoughts ... and do the people love us? ... Do they ever know that we love them? No! The people don't say anything ... not a word.

KALIAYEV: But that's what love is: to give everything, to sacrifice everything, without expecting *anything* in return.

DORA: Perhaps. ... That's what burns in me, an ideal love ... pure lonely joy; yet there are times when I wonder if love is not something else ... something more than just a lonely voice ... I wonder if there isn't some kind of response: I often picture it – the sun shining, heads humbly bowed, hearts no longer proud, arms outstretched. ... Oh, Yanek! If only we could forget, just for an hour, the ugliness of this world, and let ourselves go at last. Just one hour to ourselves! . . . Can you understand that?

KALIAYEV: Yes, Dora . . . I can . . . That's what men call . . . love.

DORA: Oh, you understand everything, darling. Yes, that is love; but does that kind of love mean anything to you? Do you love justice like that? [*Silence.*] Do you love our people with a tender, unselfish love, or with a passion for revolution and revenge? [KALIAYEV *still says nothing.*] You see? [*She goes towards him . . . very quietly and weakly.*] What about *me*, Yanek? Do you love *me*? [*He looks at her in silence.*]

KALIAYEV: No one will ever love you as I do!

DORA: I know . . . but wouldn't it be better to love like other people do?

KALIAYEV: I'm not just other people . . . I love you as I am!

DORA: Yes, but do you love me more than justice, more than the Organization?

KALIAYEV: You, justice and the Organization go together: they are a part of you!

DORA: Yes, but answer me, please answer me! Do you love me with a human love? Do you love me selfishly, possessively? . . . Would you love me if I were unjust?

KALIAYEV: If you were unjust and I could love you. . . . It would not be you that I loved.

DORA: But you're not answering me. Just tell me if you would love me if I were not part of the Organization.

KALIAYEV: Where would you be then?

DORA: I remember when I was at University . . . I was always laughing then. I was quite pretty . . . I used to spend hours wandering around, dreaming. Would you love me if I were like that – carefree and innocent? [*A pause.*]

KALIAYEV [*in a low, desperate voice*]: I'm longing to say yes!

DORA [*with a passionate cry*]: Then *say* yes, darling, if you really mean it ... if it is true ... say yes! Forget justice, and suffering and human slavery.... Please say yes! Forget the scaffold, the writhing children ... men who are whipped to death! ...

KALIAYEV: Stop it, Dora!

DORA: No! ... For once we must listen to our hearts. I'm waiting for you to tell me that you want me ... *me*, Dora! ... and that I mean more to you than this world ... this foully unjust world! ...

KALIAYEV [*brutally*]: Stop it! The only words in my heart ... are of you ... but soon ... I must not flinch!

DORA [*bewildered*]: Soon? ... Oh, yes, I'd forgotten ... [*laughing and crying at the same time*] No, it's all right, my love ... Don't be angry ... I was being unreasonable ... I'm just tired ... I couldn't have said it to you either ... I love you in the same way as you love justice and those in prison ... [*A pause.*] Do you remember what summer is like, Yanek? ... but no! ... it's always winter here. We are not of this world ... we are 'the just' ... There *is* a warmth in the world, but it is not for us ... [*Turning away.*] Oh, pity 'the just'!

KALIAYEV [*gazing at her with despair*]: Yes, that's our role here on earth — there's no place for *our* love ... [*triumphantly*] ... but I will kill the Grand Duke ... and then there will be peace for both of us!

DORA: Peace! When will we find peace?

KALIAYEV [*violently*]: Tomorrow! [ANNENKOV *and* STEPAN *enter* ... KALIAYEV *and* DORA *move away from one another.*]

ANNENKOV: Yanek!

KALIAYEV: I'm ready. [*Breathes deeply.*] At last! At last!

STEPAN [*going up to him*]: Good-bye, Yanek ... I am with you.

KALIAYEV: Good-bye, Stepan. [*Turns to face* DORA.] Good-bye, Dora ... [*They stand very close to one another but do not touch.*]

DORA: No, not good-bye ... au revoir, au revoir, my love ... we'll meet again ...

KALIAYEV: Au revoir ... [*He gazes at her in silence.*] Dora ... I ... I ... Russia will be a beautiful place!....

DORA [*in tears*]: Yes ... Russia *will* be a beautiful place ... [KALIAYEV *turns on his heels, crosses himself in front of the prie-dieu and exits with* ANNENKOV ... STEPAN *goes to the window* ... DORA *stands absolutely still, staring at the door.*]

STEPAN: How proudly he's walking. I was wrong not to trust him. I thought his enthusiasm was too romantic. Did you see him cross himself? Does he believe in God?

DORA: Well, he doesn't go to church.

STEPAN: But God is in his soul. That's the difference between us: I am more bitter than he is. For us who don't believe in God, there is nothing between total justice and utter despair.

DORA: For Yanek, there is despair even in justice.

STEPAN: Yes, he has a weak soul ... but a strong hand; he will kill him ... I know he will ... and that's the main thing: we must destroy ... but you say nothing. [*He looks at her intently.*] Do you love him? [*A pause.*]

DORA: We need time for love.... We scarcely have time for justice.

STEPAN: You're right: there's too much to do. We must blow this world to pieces, and after that ... [*at the window*]. They're out of sight ... they must be there.

DORA: And after that?

STEPAN: We shall love one another.

DORA: If we're still alive.

STEPAN: Then other people will love each other, which is the same thing. [*A pause.*]

DORA: Stepan, say 'hate'.

STEPAN: What?

DORA: I just want to hear you say that word ... 'hate'.

STEPAN: Hate.

DORA: Yes, that's right ... Yanek could never say it well.

STEPAN [*after a short silence, coming towards her*]: I see ... you despise me ... Are you sure you're right though? [*Pauses and then continues with rising passion.*] You're all the same, grudging what you do in the name of your despicable love! ... *I* don't love anything ... I *hate*, yes I hate, my fellow men. Why should I want their precious love? I knew that three years ago in prison. ... Three years I've borne its marks on me ... and you want me to turn sentimental and carry the bomb like a cross! Oh, no! I've seen too much! Look! ... [*He tears his shirt open ... DORA, horrified, shrinks away at the sight of lashmarks on his back.*] There you are! There are the marks of their love! Now ... do you still despise me? [*She quickly embraces him.*]

DORA: Who could despise suffering? I love you too.

STEPAN [*he looks at her ... murmuring*]: I'm sorry, Dora. [*A pause ... he turns away.*] Perhaps I'm just worn out. All those years of struggling and suspense, of police-spies and prisons, and finally ... [*points to the scars*] ... this. How could I have the strength to love? At least I've got the strength to hate ... that's better than feeling nothing.

DORA: Yes, it is better. [*He looks at her ... seven o'clock strikes in the distance.*]

STEPAN [*swinging round*]: The Duke will be going by ... [DORA *runs to the window and presses her forehead against it ... a long silence ... then in the distance a carriage can be heard ... it draws nearer and then goes by the window.*] Let's

hope he's alone! [*The noise of the carriage grows fainter ...
then a violent explosion ...* DORA *starts violently and buries
her head in her hands. A long silence.*] Boria hasn't thrown his
bomb ... Yanek has done it! The people have triumphed!

DORA [*in tears, she flings herself against* STEPAN]: It's *we* who
have killed him ... it's *we* who have killed him! *I* have
killed him!

STEPAN [*with a shout*]: Who have we killed? Yanek?

DORA: The Duke!

CURTAIN

ACT FOUR

Scene: A cell in the Pougatchev Tower, Boutirki prison. It is morning. When the curtain rises, KALIAYEV *is in his cell, staring at the door. Enter a guard shoving a prisoner, who is carrying a bucket.*

GUARD: Get on with it. [*He stands by the window....* FOKA, *the prisoner, begins to clean without looking at* KALIAYEV *... silence.*]

KALIAYEV: What's your name, friend?

FOKA: Foka.

KALIAYEV: Are you a prisoner?

FOKA: Looks like it.

KALIAYEV: What did you do?

FOKA: I killed a few people.

KALIAYEV: Were you hungry?

GUARD: Keep it quiet.

KALIAYEV: What?

GUARD: I said keep it quiet! You're not really meant to talk – so keep your voice down like 'im.

KALIAYEV: Were you hungry?

FOKA: No, I was thirsty.

KALIAYEV: What happened?

FOKA: Well ... there was this hatchet lying around, and I really laid about with it good and proper: I killed three people, so they tell me. [KALIAYEV *looks at* FOKA.] Aah, my young gentleman, I see you aren't calling me friend any more. Gone all 'aughty, eh?

KALIAYEV: No ... I killed someone as well.

FOKA: How many?

KALIAYEV: I'll tell you if you like, my friend ... but, tell me, you regret what you did now, don't you?

FOKA: Gawd! Do I regret it? Huh ... twenty years, it's a long time ... enough to make anyone regret it.

KALIAYEV: Twenty years! I come here when I'm twenty-three ... I'd be an old man by the time I got out.

FOKA: Well, it probably won't be so bad for you. You never can tell with these judges; depends whether he's married and what his wife's like ... and anyway, you're a gentleman, and it ain't the same for you gentlemen and us poor buggers. You'll get away with it.

KALIAYEV: I doubt it ... I don't want to get away with it anyway: being ashamed for twenty years ... I couldn't stand it.

FOKA: What yer mean, ashamed? That's just the sort of thing a gentleman like you would say.... How many people did you kill?

KALIAYEV: Only one.

FOKA: Only one? Well ... that's nothing.

KALIAYEV: I killed the Grand Duke.

FOKA: The Grand Duke, eh? Go on! Typical of you gentlemen.... You're really in trouble then, aren't you?

KALIAYEV: Yes ... but I had to do it.

FOKA: Why? You lived at Court, didn't you? A woman, eh? Was that it? Yeh ... a good-looking young lad like you ...

KALIAYEV: I'm a socialist.

GUARD: Not so loud!

KALIAYEV [louder]: I'm a revolutionary socialist!

FOKA: That's a good one! Why the hell did you have to go and be a like you say? All you had to do was to stay put and you'd've been well away. The world was made for you gentlemen.

KALIAYEV: No!... the world was made for you, my friend. Oh, there are too many crimes, too much poverty in the world today. One day, when there's less poverty there'll be fewer crimes. If Russia were free, you would not be here.

FOKA: Yes, well ... one thing's certain, whether you're free or not – it's not worth having one too many.

KALIAYEV: There's never any point. Usually a man only takes to drink because he's oppressed. A day will come when there'll be no point in drinking, when nobody will be ashamed ... neither gentleman, nor poor peasant; we'll all be brothers ... and justice will make our hearts pure and innocent ... [*A pause.*] Do you understand what I'm saying?

FOKA: Yeh, you mean the kingdom of God.

GUARD: Keep your voices down!

KALIAYEV: No, it's not that!... God can do nothing! Justice is our concern. [*Silence.*] Don't you understand? Do you know the story of St Dmitri?

FOKA: No.

KALIAYEV: Well, he'd made an appointment with God, far out on the Steppes, and on the way he met a peasant whose cart was stuck in the mud; so St Dmitri stopped to help him. The wheels had sunk so far into the mud that it took him an hour to pull the cart out. When he had done it, St Dmitri ran on to keep his appointment ... but when he got there ... God had gone.

FOKA: So?

KALIAYEV: Well, there are always some who arrive too late, because there are too many carts stuck in the mud ... too many others who need help. [FOKA *recoils uneasily.*] What's wrong?

GUARD: Not so loud ... and you!... get on with it.

FOKA: It ain't natural ... all this stuff about saints and carts and whatnot. Seems bloody silly getting put in prison for ideas like that.... Yes, and there's another thing ... [*The* GUARD *laughs.*]

KALIAYEV [*looking at him*]: What?

FOKA: What happens to people who kill Grand Dukes?

KALIAYEV: They hang.

FOKA: Yes, they do ... [*He makes his way out ... the* GUARD *laughs louder.*]

KALIAYEV: Wait? What have I done?

FOKA: You ain't done nothing.... It's just that I wouldn't like to make a fool of a fine gentleman like you. I mean, it's all right talking like that just to pass the time, but ... but if you're going to be hanged ... well, I mean, well ... it just ain't fair.

KALIAYEV: Why?

GUARD [*still laughing*]: Go on, then ... tell him.

FOKA: Well, all this talk about you and me being brothers, isn't any use ... I'm the hangman ...

KALIAYEV: I thought you were a prisoner like me.

FOKA: Yes, I am, but they've given me the job of hangman as well ... I get a year knocked off my sentence for each one I hang ... suits me.

KALIAYEV: So, to pay for your crimes ... they make you commit new ones.

FOKA: No, they're not crimes ... I'm just carrying out orders. Anyway, they don't care: it's all the same to them: if you ask me, they're not Christians.

KALIAYEV: How many people have you ... hanged ... so far?

FOKA: Two. [KALIAYEV *winces.* FOKA *and the* GUARD *reach the door ... the* GUARD *gives* FOKA *a shove.*]

KALIAYEV: So you're an executioner, are you?

FOKA [*from the doorway*]: And you, sir ... what about you?

[FOKA *and the* GUARD *exit* ... *noise of footsteps and orders can be heard* ... *enter* SKOURATOV, *Chief of Police, followed by the* GUARD ... SKOURATOV *is very elegant.*]

SKOURATOV [*to the* GUARD]: You can go now. Good morning. You don't know me, do you? I know *you*, though ... [*he laughs*] ... famous already, eh? [*He looks at* KALIAYEV.] May I introduce myself? [KALIAYEV *says nothing.*] Oh, you don't feel like talking. I quite understand. A week in solitary confinement ... wears a man down, eh? Well, we've put a stop to that: from now on you can have visitors; in fact, I've sent you one already — old Foka ... curious fellow, isn't he? I thought you'd find him interesting. You must be pleased with the change; it's good to see a human face again, after a week's solitary confinement ... isn't it?

KALIAYEV: It depends on the face.

SKOURATOV: Aha, quite ... I see you know your own mind. Unless I'm very much mistaken, my face displeases you.

KALIAYEV: Yes.

SKOURATOV: You disappoint me ... still I have hopes that you may change your mind. For one thing, the lighting's bad; these basement cells make everyone look ghastly ... and, of course, you don't know me. Sometimes a man's face puts one off at first, and then later, when one gets to know the man himself ...

KALIAYEV: Who are you?

SKOURATOV: Skouratov, Chief of Police.

KALIAYEV: A lackey.

SKOURATOV: At your service, but if I were in your position, I wouldn't be too sure of myself ... I wouldn't throw my weight around, but you'll learn. You begin by wanting justice, and in the end you set up a police force. Anyway,

the truth doesn't frighten me, I'm going to be frank with
you. . . . You interest me; I'm going to offer you a pardon.

KALIAYEV: What do you mean?

SKOURATOV: I should have thought it was obvious – I'm
offering you your life.

KALIAYEV: Who asked you for it?

SKOURATOV: One does not ask for life, my young friend;
one is given it. Haven't you ever let anyone off? [*A pause.*]
Think hard . . .

KALIAYEV: I do not want your pardon . . . and that's all
there is to it.

SKOURATOV: Well, at least listen to me. I'm not your
enemy, even if I seem to be. I won't even say that your
ideas are wrong . . . except when they lead to murder . . .

KALIAYEV: Do not use that word!

SKOURATOV [*looking at him*]: Aha, you *are* on edge, aren't
you? [*a pause*] . . . but no, really, I want to help you.

KALIAYEV: Help me? . . . I'm ready to pay for what I've
done, but I don't want you and your . . . friendliness! Get
out.

SKOURATOV: The charge you have to face . . .

KALIAYEV: There is no charge! I'm a prisoner of war . . .
not a criminal.

SKOURATOV: Very well, but harm has been done, has it
not? Let's leave politics out of it: a man has been killed,
and in a particularly horrible manner.

KALIAYEV: I threw the bomb at your tyranny, not at a
man!

SKOURATOV: No doubt, but you still killed a man, and it
wasn't a pretty sight, my friend. When they had recovered
the body, the head was missing . . . completely disappeared! The only things that could be recognized
were an arm and a bit of a leg.

KALIAYEV: I have carried out a sentence.

SKOURATOV: Perhaps, but . . . no one is blaming you for the sentence; what is a sentence, anyway? It's just a word . . . a word you can argue about for days. What you're accused of . . . of course, you don't like that word . . . is a sort of amateur job, a messy one in fact. The results — they're plain enough to see, there's no disputing *them*. Ask the Grand Duchess. . . . There was blood, you know . . . a lot of blood . . .

KALIAYEV: Be quiet!

SKOURATOV [*his tone changes*]: All right, but I just want to say that if you persist in talking about a sentence, and insist that it was the party and the party alone that tried and condemned the Grand Duke to death, in fact that he was killed not by a bomb but by an idea, then you don't need a pardon . . . but suppose we get back to the facts! Suppose we say that it was you, Ivan Kaliayev, who blew the Grand Duke's head to pieces . . . that's a different matter altogether, isn't it? You'll need to be pardoned *then*; and that's how I want to help you . . . purely out of the kindness of my heart, I assure you. [*He smiles.*] What else can you expect from me? I'm not interested in ideas, I'm interested in people.

KALIAYEV [*exploding*]: You and your employers have got no power over me! You can kill me, but you cannot pass judgement on me! Oh, I know what you're getting at: you're trying to find a chink in my armour, you're hoping to make me feel ashamed of myself and burst into tears, and repent of what you call my crime! . . . Well, you won't get anywhere. What I am is nothing to do with you. What concerns you is our hatred . . . mine and my brothers! . . . and you're welcome to it!

SKOURATOV: Hatred? That too is just an idea . . . but

murder ... is more than just an idea – it has its reper-
cussions: I mean, of course, repentance and punishment,
and that is the point; in fact, that is why I joined the
police – to be at the heart of things ... but you don't want
to hear me talking about myself. [*A pause ... he goes slowly
towards him.*] What I'm getting at is, you shouldn't
pretend to forget the Grand Duke's head. If you keep
this in mind, you'd find that a mere ideal is not enough.
To start with, you'd be ashamed of what you've done, not
proud of it; and as soon as you felt ashamed, you'd want
to live to redeem yourself. The most important thing,
therefore, is that you make up your mind to live.

KALIAYEV: And if I do?

SKOURATOV: Pardon ... for you and your friends.

KALIAYEV: Have you arrested them?

SKOURATOV: No ... not yet; but if you decide to live, we
shall arrest them.

KALIAYEV: I'm not sure that I understand you ...

SKOURATOV: I'm sure you *do*. Don't lose your temper yet;
think it over first. Your ideal cannot allow you to hand
them over to us, but from a practical point of view you'd
be doing them a service: you would be saving them from
further trouble, and at the same time you would save
them from ... the gallows, but, above all, you'd find peace
of mind. So, whichever way you look at it, it's the best
thing for you to do ... [*A pause.*] Well?

KALIAYEV: You'll find out the answer before long ... from
my brothers.

SKOURATOV: Another crime? It seems to be quite a
vocation. Well, I've had my say, and I must confess that
I'm disappointed; I see that you still cling to your ideal –
I can't tear you away from it.

KALIAYEV: You cannot tear me from my brothers!

SKOURATOV: Good-bye, then. [*He is about to go out, then turns round again.*] Why did you spare the Grand Duchess and her niece and nephew?

KALIAYEV: Who told you that?

SKOURATOV: Your informer – he was giving us a bit of information too ... but why did you spare them?

KALIAYEV: It's nothing to do with you!

SKOURATOV [*laughing*]: You think not, eh? Well, I'll tell you why you spared them.... An ideal can kill the Grand Duke, but when it comes to killing children, it's a different matter–you found that out yourself ... but let's carry it a stage further: if an ideal does not justify the killing of children, does it in fact justify the killing ... of the Grand Duke? [KALIAYEV *makes a sign of defiance.*] No, don't answer *me* ... give your answer to the Grand Duchess.

KALIAYEV: The Grand Duchess?

SKOURATOV: Yes, she wants to see you, and the main reason for my coming here was to make it possible for her to speak to you ... which she will do in a minute. She might even make you change your mind; the Grand Duchess is a Christian ... in fact, she's an expert ... on the soul. [*He laughs.*]

KALIAYEV: I refuse to see her!

SKOURATOV: I'm sorry, but she insists on seeing you. After all, you owe her some consideration. What is more, since her husband's death, I am told she has become ... mentally unbalanced, so we didn't want to stand in her way. [*He is at the door.*] If you *do* change your mind, don't forget my offer: I'll be seeing you again. [*A pause ... he listens.*] She's coming now. First the police ... and now ... religion! You *are* being spoilt, aren't you? But everything holds together. Imagine God without prisons!... What solitude! [*Exit* SKOURATOV . . . *voices and words of command ring out . . . enter the* GRAND DUCHESS . . . *she stands quite still . . . she does not speak . . . the door is open.*]

KALIAYEV: What do you want?

GRAND DUCHESS [*uncovering her face*]: Look . . . [KALIAYEV *says nothing.*] Many things die with a man . . .

KALIAYEV: I realized that.

GRAND DUCHESS: No. . . . Murderers do not know that; if they did, how could they kill? [*She speaks naturally, but her voice is strained . . . a pause.*]

KALIAYEV: I have seen you . . . and now I want to be alone.

GRAND DUCHESS: No, I must look at you. [*He recoils . . . she sits . . . she seems worn out . . .*] I can't stay by myself any longer. . . . Before, when I was miserable, he used to share my sorrow . . . I didn't mind suffering then, but now. . . . No, I can't bear it any longer. . . . Loneliness . . . silence . . . but whom can I talk to? The others don't know what it's like. They pretend to be distressed! . . . and they really are . . . for an hour or so; then they go off to eat . . . or sleep – yes, sleep. I thought that you must be like me. . . . You don't sleep, do you? Whom could I speak to about the crime except to the murderer?

KALIAYEV: What crime? I remember only an act of justice.

GRAND DUCHESS: The same voice! Your voice is exactly like his; but then all men sound the same when they speak of justice. . . . He used to say: 'That is just', and nobody could question it, and yet . . . perhaps he was wrong . . . perhaps you are wrong too . . .

KALIAYEV: He was the living, human symbol of the supreme injustice which the Russian people have suffered for centuries! In return for that . . . he received only privileges! But I . . . even if I am wrong . . . *my* wages are prison and death . . .

GRAND DUCHESS: I know that you are suffering, but what about him? You killed him!

KALIAYEV: He died suddenly.... A death like that is nothing.

GRAND DUCHESS: Nothing!... [*quieter*]. Yes, I suppose so. They took you away immediately. They tell me you made speeches while you were surrounded by the police; yes ... that must have helped you ... but I ... I arrived a few minutes later, and I saw it all ... I picked up what I could ... all that blood ... [*A pause.*] I was wearing a white dress ...

KALIAYEV: Stop!

GRAND DUCHESS: Why? It's only the truth! Do you know what he was doing two hours before he died? He was sleeping ... in an armchair, with his feet up – he often used to do that .... He was sleeping ... and *you* ... you were waiting for him in the ... cruel twilight.... Oh, please help me; you are young, you cannot be wicked. [*She is in tears ...* KALIAYEV *recoils and stiffens.*]

KALIAYEV: I never had time ... to be young.

GRAND DUCHESS: Why do you stiffen like that? Have you never felt sorry for yourself?

KALIAYEV: No.

GRAND DUCHESS: You are wrong – it comforts you. I no longer pity anyone but myself ... [*A pause.*] I am ill.... You should have killed me with him, instead of sparing me.

KALIAYEV: I didn't spare *you* ... I spared the children you had with you.

GRAND DUCHESS: Yes ... I know. I didn't like them much. They are the Grand Duke's niece and nephew – aren't they as guilty as their uncle?

KALIAYEV: No!

GRAND DUCHESS: Do you know them? My niece is a heartless little girl; she always refuses to give anything to the poor when she's asked to. She won't go near them. Isn't *she* unjust? Of course she is! But he ... he used to love the peasants ... he used to drink with them ... and you killed him. You're unjust as well! The world is empty and cruel ...

KALIAYEV: You're wasting your time. You're just trying to wear me down and make me give in. ... Well, you won't do it, so leave me alone.

GRAND DUCHESS: Won't you pray with me and repent? We wouldn't be so lonely then.

KALIAYEV: Let me prepare for death. ... If I didn't die, then I *would* be a murderer!

GRAND DUCHESS [*she stands up*]: Die? You really want to die? No! [*She goes towards him ... she is very worried.*] You must live ... and face up to being a murderer. After all, you did kill him, didn't you. Only God can justify you.

KALIAYEV: What God? Yours ... or mine?

GRAND DUCHESS: The God of the Holy Church.

KALIAYEV: The Church has got nothing to do with it!

GRAND DUCHESS: The Church serves a master, who was imprisoned ... just like you.

KALIAYEV: Times have changed: the Church has just chosen what it wants from its master's suffering.

GRAND DUCHESS: What do you mean, chosen?

KALIAYEV: The Church has kept grace for itself ... and it's left us to exercise charity!

GRAND DUCHESS: Whom do you mean by us?

KALIAYEV [*shouting*]: All those you hang! [*Silence.*]

GRAND DUCHESS [*gently*]: I'm not your enemy.

KALIAYEV [*he is desperate*]: Yes you are! You are! ... and so are all the rest of you! There's something even fouler than *being* a criminal, and that is forcing a man into crime who wasn't made for it. . . . Look at me . . . I swear to you I wasn't born a murderer.

GRAND DUCHESS: Don't talk to me as if I were your enemy . . . [*She closes the door.*] Look! I'm at your mercy . . . we are separated by blood, but we can be united in God . . . in a common tragedy. Please, just pray with me . . . [*She is crying.*]

KALIAYEV: No! [*He goes towards her.*] I feel only pity for you . . . and you have touched my heart – and now I'll hide nothing from you . . . I want you to understand: I no longer expect to see God, but when I die, I shall keep the promise I made to those I love . . . my brothers, who will be thinking of me at this moment. . . . If I were to pray now . . . I would betray them!

GRAND DUCHESS: What do you mean?

KALIAYEV [*triumphantly*]: Nothing . . . except that soon . . . I shall be happy! A long ordeal lies ahead for me, but I shall see it through . . . and then . . . when they've pronounced the sentence, and they're all ready for the execution . . . then . . . at the foot of the scaffold . . . I shall turn away from you and this vile world. [*Quieter and in an intense whisper.*] And at last my heart will be filled with love! . . . Can you understand?

GRAND DUCHESS: There is no love except with God.

KALIAYEV: Yes, there is. . . . Love for people . . . love for mankind!

GRAND DUCHESS: But men are vile. . . . You can either forgive them or destroy them. What else can you do?

KALIAYEV: You can . . . die with them!

GRAND DUCHESS: But you die alone. . . . *He* died alone.

KALIAYEV [*desperately*]: No . . . no, you *can* die with them. Those who love one another today must die together if

215

they are to be re-united. In life ... they are cut off by injustice, sorrow, shame ... by the evil that men do to one another, by crime. ... Living is agony ... because living is separation!

GRAND DUCHESS: God reunites us.

KALIAYEV: But not on this earth, and it is this earth that counts!

GRAND DUCHESS: This is a world full of dogs, their noses fixed to the ground, sniffing everywhere ... but they never find what they want.

KALIAYEV: Soon I shall know! ... [a pause] ... and yet ... can't you imagine a love ... a love between two people, who have given up all hope of joy and who love each other in sorrow ... two people whose only link ... is sorrow! [He looks at her.] Can't you imagine that same bond uniting them in death as well?

GRAND DUCHESS: What is this terrible love?

KALIAYEV: The only kind of love that you and the rest of you have ever allowed us!

GRAND DUCHESS: I too loved. The man you killed ...

KALIAYEV: I know. ... That is why I forgive you for the wrong you have done me. [A pause.] Now please go. [A long silence.]

GRAND DUCHESS [getting up]: Yes, I shall go now. I came here to bring you back to God. I realize that now. But you wish to be your own judge and save yourself alone. That is beyond your power ... but God can do it, if you live; I will ask that you be granted a pardon.

KALIAYEV: No, no! ... Don't do that ... please! Let me die, or I shall hate you mortally.

GRAND DUCHESS [at the door]: I shall ask your pardon ... from man and from God.

KALIAYEV: No! You can't do that! [The GRAND DUCHESS

exits ... KALIAYEV *runs to the door ...* SKOURATOV *suddenly appears ...* KALIAYEV *starts, closes his eyes, then looks at* SKOURATOV *again.*] Thank God you're here!

SKOURATOV: Delighted. ... Why?

KALIAYEV: Because I need someone ... to despise again.

SKOURATOV: Oh, that's a pity. ... Well, I have come for your answer.

KALIAYEV: You've had my answer already.

SKOURATOV [*changing his tone*]: No, not yet I haven't! Now just you listen. I arranged this meeting between you and the Grand Duchess so that I could put an account of it in the papers tomorrow. The report will be perfectly correct except on one point. ... It will contain a statement saying that you have repented of your crime. Your friends will think that you have betrayed them!

KALIAYEV [*calmly*]: They will not believe it.

SKOURATOV: I shall withdraw this statement only if you make a full confession – you have got all night to make up your mind. [*He turns to the doorway.*]

KALIAYEV [*louder*]: They will not believe it!

SKOURATOV [*turning round*]: Why not? Have they never faltered? [*A pause.*]

KALIAYEV: You do not know ... their love!

SKOURATOV: No, but I know that a man cannot believe in 'brotherhood' for a whole night ... without a single moment of doubt. ... So, I shall wait for that moment. [*He closes the door, his back pressed against it.*] Take your time, my friend ... I'm very patient. [*They stand face to face, quite still. ...*]

CURTAIN

ACT FIVE

Scene: Another flat, similar in style. . . . A week later. It is midnight. Silence . . . DORA *is walking up and down.*

ANNENKOV: You must try to relax, Dora.

DORA: I'm cold.

ANNENKOV: Come and lie down here . . . cover yourself up.

DORA [*still walking up and down*]: How the night drags . . . I'm so cold, Boria. [*There is a knock on the door, then two knocks . . .* ANNENKOV *gets up and goes to open the door . . .* STEPAN *and* VOINOV *enter . . .* VOINOV *goes to* DORA *and embraces her. She presses him close to her.*] Oh, Alexis!

STEPAN: Orlov says that it may be tonight. All the junior officers who aren't on duty have been told to report to the prison. That'll be the excuse for him being there.

ANNENKOV: Where are you going to meet him?

STEPAN: He's going to wait for Voinov and me at the restaurant in Sophiskaia Street.

DORA: So, it's tonight, Boria . . . [*She sits . . . exhausted.*]

ANNENKOV: There's still a chance. The decision rests with the Tsar.

STEPAN: Yes . . . the decision will rest with the Tsar, if Yanek has asked for a pardon.

DORA: He hasn't.

STEPAN: Why should he see the Grand Duchess if he didn't want a pardon? Besides, she says that he repented. How can we be sure?

DORA: We know what he said at the trial and what he said in his letter. Didn't he say that his only regret was that he

didn't have *another* life to hurl in the face of tyranny?
Could the man who said that beg for a pardon, or repent?
No!... He wanted to die, and he still does. There's no
going back on what he's done.

STEPAN: He shouldn't have seen the Grand Duchess.

DORA: He was the judge of that.

STEPAN: No... it was against our principles that he saw her.

DORA: Our only principle is to kill. Now at last he's free...
Quite free!

STEPAN: No, not yet.

DORA: He is, he is! And now that he is so close to death,
he has a right to do what he wants. Yes, he *will* die...
you won't be disappointed.

ANNENKOV: Dora!...

DORA: Yes, you'd be pleased if he was pardoned! It would
prove that the Grand Duchess was telling the truth,
wouldn't it? He would have repented ... he would have
betrayed us; but if he dies, you will believe in him, and
you can still love him ... [*She looks at them.*] Your love
demands a lot.

VOINOV [*going towards her*]: No, Dora, you're wrong. We
never doubted him.

DORA [*pacing up and down*]: Didn't you?... No, perhaps not,
I'm sorry. But anyway what does it matter, we'll know
for certain tonight. Oh, Alexis, what did you come back
for?

VOINOV: To replace him. I was so proud when I read
what he said at the trial; I cried. You remember what
he said: 'Death will be my supreme protest against a
world of blood and tears.'... My hands shook when I read
that.

DORA: 'A world of blood and tears.'... Yes he said that,
didn't he?

VOINOV: Oh, Dora, what courage. And then his last great cry: 'If I have proved equal to man's protest against violence in the world, then may death crown my work by the purity of the ideal.' That was when I decided to come back.

DORA [*her head in her hands*]: Yes . . . he always longed for purity, but oh, what a cruel fulfilment!

VOINOV: Don't cry, Dora. He asked that nobody should cry when he died. Oh, I understand him so well now; I couldn't mistrust him. I suffered because I was a coward, then I threw the bomb at Tiflis, and now I'm no different from Yanek. When I heard that he'd been sentenced to death, the only thing I could think of was taking his place . . . as I wasn't able to be beside him.

DORA: Who can take his place tonight? He will be alone, Alexis.

VOINOV: We must support him with our pride, as he supports us with his example. Don't cry.

DORA: Look. . . . My eyes are dry, but proud. . . . Oh, no . . . I can never be proud again!

STEPAN: Don't judge me too harshly, Dora; I would like Yanek to live. We need men like him.

DORA: But he doesn't want to live! . . . and so we must want him to die too.

ANNENKOV: You're mad.

DORA: We must . . . I know him. That's the only way he'll find peace . . . in death. So let him die . . . [*softer*] but quickly . . .

STEPAN: I'm off, Boria. Come on, Alexis – Orlov is waiting for us.

ANNENKOV: Yes, you'd better go. Hurry back. [STEPAN *amd* VOINOV *go to the door* . . . STEPAN *turns and looks at* DORA.]

STEPAN: In a few minutes we shall know everything. . . . Look after her, Boria. [*Exit* STEPAN *and* VOINOV . . . DORA *goes to the window, watched by* ANNENKOV.]

DORA: Death! The gallows! Oh, Boria, it's always death!

ANNENKOV: Yes, Dora . . . but there's no other way.

DORA: Don't say that! If death is the only way, then we have chosen the wrong path. The right path leads to life . . . a life where the sun shines. You can't be cold all the time . . .

ANNENKOV: Our path leads to life as well. Life for others . . . Russia will live, our grandchildren will *live*. Do you remember what Yanek used to say? 'Russia will be beautiful.'

DORA: Others . . . our grandchildren . . . yes, but Yanek is in prison and the rope is cold. . . . He is going to die . . . perhaps he's dead already . . . dead so that others may live. But, Boria, suppose the others don't live! Suppose he's dying for nothing!

ANNENKOV: Be quiet! [*Silence.*]

DORA: It's so cold . . . but the spring is here. . . . There are trees in the prison yard . . . I know there are. He must see them . . .

ANNENKOV: Wait until we know, Dora . . . and try to stop shivering.

DORA: I'm so cold . . . I feel as though I'm dead already. [*A pause.*] I feel so old: we shall never be young again, Boria. We lose sight of childhood at the first murder; I throw the bomb and then in one second a whole lifetime goes by, and all that remains . . . is death: we have gone through one age of man.

ANNENKOV: Then we must go down fighting like men.

DORA: We've gone too fast . . . we're no longer men.

ANNENKOV: Misery and injustice also move fast. There's

no time for patience any more, no time to mature gradually. Russia is in a hurry.

DORA: I know. We bear the world's suffering. He did it too. . . . It takes great courage . . . but sometimes I wonder if we will be punished for our pride.

ANNENKOV: It's a pride that we pay for with our lives. No one can go further; we have a right to it.

DORA: Can we be sure that no one will go any further? Sometimes when I listen to Stepan, I'm afraid: perhaps others will come and justify themselves by our example and not pay with their lives!

ANNENKOV: Then they would be cowards.

DORA: Who knows? Perhaps that's what justice is. . . . Then no one would dare look justice in the face again.

ANNENKOV: Dora! [*Silence.*] Are you losing faith? You've never been like this before.

DORA: I'm so cold. I keep thinking how he must not shiver, in case he seems to be afraid.

ANNENKOV: Aren't you with us any more, Dora?

DORA [*throwing herself into his arms*]: Oh, Boria, of course I am! I'm with you to the end. I hate tyranny and I know that this is the only way . . . but when I chose it I was happy . . . not any more: that's the difference. . . . We are prisoners.

ANNENKOV: The whole of Russia is in chains, but we will break them.

DORA: Just give me the bomb and you'll see; I shall walk straight into the flames and I shall not flinch. . . . Oh, it's so much easier to die with one's conflicts than to live with them! [*A pause.*] Boria? . . . have you ever been in love?

ANNENKOV: Yes . . . but it was so long ago, I can't really remember.

DORA: How long ago?

ANNENKOV: Four years.

DORA: How long have you been leader of the Organization?

ANNENKOV: Four years. [*A pause.*] Now it's the Organization I love.

DORA [*going towards the window*]: To love, yes ... but to *be* loved, no! ... no, we must keep going, keep going on and on. If only we could pause just for a little while. No, go on, keep on. ... If only we could hold out our arms and be ourselves! ... but vile injustice clings to us like a leech – keep on! We are condemned to be greater than ourselves. People, faces ... they are what we'd like to love: love instead of justice! No, we must go on ... [*She is in tears.*] Keep going ... Dora ... keep ... going ... Yanek. ... But the end is coming for him ...

ANNENKOV [*taking her in his arms*]: He'll get a pardon.

DORA [*looking at him*]: You know that he won't. ... You know that he musn't! [*He looks away.*] Perhaps he's already standing in the prison yard. ... There is a sudden hush when he appears. As long as he isn't cold ... Boria! Do you know how they hang people?

ANNENKOV: No, Dora!

DORA [*wildly*]: The hangman jumps on to your shoulders and your neck ... cracks! [*A pause ... with a shriek.*] Isn't it ghastly?

ANNENKOV: Yes, in a way ... and in another way it's rather wonderful.

DORA: Wonderful?

ANNENKOV: Yes ... to feel a man's hand just before you die. [DORA *turns and throws herself into a chair ... silence.*] You must go away and have a rest as soon as it's all over, Dora.

DORA [*distraught*]: Go away? Who with?

ANNENKOV: With me, Dora.

DORA [*she looks at him*]: Go away? . . . [*Turns to the window.*] Ah, it's morning: Yanek's dead already! . . . I can feel it. [*Silence.*]

ANNENKOV: I am your brother.

DORA: Yes . . . you're my brother, you're all my brothers, my brothers whom I love . . . but what a foul taste brotherhood sometimes has! [*It is raining . . . day is breaking . . . there is a knock at the door, followed by two more . . .* STEPAN *and* VOINOV *enter . . . no one moves . . .* DORA *staggers, but recovers herself.*]

STEPAN: [*A pause . . . in a low voice.*] Yanek . . . hasn't betrayed us.

ANNENKOV: Did Orlov see what happened?

STEPAN: Yes.

DORA [*going steadily towards* STEPAN]: Sit down, Stepan. . . . Tell me what happened.

STEPAN: What's the use?

DORA: Tell me everything; I have a right to know. . . . You've got to tell me . . . every detail . . .

STEPAN: I can't tell you. Anyway we've got to leave now.

DORA: No, you must tell me first. When was he told?

STEPAN: Ten o'clock last night.

DORA: When did they hang him?

STEPAN: Two o'clock this morning.

DORA: So he waited in his cell for four hours . . .

STEPAN: Yes . . . without a word. Then suddenly everything happened; and now it's all over.

DORA: Four hours without speaking. What was he wearing? Did he have on his fur-lined coat?

STEPAN: No. He had a black suit on, and his black felt hat, but he wasn't wearing a coat.

DORA: Was it cold?

STEPAN: Well, it was pitch dark ... and there was snow on the ground ... then the rain came and turned it to slush.

DORA [*looking at him intently*]: Was he shivering?

STEPAN: No.

DORA: Did Orlov catch his eye?

STEPAN: No.

DORA: Who was he looking at?

STEPAN: Orlov says he was looking at everyone ... but he didn't seem to see anyone.

DORA: And then? What happened next?

STEPAN: That's enough, Dora.

DORA: No! I want to know; his death belongs to me, if nothing else does!

STEPAN: They read the verdict.

DORA: What did he do while it was being read?

STEPAN: Nothing ... but just once, he shook his leg to get rid of a bit of mud stuck to his shoe.

DORA [*her head in her hands*]: A bit of mud!

ANNENKOV [*sharply*]: How do you know all this? You asked Orlov to tell you every detail ... why? [STEPAN *says nothing.*]

STEPAN [*quietly ... looking away*]: There was something between me and Yanek.

ANNENKOV: What do you mean? [*A pause.*]

STEPAN: I ... envied him.

DORA: Go on, Stepan! What happened next?

STEPAN: Father Florentski held the crucifix out to him. ... He refused to kiss it. He said: 'I've already told you that I've finished with life, and have come to terms with death.'

DORA: What was his voice like?

STEPAN: The same as always ... but not so intense, not so impatient.

DORA: Did he look happy?

ANNENKOV: Are you mad?

DORA: Yes, he *did* look happy ... I know he did! It would be too unfair if he did not find happiness in death when he had rejected it in life; he *was* happy ... and he walked quite calmly to the scaffold, didn't he?

STEPAN: Yes.... Someone was singing to an accordion down on the river; just then a dog barked.

DORA: Then he ...

STEPAN: He climbed the steps and was swallowed up by the darkness. You could just see the shroud which the hangman put over his head.

DORA: And then? [*A pause.*] What then? [*A pause.*]

STEPAN: Muffled sounds.

DORA: Muffled sounds! Oh, Yanek! And then? ... [STEPAN *says nothing ... violently.*] Tell me what happened next! ... go on ... [STEPAN *still says nothing.*] *You* tell me Alexis!

VOINOV: A ... a horrible thud.

DORA: Aah! [*She flings herself against the wall* ... STEPAN *turns away* ... ANNENKOV *weeps, expressionless* ... DORA *turns round and looks at them ... leaning against the wall ... in a changed, distraught voice.*] Don't cry ... no, no, don't cry. Don't you realize ... that today is the day of our justification! Something has been born today which is our testimony, the testimony of us revolutionaries. Yanek is no longer a murderer! A horrible thud! That's all it took ... one thud and he was plunged back into the joys of childhood! Do you remember his laugh? He used to laugh sometimes ... for no reason at all.... How young he was! He's laughing now ... I know he is, his face pressed to the earth ... [*She goes towards* ANNENKOV.] Boria? ... you are my brother ... you'll help me ...

ANNENKOV: Yes, of course I will.

DORA: Then do this for me: let me throw the bomb ...
[ANNENKOV *looks at her.*] Yes ... the next time, I want to
throw the bomb ... I want to be the first to throw it!

ANNENKOV: We don't let women throw the bombs.

DORA [*with a shriek*]: Am I a woman ... now? [*They all look
at her in silence.*]

VOINOV [*very quietly*]: Let her, Boria.

STEPAN: Yes, let her.

ANNENKOV: It's your turn, Stepan ...

STEPAN [*looking at* DORA]: Let her.... She's ... like me
... now.

DORA: You will let me, won't you?

ANNENKOV: Yes, Dora.

DORA: I shall throw the bomb ... and then one cold night
... [*She cries uncontrollably.*] Oh, Yanek! ... yes ... one
cold night ... the same rope ... everything will be easier
... now....

CURTAIN

THE POSSESSED

Based on the novel by
FYODOR DOSTOYEVSKY

Foreword

The Possessed is one of the four or five works that I rank
above all others. In many ways I can claim that I grew up
on it and took sustenance from it. For almost twenty years,
in any event, I have visualized its characters on the stage.
Besides having the stature of dramatic characters, they have
the appropriate behaviour, the explosions, the swift and
disconcerting gait. Moreover, Dostoyevsky uses a theatre
technique in his novels: he works through dialogues with
few indications as to place and action. A man of the theatre
– whether actor, producer, or author – always finds in him
all the suggestions he needs.

And now *The Possessed* has reached the stage after
several years of labour and persistence. And yet I am well
aware of all that separates the play from that amazing novel!
I merely tried to follow the book's undercurrent and to
proceed as it does from satiric comedy to drama and then to
tragedy. Both the original and the dramatic adaptation
start from a certain realism and end up in tragic stylization.
As for the rest, I tried, amidst this vast, preposterous,
panting world full of outbursts and scenes of violence, never
to lose the thread of suffering and affection that makes
Dostoyevsky's universe so close to each of us. Dostoyevsky's
characters, as we know well by now, are neither odd nor
absurd. They are like us; we have the same heart. And if
The Possessed is a prophetic book, this is not only because
it prefigures our nihilism, but also because its protagonists
are torn or dead souls unable to love and suffering from that
inability, wanting to believe and yet unable to do so – like

those who people our society and our spiritual world today. The subject of this work is just as much the murder of Shatov (inspired by a real event – the assassination of the student Ivanov by the nihilist Nechayev) as the spiritual adventure and death of Stavrogin, a contemporary hero. Hence we have dramatized not only one of the masterpieces of world literature but also a work of current application.

Albert Camus

N.b. The adaptation of *The Possessed* reintegrates into the work Stavrogin's confession (which was not published because of censorship, though its place in the narrative is known to us) and utilizes the several hundred pages that make up the *Notebooks* of *The Possessed* kept by the author while he was writing the novel.

Characters

GRIGORIEV, *the narrator*

STEPAN TROFIMOVICH
VERKHOVENSKY

VARVARA PETROVNA
STAVROGIN

LIPUTIN

SHIGALOV

IVAN SHATOV

VIRGINSKY

GAGANOV

ALEXEY YEGOROVICH

NICHOLAS STAVROGIN

PRASCOVYA DROZDOV

DASHA SHATOV

ALEXEY KIRILOV

LISA DROZDOV

MAURICE NICOLAEVICH

MARIA TIMOFEYEVNA
LEBYATKIN

CAPTAIN LEBYATKIN

PETER STEPANOVICH
VERKHOVENSKY

FEDKA

THE SEMINARIST

LYAMSHIN

BISHOP TIHON

GAGANOV'S SON

MARIA SHATOV

NOTE: *The necessities of stage production called for fairly numerous cuts in the text of the adaptation. This edition contains all the passages and scenes cut in the production. They have been set between parallel rules.*

Sets

1. At Varvara Stavrogin's. A luxurious period drawing-room.
2. Filipov's poor lodgings. Double set, representing a living-room and a small bedroom.
3. The street.

4. Lebyatkin's dwelling. A wretched living-room in the suburb.
5. The forest.
6. At Tihon's. A vast hall in the Convent of the Virgin.
7. The main drawing-room in the Stavrogin country house, at Skvoreshniki.

FIRST PART

When the theatre is altogether dark, a spotlight picks out the NARRATOR *standing in front of the curtain with hat in hand.*

ANTON GRIGORIEV, *the* NARRATOR [*courteous, calm and ironic*]:

Ladies and Gentlemen,

The strange events you are about to witness took place in our provincial city under the influence of my esteemed friend Professor Stepan Trofimovich Verkhovensky. The Professor had always played a thoroughly patriotic role among us. He was liberal and idealistic, loving the West, progress, justice, and generally everything lofty. But on those heights he unfortunately fell to imagining that the Tsar and his Ministers had a particular grudge against him, and he settled among us to play the part of the persecuted thinker in exile. It must be said that he did so with great dignity. Simply, three or four times a year he had attacks of patriotic melancholy that kept him in bed with a hot-water bottle on his belly.

He lived in the house of his friend Varvara Stavrogin, the widow of the General, who, after her husband's death, had entrusted to him the upbringing of her son, Nicholas Stavrogin. Oh, I forgot to tell you that Stepan Trofimovich was twice widowed and once a father. He had shipped his son abroad. Both his wives had died young, and, to tell the truth, they hadn't been very happy with him. But it is hardly possible to love one's wife and justice at the same time. Consequently, Stepan Trofimovich transferred all his affection to his pupil Nicholas Stavrogin, to whose moral education he applied himself most rigorously until Nicholas fled home and took to indulging in wild debauch. Hence, Stepan Trofimovich remained alone with Varvara Stavrogin, who felt an unlimited friendship for him – in other words, she often hated him. That is where my story begins.

SCENE ONE

The curtain rises on Varvara Stavrogin's drawing-room. The NARRATOR *goes over and sits down at the table to play cards with* STEPAN TROFIMOVICH.

STEPAN: Oh, I forgot to ask you to cut the cards. Forgive me, Anton, but I didn't sleep well at all last night. How I regretted having complained to you of Varvara!

GRIGORIEV: You merely said she was keeping you out of vanity and that she was jealous of your education.

STEPAN: That's what I mean. But it's not true! Your turn. You see, she's an angel of honour and sensitivity, and I'm just the reverse.

[VARVARA STAVROGIN *comes in, but stops at the door.*]

VARVARA: Cards again! [*They rise.*] Sit down and go on. I am busy. [*She goes over to look at some papers on a table at the left. They continue playing, but* STEPAN TROFIMOVICH *keeps glancing at* VARVARA STAVROGIN, *who finally speaks, avoiding his eyes.*] I thought you were to work on your book this morning.

STEPAN: I took a walk in the garden. I had taken Tocqueville under my arm –

VARVARA: And you read Paul de Kock instead. But you have been announcing your book for fifteen years now.

STEPAN: Yes, I have gathered the material, but I have to put it together. It doesn't matter anyway! I am forgotten. No one needs me.

VARVARA: You would be less forgotten if you played cards less often.

STEPAN: Yes, I play cards. And it's unworthy of me. But who is responsible? Who nipped my career in the bud? *Ah, que meure la Russie!* I'll trump that.

VARVARA: Nothing keeps you from working and from proving by your work that people were wrong to neglect you.

STEPAN: You are forgetting, *chère amie,* that I have published a great deal.

VARVARA: Indeed? Who remembers that now?

STEPAN: Who? Why, our friend here certainly remembers it.

GRIGORIEV: Of course I do. To begin with, your lectures on the nature of the Arabs, then the start of your study on the exceptional moral nobility of certain knights at a certain period, and, above all, your thesis on the importance that the small city of Hanau might have achieved between 1413 and 1428 if it had not been prevented from doing so by half-hidden causes, which you analysed brilliantly.

STEPAN: You have a memory like a steel trap, Anton. Thank you.

VARVARA: That is not the point. The point is that for fifteen years you have been announcing a book and you haven't written a single word of it.

STEPAN: Of course not, that would be too easy! I want to be sterile and solitary! That will teach them what they have lost. I want to be a living reproach!

VARVARA: You would be if you spent less time in bed.

STEPAN: What?

VARVARA: Yes, to be a living reproach one has to stand on one's feet.

STEPAN: Standing up or lying down, the important thing is to personify the idea. Besides, I am active, I am active, and always according to my principles. This very week I signed a protest.

VARVARA: Against what?

STEPAN: I don't know. It was ... oh, I've forgotten. *Il fallait protester, voilà tout.* Oh, in my time everything was different. I used to work twelve hours a day ...

VARVARA: Five or six would have been enough ...

STEPAN: I used to spend hours in the library gathering mountains of notes. We had hope then! We used to talk until daybreak, building the future. Oh, how noble we were then, strong as steel, firm as the Rock of Gibraltar! Those were evenings truly worthy of Athens: music, Spanish melodies, love of humanity, the Sistine Madonna. ... *O ma noble et fidèle amie,* have you any idea of all I gave up?

VARVARA: No. [*She rises.*] But I know that if you talked until dawn you couldn't work twelve hours a day. Besides, all this is mere talk! You know that at long last I am expecting my son, Nicholas, any moment. ... I must have a word with you. [GRIGORIEV *gets up, comes over, and kisses her hand.*] Thank you, Anton, you are discreet. Stay in the garden and you can come back later.

[GRIGORIEV *leaves.*]

STEPAN: *Quel bonheur, ma noble amie, de revoir notre Nicolas!*

VARVARA: Yes, I am very happy. He is my whole life. But I am worried.

STEPAN: Worried?

VARVARA: Yes – don't act like a male nurse – I am worried. By the way, since when have you been wearing red neckties?

STEPAN: Why, just today I –

VARVARA: It doesn't suit your age, in my opinion. Where was I? Yes, I am worried. And you know very well why. All those rumours . . . I can't believe them, and yet I can't forget them. Debauchery, violence, duels, he insults everybody, he frequents the dregs of society! Absurd, absurd! And yet, suppose it were true?

STEPAN: But it isn't possible. Just remember the dreamy, affectionate child he was. Just remember the touching melancholies he used to fall into. No one but an exceptional soul can feel such melancholy . . . as I am well aware.

VARVARA: You are forgetting that he is no longer a child.

||STEPAN: But his health is poor. Just remember; he used to weep for nights on end. Can you imagine him forcing men to fight?

VARVARA: He was in no way weak! What has made you imagine that? He was simply high-strung, that's all. But you got it into your head to wake him up in the middle of the night, when he was twelve years old, to tell him your troubles. That's the kind of tutor you were.

STEPAN: *Le cher ange* loved me. He used to ask me to confide in him and would weep in my arms.

VARVARA: The angel has changed. I am told that I wouldn't recognize him now, that his physical strength is exceptional. ||

STEPAN: But what does he tell you in his letters?

VARVARA: His letters are few and far between but always respectful.

STEPAN: You see?

VARVARA: I see nothing. You should get out of the habit of talking without saying anything. And, besides, the facts speak for themselves. Did he or didn't he have his commission taken away from him because he had seriously wounded another officer in a duel?

STEPAN: That's not a crime. He was motivated by the warmth of his noble blood. That's all very chivalrous.

VARVARA: Yes. But it is less chivalrous to live in the vilest sections of St Petersburg and to enjoy the company of cut-throats and drunkards.

STEPAN [*laughing*]: Oh, that's simply Prince Harry's youth all over again!

VARVARA: What do you mean by that?

STEPAN: Why, Shakespeare, *ma noble amie,* immortal Shakespeare, the genius of geniuses, great Will, in short, who shows us Prince Harry indulging in debauch with his friend Falstaff.

VARVARA: I shall re-read the play. By the way, are you taking any exercise? You are well aware that you should walk six versts a day. Good. In any case, I asked Nicholas to come home. I want you to sound him out. I plan to keep him here and to arrange his marriage.

STEPAN: His marriage! Oh, how romantic that is! Have you anyone in mind?

VARVARA: Yes, I am thinking of Lisa, the daughter of my friend Prascovya Drozdov. They are in Switzerland with my ward, Dasha. . . . But what does it matter to you?

STEPAN: I love Nicholas as much as my own son.

VARVARA: That isn't much. Altogether, you have seen your son only twice, including the day of his birth.

STEPAN: His aunts brought him up and I sent him regularly the income from the little estate his mother left him, and all the time I suffered bitterly from his absence. Moreover, he's a complete dud, poor in spirit and poor in heart. You should see the letters he writes me! You would think he was speaking to a servant. I asked him with all my paternal love if he didn't want to come and see me. Do you know what he replied? 'If I come home, it will be to check my accounts, and to settle accounts too.'

VARVARA: Why don't you learn once and for all to make people respect you? Well, I shall leave you. It is time for your little gathering. Your friends, your little spree, cards, atheism, and, above all, the stench, the stench of tobacco and of men ... I am leaving. Don't drink too much, you know it upsets you.... Good-bye! [*She looks at him; then shrugging her shoulders:*] A red necktie! [*She leaves.*]

STEPAN [*follows her with his eyes, starts to stammer, then looks towards the desk*]: O femme cruelle, implacable! And I can't talk to her! I shall write her a letter! [*He goes towards the table.*]

VARVARA [*thrusting her head in the door*]: And, by the way, stop writing me letters. We live in the same house; it is ridiculous to exchange letters. Your friends are here.
    [*She leaves.* GRIGORIEV, LIPUTIN, *and* SHIGALOV *come in.*]

STEPAN: Good day, my dear Liputin, good day. Forgive my emotion.... I am hated.... Yes, I am literally hated. But I don't care! Your wife is not with you?

LIPUTIN: No. Wives must stay at home and fear God.

STEPAN: But aren't you an atheist?

LIPUTIN: Yes. Shhhh! Don't say it so loud. That's just it. A husband who is an atheist must teach his wife the fear of God. That liberates him even more. Look at our friend Virginsky. I met him just now. He had to go out and do his marketing himself because his wife was with Captain Lebyatkin.

STEPAN: Yes, yes, I know what people say, but it's not true. His wife is a noble creature. Besides, they all are.

LIPUTIN: What, not true? I was told it by Virginsky himself. He converted his wife to our ideas. He convinced her that man is a free creature, or ought to be such. So she freed herself and, later on, simply told Virginsky that she was dismissing him as her husband and taking Captain Lebyatkin in his place. And do you know what Virginsky said to his wife when she announced this news? He said: 'My dear, up to now I merely loved you; from now on, I esteem you.'

STEPAN: He's a true Roman.

GRIGORIEV: I was told, on the contrary, that when his wife dismissed him, he burst into sobs.

STEPAN: Yes, yes. He's an affectionate soul. [SHATOV comes in.] But here's our friend Shatov. Any news of your sister?

SHATOV: Dasha is about to come home. Since you ask me, I shall tell you that she is bored in Switzerland with Prascovya Drozdov and Lisa. I am telling you, although in my opinion it is no concern of yours.

STEPAN: Of course not. But she is coming home, and that is the main thing. Oh, my dear friends, it's impossible to live far from Russia —

LIPUTIN: But it's impossible to live in Russia, too. We need something else, and there is nothing.

STEPAN: What do you suggest?

LIPUTIN: Everything must be made over.

SHIGALOV: Yes, but you don't draw the conclusions. [SHATOV goes over and sits down gloomily and places his cap beside him. VIRGINSKY and then GAGANOV come in.]

STEPAN: Good day, my dear Virginsky. How is your wife?

... [VIRGINSKY *turns away.*] Good, we're fond of you, you know, very fond of you!

GAGANOV: I was just going by and I came in to see Varvara Stavrogin. But perhaps I am in your way?

STEPAN: No, no! *Au banquet de l'amitié* there is always room. We were just beginning to discuss things. I know you are not afraid of a few paradoxes.

GAGANOV: Aside from the Tsar, Russia, and the family, everything is open to discussion. [*To* SHATOV] Don't you agree?

SHATOV: Everything is open to discussion. But certainly not with you.

STEPAN [*laughing*]: We must drink to the conversion of our good friend Gaganov. [*He rings a bell.*] That is, if Shatov, irascible Shatov, allows us to. For our good Shatov is irascible; he boils over at nothing at all. And if you want to discuss with him, you have to tie him down first. You see, he's already leaving. He has taken offence. Come, come now, my good friend, you know how fond we are of you.

SHATOV: Then don't insult me.

STEPAN: But who is insulting you? If I did so, I beg your pardon. I am well aware that we talk too much. We talk when we ought to act. Act, act ... or, in any case, work. For twenty years now I have been sounding the alarm and urging people to work. Russia can't arise without ideas. And we can't have ideas without working. Let's get down to work, then, and eventually we'll have an original idea ...

[ALEXEY YEGOROVICH, *the butler, brings in drinks and leaves.*]

LIPUTIN: Meanwhile, we should suppress the army and the navy.

GAGANOV: Both at once?

LIPUTIN: Yes, in order to have universal peace!

GAGANOV: But if others don't suppress theirs, wouldn't they be tempted to invade us? How can we know?

LIPUTIN: By suppressing ours. In that way we shall know.

STEPAN [*quivering with excitement*]: Ah! *C'est un paradoxe!* But there is truth in it . . .

VIRGINSKY: Liputin goes too far because he despairs of ever seeing our ideas dominate. *I* think we should begin at the beginning and get rid of priests and the family at the same time.

GAGANOV: Gentlemen, I can take any joke whatever . . . but to suppress at one and the same time the army, the navy, the family, the priests – no, no, no.

STEPAN: There's no harm in talking about it. One can talk of anything.

GAGANOV: But to suppress everything like that all at once – no. Ah, no. No . . .

LIPUTIN: Come, now. Don't you think Russia needs reform?

GAGANOV: Yes, probably. Everything isn't perfect in our country.

LIPUTIN: Then it must be dismembered.

STEPAN *and* GAGANOV: What?

LIPUTIN: Yes, of course. To reform Russia, it has to be made into a federation. But before it can be federated, it has to be dismembered. It's mathematically simple.

STEPAN: It deserves reflection.

GAGANOV: I. . . . Oh, no, I won't let anyone lead me around by the nose . . .

VIRGINSKY: Reflection calls for time, and abject poverty can't wait.

LIPUTIN: We must think of the most urgent first. The most urgent need is for everyone to be able to eat. Books, art galleries, theatres are for later on, later on.... A pair of shoes is worth more than Shakespeare.

STEPAN: Oh, I can't admit this. No, no, my good friend, immortal genius shines over all mankind. Let everyone go barefoot and long live Shakespeare ...

SHIGALOV: You don't any of you draw the conclusions. [*He leaves.*]

LIPUTIN: Allow me –

STEPAN: No, no, I cannot accept that. *Nous qui aimons le peuple* –

SHATOV: You don't love the masses.

VIRGINSKY: What? I –

SHATOV [*rising in anger*]: You don't love either Russia or the masses. You have lost contact with the masses. You talk about them as if they were a distant tribe with exotic customs that move you to pity. You have lost track of them, and without the masses, there is no god. This is why all of you and all of us, yes, all of us, are so wretchedly cold and indifferent. We are merely out of step, nothing else. You yourself, Stepan Trofimovich, I make no exception for you, let it be known, although you taught us all. In fact, I am speaking especially to you.

[*He seizes his cap and rushes towards the door. But* STEPAN TROFIMOVICH *calls out to stop him.*]

STEPAN: All right, Shatov, since you insist, I am angry with you. Now let us make it up. [*He holds out his hand, and* SHATOV *reluctantly shakes it.*] Let's drink to universal reconciliation!

GAGANOV: Let's drink. But I won't let anyone lead me around by the nose.

[*Toast.* VARVARA STAVROGIN *enters.*]

VARVARA: Please don't get up. Drink to the health of my son, Nicholas, who has just arrived. He has gone up to change, and I have asked him to come and say hello to your friends.

STEPAN: How did he seem to you, *ma noble amie?*

VARVARA: His appearance and good health delighted me. [*She looks at them.*] Yes, why not say so? There have been so many rumours recently that I am glad to have a chance to show what my son is.

GAGANOV: We are delighted to see him, my dear!

VARVARA [*looking at* SHATOV]: And you, Shatov, are you happy to see your friend again? [SHATOV *gets up and, as he does so, awkwardly knocks over a small intarsia table.*] Pick up that table, please. It will be chipped, but there's no use crying over that. [*To the others.*] What were you talking about?

STEPAN: Of hope, *ma noble amie,* and of the luminous future already visible at the end of our dark way.... Oh, we shall be consoled for such sufferings and persecutions. Exile will come to an end, for dawn is already in sight ...

[NICHOLAS STAVROGIN *appears upstage and stands still on the threshold.*]

STEPAN: *Ah, mon cher enfant!*

[VARVARA *makes a move towards* STAVROGIN, *but his unemotional manner stops her. She looks at him with anguish. A few seconds of general embarrassment.*]

GAGANOV: How are you, my dear Nicholas?

STAVROGIN: I am well, thank you.

[*A merry scene of greeting ensues.* STAVROGIN *steps towards his mother and kisses her hand.* STEPAN TROFIMOVICH *goes up to him and embraces him,* STAVROGIN *smiles at* STEPAN *and resumes his unemotional manner while the others, except* SHATOV, *greet him. But his prolonged silence dampens the enthusiasm.*]

VARVARA [*looking at* NICHOLAS]: Dear, dear child, you are sad, you are bored. That is right.

STEPAN [*bringing him a glass*]: My good Nicholas!

VARVARA: Go on, I beg you. We were talking of the dawn. I believe.

[STAVROGIN *lifts his glass as a toast in the direction of* SHATOV, *who leaves the room without saying a word.* STAVROGIN *sniffs the contents of his glass and sets it down on the table without drinking it.*]

LIPUTIN [*after a moment of general embarrassment*]: Good. Did you know that the new governor had already arrived? [*In his corner on the left,* VIRGINSKY *says something to* GAGANOV, *who answers:*]

GAGANOV: I won't let anyone lead me around by the nose.

LIPUTIN: It seems that he wants to upset everything. But it would surprise me if he did.

STEPAN: It won't last. Just a touch of administrative intoxication!

[STAVROGIN *has gone over to the spot vacated by* SHATOV. *Standing very upright with a far-away, gloomy look on his face, he is watching* GAGANOV.]

VARVARA: What do you mean now?

STEPAN: Why, you know the symptoms, don't you? For instance, just entrust any old nitwit with selling tickets behind the window of the most insignificant station and immediately, when you go to get a ticket, that nitwit will look at you as if he were Jupiter, just to show his power. The nitwit is drunk, you see. He is suffering from administrative intoxication.

VARVARA: Come to the point, I beg you.

STEPAN: I simply meant. . . . However that may be, I know the new governor somewhat. A very handsome man, isn't he – about forty years old?

VARVARA: Where did you get the idea that he is a handsome man? He has pop eyes.

STEPAN: That's true, but. . . .Well, in any case, I accept the opinion of the ladies.

GAGANOV: We can't criticize the new governor before seeing him at work, can we?

LIPUTIN: And why shouldn't we criticize him? He's the governor; isn't that enough?

GAGANOV: Allow me –

VIRGINSKY: It's through reasoning like Gaganov's that Russia is sinking into ignorance. If a horse were named governor, Gaganov would wait to see him at work.

GAGANOV: Oh! But, allow me, you are insulting me, and I won't permit it. I said . . . or, rather . . . I repeat: I won't let anyone lead me around by the nose . . . [STAVROGIN *crosses the stage amid the silence that sets in with his first step, advances like a sleepwalker towards* GAGANOV, *slowly raises his arm, seizes* GAGANOV's *nose, and, gently pulling it, makes* GAGANOV *step towards the centre of the stage. With anguish in her voice,* VARVARA STAVROGIN *shouts:* 'Nicholas!' NICHOLAS *lets go of* GAGANOV, *steps backwards a few steps, and looks at him, smiling absent-mindedly. After a second of stupor, general tumult. The others surround* GAGANOV *and lead him to a chair, into which he sinks.* NICHOLAS STAVROGIN *turns on his heels and leaves the room.* VARVARA STAVROGIN, *hardly knowing what she is doing, takes up a glass and carries it over to* GAGANOV.] He. . . . How could he . . . ? Help, help!

VARVARA [*to* STEPAN TROFIMOVICH]: Oh, my God, he's mad, he's mad!

STEPAN [*hardly knowing what he is doing either*]: No, *très chère,* mere thoughtlessness, youth . . .

VARVARA [*to* GAGANOV]: Forgive Nicholas, my friend, I beg of you.

[STAVROGIN *enters. After a brief hesitation he walks firmly towards* GAGANOV, *who gets up, frightened. Then rapidly and with a frown:*]

STAVROGIN: Of course you will forgive me! A sudden whim. ... A stupid distraction ...

STEPAN [*stepping up to the other side of* STAVROGIN, *who is looking vacantly ahead of him*]: That's not an acceptable apology, Nicholas. [*With anguish*] *Je vous en prie, mon enfant.* You have a noble heart, you are well brought up and cultured, and suddenly you seem to us enigmatic – a dangerous person. At least have pity on your mother.

STAVROGIN [*looking at his mother, then at* GAGANOV]: All right. I shall apologize. But I shall do so secretly to Mr Gaganov, who will understand me.

[GAGANOV *steps forward hesitantly.* STAVROGIN *leans over and seizes* GAGANOV's *ear in his teeth.*]

GAGANOV [*in pain*]: Nicholas! Nicholas!

[*The others, who haven't yet understood the situation, look at him.*]

GAGANOV [*in terror*]: Nicholas, you are biting my ear! [*Screaming.*] He's biting my ear! [STAVROGIN *lets go of him and stands staring at him with a dull look on his face.* GAGANOV *rushes out, screaming with fright.*] Watch out! Watch out!

VARVARA [*going to her son*]: Nicholas, for the love of God!

[NICHOLAS *looks at her, laughs weakly, then collapses on the floor in a sort of fit.*]

BLACKOUT

THE NARRATOR: Gaganov stayed in bed several weeks. Nicholas Stavrogin likewise. But he eventually got up, made his apologies most honourably, and set out for a rather long trip. The only place where he stayed for a time was Geneva – not because of the hectic charm of that city, but because there he found the Drozdov ladies.

SCENE TWO

Varvara Stavrogin's drawing-room. VARVARA STAVROGIN *and* PRASCOVYA DROZDOV *are on the stage.*

PRASCOVYA: Oh, my dear, I can say that I am pleased to return Dasha Shatov to you. I have no criticism to make, for my part, but it seems to me that if she hadn't been there, there would not have been that little misunderstanding between your Nicholas and my Lisa. I assure you that I know nothing, for Lisa is much too proud, too obstinate, to have spoken to me. But the fact is that they are at odds with each other, that Lisa was humiliated, God alone knows why, and that perhaps your Dasha would have something to say about it, although . . .

VARVARA: I don't like insinuations, Prascovya. Tell all you have to tell. Are you trying to imply that Dasha had an intrigue with Nicholas?

PRASCOVYA: An intrigue, dear – what a word! Besides, I don't want to imply . . . I love you too much. . . . How can you imagine? . . . [*She dries a tear.*]

VARVARA: Don't weep. I'm not hurt. Just tell me what took place.

PRASCOVYA: Why, nothing at all. He is in love with Lisa, that's certain. I couldn't be mistaken on that point. Feminine intuition! . . . But you know Lisa's character. I suppose one might say obstinate and scornful – yes, that's it! And Nicholas is proud. What pride – oh, he is indeed your son! Well, he couldn't put up with her little jokes. And, in return, he bantered.

VARVARA: Bantered?

PRASCOVYA: Yes, that's the word. In any case, Lisa constantly tried to start a quarrel with Nicholas. Sometimes when she was aware that he was talking with Dasha, you couldn't hold her back. Really, my dear, it was unbearable. The doctors forbade me to get excited, and, furthermore, I was so bored on the shores of that lake, and I had a toothache. Since then I have learned that the Lake of Geneva predisposes people to toothaches, and that that's one of its peculiarities. Finally Nicholas left. In my opinion, they will make it up.

VARVARA: Such a slight misunderstanding doesn't mean a thing. Besides, I know my Dasha too well. It's utterly absurd. Moreover, I shall get at the facts of the matter. [She rings.]

PRASCOVYA: No, I assure you . . .

[ALEXEY YEGOROVICH enters.]

VARVARA: Tell Dasha that I am waiting for her.

[ALEXEY YEGOROVICH leaves.]

PRASCOVYA: I was wrong, dear, to speak to you of Dasha. There was nothing but the most ordinary conversations between her and Nicholas, and there was no whispering. At least in my presence. But I felt Lisa's irritation. And then that lake – you have no idea! It does calm you, to be sure, but only because it bores you. Yet, if you know what I mean, simply by boring you it irritates you . . . [DASHA enters.] My Dashenka, my little one! How I hate giving you up. We shall miss our good evening conversations in Geneva. Oh! Geneva! *Au revoir, chère!* [*To* DASHA] *Au revoir, ma mignonne, ma chérie, ma colombe.* [She leaves.]

VARVARA: Sit down there. [DASHA *sits down.*] Embroider. [DASHA *picks up an embroidery frame from the table.*] Tell me about your trip.

DASHA [*in a steady, dull voice, somewhat tired*]: Oh! I had a good time, and I learned a great deal. Europe is very instructive – yes, instructive. We are so far behind them. They –

VARVARA: Forget Europe. You have nothing particular to tell me?

DASHA [*looks at her*]: No, nothing.

VARVARA: Nothing on your mind, or on your conscience, or in your heart?

DASHA [*with a sort of colourless conviction*]: Nothing.

VARVARA: I was sure of it. I never had the slightest doubt about you. I have treated you as my daughter, and I am aiding your brother. You wouldn't do anything that might hurt me, would you?

DASHA: No, nothing, God bless you.

VARVARA: Listen. I have been thinking about you. Drop your embroidery and come over near me. [DASHA *moves closer to her.*] Do you want to get married? [DASHA *looks at her.*] Wait a moment, don't answer. I am thinking of someone older than you. But you are a reasonable girl. Besides, he is still very presentable. I am thinking of Stepan Trofimovich who was your professor and whom you have always esteemed. Well? [DASHA *keeps on looking at her fixedly.*] I know, he is frivolous. He whimpers and he thinks about himself too much. But he has decided qualities that you will appreciate, particularly because I ask it of you. He deserves to be loved because he is defenceless. Do you understand that? [DASHA *nods affirmatively. Bursting out*] I was sure of it; I was sure of you. As for him, he will love you because he is under an obligation! He must adore you! Listen, Dasha. He will obey you. Unless you are an idiot, you can force him to. But never push him to extremes – that is the first rule of conjugal life. Oh, Dasha, there is no greater happiness than sacrificing oneself. Besides, you will be doing me a great favour, and that is the important thing. But I am not forcing you in any way. It is up to you to decide. Speak.

DASHA [*slowly*]: If it is absolutely necessary, I shall do it.

VARVARA: Absolutely? What are you alluding to, my child? [DASHA *lowers her head in silence.*] What you have just said is a stupidity. I am going to marry you off, to be sure, but not out of necessity, you understand. The idea just came to me, that's all. There's nothing to hide, is there?

DASHA: No. I shall do as you wish.

VARVARA: Hence you consent. So let's get to the details. Directly after the ceremony, I shall give you fifteen thousand roubles. Out of those fifteen thousand, you will give eight thousand to Stepan Trofimovich. Allow him to receive his friends once a week. If they should come more often, put them out. Moreover, I shall be there to keep an eye on things.

DASHA: Has Stepan Trofimovich said anything to you about this?

VARVARA: No, he hasn't said anything. But he will. [*She rises suddenly and throws her black shawl over her shoulders.* DASHA *continues to stare at her.*] You are an ungrateful girl! What are you thinking of? Do you think I am going to compromise you? Why, he will come on his knees to beg you to marry him! He will be bursting with happiness, that's how it will be!

[STEPAN TROFIMOVICH *enters.* DASHA *rises.*]

STEPAN: Oh! Dashenka, my pretty girl, what a delight to

find you among us again. [*He kisses her.*] Here you are at last!

VARVARA: Leave her alone. You have all of life ahead of you to caress her. And I have something to say to you. [DASHA *leaves.*]

STEPAN: *Soit, mon amie, soit.* But you know how much I love my little pupil.

VARVARA: I know. But don't keep calling her 'my little pupil'. She is grown-up! It's irritating! Hum, you have been smoking.

STEPAN: *C'est-à-dire* ...

VARVARA: Sit down. That's not the question. The question is that you must get married.

STEPAN [*stupefied*]: Get married? A third time, and at the age of fifty-three!

VARVARA: Well, what difference does that make? At fifty-three we are at the peak of life. I know what I am saying, for I am almost there. Besides, you are a handsome man.

STEPAN: You have always been indulgent towards me, *mon amie. Mais je dois vous dire ... je ne m'attendais pas. ...* Yes, at the age of fifty we are not yet old. That is obvious. [*He looks at her.*]

VARVARA: I shall help you. She will not be without a dowry. Oh! I forgot: you are marrying Dasha.

STEPAN [*giving a start*]: Dasha. ... But I thought ... Dasha! But she's only a child!

VARVARA: A twenty-year-old child, *grâce à Dieu!* Don't roll your eyes that way, please; you're not in the circus. You are intelligent, but you don't understand anything. You need someone to take care of you constantly. What will you do if I die? Dasha will be an excellent housekeeper for you. Moreover, I shall be there; I'm not going to die right away. Besides, she is an angel of kindness. [*Bursting out in anger*] You understand, I am telling you that she is an angel of kindness!

STEPAN: I know, but such a difference in age ... I was thinking.... If necessary, you see, someone of my own age ...

VARVARA: Well, you will educate her, you will develop her heart. You will give her an honourable name. Perhaps you will be her saviour – yes, her saviour ...

STEPAN: But what about her? ... Have you talked to her?

VARVARA: Don't worry about her. Of course, it is up to you to urge her, to beg her to do you that honour, you understand. But don't worry, for *I* shall be there. Besides you love her. [STEPAN TROFIMOVICH *rises and staggers.*] What's the matter with you?

STEPAN: I ... I accept, of course, of course, because you wish it, but I should never have thought that you would agree ...

VARVARA: What do you mean?

STEPAN: Without an overriding reason, without an urgent reason ... I should never have thought that you could accept seeing me married to ... to another woman.

VARVARA [*rises suddenly*]: Another woman! [*She looks at him with flashing eyes, then heads towards the door. Before reaching it, she turns to him.*] I shall never forgive you, never, you understand, for having imagined for one second that between you and me ... [*She is on the point of leaving, but* GRIGORIEV *enters.*] I.... Good day, Grigoriev. [*To* STEPAN TROFIMOVICH] So you have accepted. I shall arrange the details myself. Moreover, I am on my way to Prascovya's to tell her about the plan. And take care of yourself. Don't let yourself get any older! [*She leaves.*]

GRIGORIEV: Our friend seems thoroughly upset.

STEPAN: In other words. . . . Oh, I shall eventually lose all patience and cease wanting . . .

GRIGORIEV: Wanting what?

STEPAN: I agreed because I am bored with life and nothing matters to me. But if she exasperates me, things might begin to matter to me. I shall be aware of the insult and I shall refuse.

GRIGORIEV: You will refuse?

STEPAN: To get married. Oh, I shouldn't have talked about it! But you are my friend; it is as if I were talking to myself. Yes, I am asked to marry Dasha, and I accepted in principle, I accepted. At my age! Oh, my dear friend, for any soul that is the least bit proud, the least bit free, marriage is death itself. Marriage will corrupt me and sap my energy; I shall no longer be able to serve the cause of humanity. Children will come, and God alone will know whether they are mine. No, after all, they won't be mine; the wise man can face the truth. And I have accepted! Because I am bored. No, it's not because I am bored that I accepted. But there's that debt . . .

GRIGORIEV: You are doing yourself an injustice. A man doesn't have to need money to marry a pretty young girl.

STEPAN: Alas, I need money more than I need a pretty girl. . . . You know that I didn't manage very well that property my son inherited from his mother. He is going to demand the eight thousand roubles I owe him. He is accused of being a revolutionary, a socialist, of aiming to destroy God and property, and so forth. I don't know about God, but as for property, he clings to his own, I assure you. . . . Besides, it's a debt of honour for me. I must sacrifice myself.

GRIGORIEV: But all this does you honour. Why are you complaining?

STEPAN: There's something else in it. I suspect. . . . Well. . . . Oh, I am not as stupid as I seem in her presence! Why this marriage in haste? Dasha was in Switzerland. She saw Nicholas. And now . . .

GRIGORIEV: I don't understand.

STEPAN: Yes, there's a mystery about it. Why such a mystery? I don't want to cover up the sins of others. Yes, the sins of others! O God who art so great and so good, who will console me!

[LISA *and* MAURICE NICOLAEVICH *enter.*]

LISA: Here he is at last, Maurice, this is he, this is the man. [*To* STEPAN TROFIMOVICH] You recognize me, don't you?

STEPAN: *Dieu! Dieu! Chère Lisa!* At last a minute of happiness!

LISA: Yes. It's been twelve years since we have seen each other. And you are happy, aren't you, to see me again? You haven't forgotten your little pupil?

[STEPAN TROFIMOVICH *rushes towards her, seizes her hand, and stares at her, unable to speak.*]

LISA: Here are some flowers for you. I wanted to bring you a cake, but Maurice Nicolaevich advised flowers. He has such a sense of propriety. This is Maurice: I should like you to become good friends. I like him very much. Yes, he is the man I like most in the world. Maurice, I want you to meet my dear old professor.

MAURICE: I feel most honoured.

LISA [*to* STEPAN]: What a delight to see you again! And yet I am sad. Why do I always feel sad at such moments? You are such a learned man – can't you tell me? I always imagined that I should be madly happy when I saw you again and that I should remember everything, and here I am not at all happy – and, yet, I love you.

STEPAN [*with the flowers in his hand*]: It doesn't matter. Here I am too, loving you dearly, and you see I'm on the point of weeping.

LISA: Why, you have my portrait on the wall! [*She goes and takes down a miniature.*] Can this be I? Was I really so pretty? But I won't look at it! One life ends, another begins, then it yields to still another, and so on *ad infinitum*. [*Looking at* GRIGORIEV] You see how all this calls up the past!

STEPAN: Forgive me, I was forgetting to introduce Grigoriev, an excellent old friend.

LISA [*with a touch of coquetry*]: Oh, yes, you are the confidant! I like you very much.

GRIGORIEV: I don't deserve such an honour.

LISA: Come, now, don't be ashamed of being a good man. [*She turns her back on him and he looks at her with admiration.*] Dasha came back with us. But you know that already, of course. She's a dear, I should like her to be happy. By the way, she told me a lot about her brother. What is Shatov like?

STEPAN: Well, he's a dreamer! He was a socialist, then he abjured his ideas, and now he lives according to God and Russia.

LISA: Yes, someone told me that he was a bit odd. I want to know him. I should like to give him some work to do.

STEPAN: Indeed, that would be a godsend for him.

LISA: A godsend – why? I want to know him; I am interested. ... I mean, I really need someone to help me.

GRIGORIEV: I know Shatov rather well, and, if I can help you, I'll go and see him at once.

LISA: Yes, yes. I may even go myself. Although I don't want

to disturb him, nor anyone else in that house. But we will have to be back home in a quarter of an hour. Are you ready, Maurice?

MAURICE: I am at your beck and call.

LISA: Splendid. You are good. [*To* STEPAN TROFIMOVICH *as she goes towards the door*] I imagine you are like me: I detest men who are not good, even if they are very handsome and very intelligent. The important thing is a good heart. By the way, let me congratulate you on your marriage.

STEPAN: What, you know?

LISA: Of course. Varvara has just told us. What good news! And I am sure that Dasha was not expecting it. Come, Maurice...

BLACKOUT

THE NARRATOR: So I went to see Shatov because Lisa wanted me to and it already seemed to me that I could refuse her nothing, although I did not for a moment believe the explanations she gave for her sudden whim. This took me, and takes you likewise, to a less elegant section of town where the landlady Filipov let out rooms and a common living-room to odd individuals such as Lebyatkin and his sister Maria, Shatov, and, above all, the engineer Kirilov.

SCENE THREE

The scene shows a living-room and a small bedroom, Shatov's, on the right. The living-room has a door on the left opening into Kirilov's room and two doors upstage, one for the outer entrance and the other opening on to the stairs leading to the upper storey. In the centre of the living-room KIRILOV, *facing the audience, is doing his exercises with a most serious look on his face.*

KIRILOV: One, two, three, four ... One, two, three, four ...
[*He takes a deep breath.*] One, two, three, four ...
   [GRIGORIEV *enters.*]

GRIGORIEV: Am I disturbing you? I was looking for Ivan
Shatov.

KIRILOV: He is out. You are not disturbing me, but I still
have one exercise to do. Allow me. [*He goes through his
exercise, muttering numbers as he does so.*] There, Shatov will
be back soon. May I give you some tea? I like drinking
tea at night. Especially after my exercises. I walk a great
deal, up and down, and I drink tea until dawn.

GRIGORIEV: Do you go to bed at dawn?

KIRILOV: Always. I have for a long time. At night I reflect.

GRIGORIEV: All night long?

KIRILOV [*calmly*]: Yes, it is essential. You see, I am
concerned with the reasons why men don't dare kill
themselves.

GRIGORIEV: Don't dare? In your opinion, there are not
enough suicides?

KIRILOV [*absent-minded*]: Normally, there ought to be many
more.

GRIGORIEV [*ironically*]: And what, in your opinion, keeps
people from killing themselves?

KIRILOV: The pain. Those who kill themselves through
madness or despair don't think of the pain. But those who
kill themselves through reason obviously think of it.

GRIGORIEV: What, are there people who kill themselves
through reason?

KIRILOV: Many. Were it not for the pain and the prejudice,
there would be many more, a very large number,
probably all men.

GRIGORIEV: What?

KIRILOV: But the idea that they will suffer keeps them from killing themselves. Even when one knows there is no pain, the idea remains. Just imagine a stone as big as a house falling on you. You wouldn't have time to feel anything, to suffer at all. Well, even so, men are afraid and hesitate. It is interesting.

GRIGORIEV: There must be another reason.

KIRILOV: Yes. . . . The other world.

GRIGORIEV: You mean punishment.

KIRILOV: No, the other world. People think there is a reason for going on living.

GRIGORIEV: And there isn't any?

KIRILOV: No, there is none, and that's why we are free. It is a matter of indifference whether we live or die.

GRIGORIEV: How can you say that so calmly?

KIRILOV: I don't like getting into disputes, and I never laugh.

GRIGORIEV: Man is afraid of death because he likes life, because life is good, that's all.

KIRILOV [*suddenly bursting out*]: But that's cowardice, just cowardice! Life isn't good. And the other world does not exist! God is simply a ghost conjured up by fear of death and suffering. In order to be free, it is essential to overcome pain and terror, it is essential to kill oneself. Then there will no longer be any God, and man will at last be free. Then history will be divided into two parts: from the ape to the destruction of God, and from the destruction of God . . .

GRIGORIEV: To the ape.

KIRILOV: To the divinity of man. [*Suddenly calm*] The man who dares to kill himself is God. No one had ever thought of that. But *I* have.

GRIGORIEV: There have been millions of suicides.

KIRILOV: Never for that reason. Always from fear. Never to kill fear. The man who kills himself to kill fear will at that very moment become God.

GRIGORIEV: I am afraid he won't have time.

KIRILOV [*rising and slowly with scorn in his voice*]: I am sorry that you seem to be laughing.

GRIGORIEV: Forgive me; I wasn't laughing. But it is all so strange.

KIRILOV: Why strange? The strange thing is that people can live without thinking of that. *I* can't think of anything else. All my life I have thought of nothing else. [*He gestures to* GRIGORIEV, *who leans forward*.] All my life I have been tormented by God.

GRIGORIEV: Why do you speak to me like this? You don't know me.

KIRILOV: You look like my brother, who died seven years ago.

GRIGORIEV: Did he exert a great influence over you?

KIRILOV: No. He never said anything. But you look very much like him, extraordinarily like him. [SHATOV *comes in.* KIRILOV *rises.*] I beg to inform you that Mr Grigoriev has been waiting for you for some time. [*He leaves.*]

SHATOV: What's the matter with him?

GRIGORIEV: I don't know. If I understood what he was saying, he wants all of us to commit suicide to prove to God that He doesn't exist.

SHATOV: Yes, he's a nihilist. He caught the bug in America.

GRIGORIEV: In America?

SHATOV: That's where I met him. We starved together and slept together on the bare ground. ‖That was the time when I felt the same as all those thwarted people. We wanted to go there to experience directly how it feels to be placed in the worst social conditions.

GRIGORIEV: Good Lord! Why go so far? All you had to do was sign up for the harvest twenty kilometres from here.

SHATOV: I know. But that's how mad we were. Kirilov hasn't changed, although there is in him a deep passion and a resistance that I respect. In America he starved without a word of complaint. || Fortunately, a generous friend sent us money to get back home. [*He looks fixedly at the* NARRATOR.] You don't ask who that man was?

GRIGORIEV: Who?

SHATOV: Nicholas Stavrogin. [*Silence.*] And you probably think you know why he did it?

GRIGORIEV: I pay no attention to gossip.

SHATOV: Well, even if he did have an affair with my wife? [*He stares at him.*] I haven't yet paid him back. But I shall do so. I don't want to have anything to do with such people. [*Pause.*] You see, Grigoriev, all those people, Liputin, Shigalov, and so many others, like Stepan Trofimovich's son and even Stavrogin – you know what motivates them? Hatred. [*The* NARRATOR *makes a gesture of protest.*] Yes. They hate their country. They would be the first to suffer dreadfully if their country could be suddenly reformed, if it became exceptionally prosperous and happy. They wouldn't have anyone to spit on any more. Whereas now they can spit on their country and wish her all kinds of misfortune.

GRIGORIEV: And you, Shatov?

SHATOV: I love Russia now, although I am not worthy of her. That is why I am saddened by her misfortune and my own unworthiness. And they, my former friends, accuse me of having betrayed them. [*He turns away.*]

Meanwhile, I ought to earn some money to repay Stavrogin. I absolutely must.

GRIGORIEV: It so happens —

[*There is a knock at the door.* SHATOV *goes to open it.* LISA *enters with a bundle of newspapers under her arm.*]

LISA [*to* GRIGORIEV]: Oh, you are already here! [*She goes towards him.*] So I was right when I thought yesterday at Stepan Trofimovich's that you would help me. Have you had a chance to talk to this Mr Shatov? [*Meanwhile, she has been looking eagerly around her.*]

GRIGORIEV: Here he is. But I haven't had time.... Shatov, Elizabeth Drozdov, whom you know by name, has asked me to talk to you about something.

LISA: I am happy to know you. I have heard about you. Peter Verkhovensky told me you were intelligent. Nicholas Stavrogin also told me about you. [SHATOV *turns away.*] In any case, here is my idea. In my opinion, and I think that you will agree with me, our country isn't sufficiently known. So I thought it would be worth while to gather in a single book all the significant events our newspapers have reported in several years. Such a book would automatically *be* Russia. If you would only help me... I need someone highly competent, and of course your work would be paid for.

‖SHATOV: It's an interesting idea, even intelligent.... It deserves thinking about....Yes, it does.

LISA. [*delighted*]: If the book sells, we shall share the profits. You would provide the outline and the work, and I the initial idea and the necessary funds.

SHATOV: But what makes you think that I can do this work? Why I rather than someone else?

LISA: Well, what I heard of you made me like you. Will you accept?

SHATOV: Maybe. Yes. Can you leave me your newspapers? I shall think about it.

LISA [*claps her hands with joy*]: Oh! How happy I am! How proud I shall be when the book comes out!‖ [*All this time she has been looking around her.*] By the way, doesn't Captain Lebyatkin live here?

GRIGORIEV: Yes, of course. I thought I told you so. Are you interested in him?

LISA: In him? Yes, but not only.... In any case, he is interested in me ... [*She looks at* GRIGORIEV.] He wrote me a letter with a poem in it, and he says that he has things to tell me. I didn't understand it at all. [*To* SHATOV] What do you think of him?

SHATOV: He's a drunkard and a dishonest man.

LISA: But I have heard that he lives with his sister.

SHATOV: Yes.

LISA: It is said that he bullies her. [SHATOV *looks at her fixedly without answering.*] But people say so many things, after all. I shall ask Nicholas Stavrogin, who knows her well, who knows her even very well, according to what I have heard ... [SHATOV *keeps on staring at her. With a sudden outburst of enthusiasm*] Oh, listen, I want to see her at once. I must see her in the flesh. Please help me. I really must.

SHATOV [*goes and picks up the newspapers*]: Take back your newspapers. I cannot accept this work.

LISA: Why not? Have I hurt you?

SHATOV: That's not it. You mustn't count on me for this chore, that's all.

LISA: What chore? This job is not imaginary. I want to do it.

SHATOV: Yes. You had better go home now.

GRIGORIEV [*affectionately*]: Yes. Please go home. Shatov will think about it. I shall come and see you and keep you informed. [LISA *looks at them, whimpers, then goes off in a hurry.*]

SHATOV: It was a pretext. She wanted to see Maria Timofeyevna, and I haven't sunk low enough to play a part in such a comedy. [MARIA TIMOFEYEVNA *has come in behind him. She is holding a roll in her hand.*]

MARIA: Good day, Shatoushka!

[GRIGORIEV *bows.* SHATOV *goes towards* MARIA TIMOFEYEVNA *and takes her arm. She walks towards the table in the centre, and places her roll on the table, pulls out a drawer, and takes out a deck of cards without paying any attention to* GRIGORIEV.] MARIA [*shuffling the cards*]: I was fed up with staying alone in my room.

SHATOV: I am pleased to see you.

MARIA: I am too. That man . . . [*She points to* GRIGORIEV.] I don't know him. Let us honour all visitors! Yes, I always enjoy talking with you, even though you are always dishevelled. You live like a monk; let me comb your hair. [*She takes a little comb from her pocket.*]

SHATOV [*laughing*]: But I have no comb.

[MARIA TIMOFEYÉVNA *combs his hair.*]

MARIA: Really? Well, later on, when my Prince comes back, I'll give you mine. [*She makes a parting, steps back to judge the impression it makes, and puts the comb in her pocket.*] Shall I tell you, Shatoushka? [*She sits down and begins to play solitaire.*] You are intelligent and yet you are bored. After all, you are all bored. I can't understand anyone being bored. Being sad doesn't amount to being bored. *I* am sad, but I enjoy myself hugely.

SHATOV: Even when your brother is here?

MARIA: You mean my lackey? He is my brother, to be sure,

but, above all, he is my lackey, I order him about: 'Lebyatkin, water!' He goes and gets it. Sometimes I make the mistake of laughing at him, and when he is drunk he beats me. [*She goes on playing solitaire.*]

SHATOV [to GRIGORIEV]: That is true. She treats him like a lackey. He beats her, but she is not afraid of him. Besides, she hasn't the slightest notion of time – she forgets everything that has just happened. [GRIGORIEV *points towards her.*] No, I can talk in her presence; she has already forgotten us because very soon she stops listening and falls back into her daydreams. Do you see that roll? Probably she has nibbled it only once since this morning and won't finish it until tomorrow.

[MARIA TIMOFEYEVNA *picks up the roll without ceasing to look at her cards, but she holds it in her hand without biting into it. During the course of the conversation she puts it down on the table again.*]

MARIA: A move, a wicked man, a betrayal, a deathbed. . . . Why, these are all lies! If people can lie, why can't cards also? [*She scatters them over the table and gets up.*] Everyone lies except the Mother of God! [*She smiles as she looks at her feet.*]

SHATOV: The Mother of God?

MARIA: Why, yes, the Mother of God, nature, great mother earth! She is good and true. Do you remember what is written, Shatoushka? 'When you have wet the earth with your tears to the depth of a foot, then you will take joy in everything.' That's why I weep so often, Shatoushka. There is no harm in these tears. All tears are tears of joy or promises of joy. [*Her face is bathed in tears. She puts her hands on* SHATOV's *shoulders.*] Shatoushka, is it true that your wife left you?

SHATOV: It is true. She forsook me.

MARIA [*caressing his face*]: Don't be angry. I too am grieving. I had a dream, you know. He returned. He, my Prince, returned, and called me in a sweet voice: 'My dear one,' he said, 'my dear one, come and join me.' And I was happy. I kept repeating: 'He loves me, he loves me.'

SHATOV: Perhaps he will really come.

MARIA: Oh, no, it was only a dream! My Prince will not come. I shall remain alone. Oh, my dear friend, why don't you ever question me about anything?

SHATOV: Because I know that you will never tell me anything.

MARIA: No, oh, no, I won't tell anything! They can kill me, they can burn me alive, but I won't tell anything. They'll never know anything!

SHATOV: See!

MARIA: Yet if you who are so kindhearted asked me, then perhaps. . . . Why don't you ask me? Ask me, ask properly, Shatoushka, and I shall tell you. Beg me to talk, Shatoushka. And I shall talk, I shall talk. . . .

[SHATOV *says nothing and* MARIA TIMOFEYEVNA *faces him with her face bathed in tears. Then a fracas and oaths are heard at the door.*]

SHATOV: Here is your brother. Go back to your room or he will beat you again.

MARIA [*bursting out laughing*]: Oh, it's my lackey? Well, what does it matter? We'll send him to the kitchen. [*But* SHATOV *draws her towards the door upstage.*] Don't worry, Shatoushka, don't worry. If my Prince comes back, he will defend me.

[LEBYATKIN *comes in and slams the door.* MARIA TIMO-FEYEVNA *remains upstage with a frozen smile of scorn on her face.*]

LEBYATKIN [*singing drunkenly*]:

> I have come to tell you
> That the sun is up,
> That the woods are swooning
> Under his ardent kisses.

Who goes there? Friend or foe? [*To* MARIA TIMO-FEYEVNA] You get back in your room!

SHATOV: Leave your sister alone.

LEBYATKIN [*bowing to* GRIGORIEV]: Retired Captain Ignatius Lebyatkin, in the service of the whole world and of his friends, just so long as they are faithful friends! Oh, the swine! And, first of all, I want you all to know that I am in love with Lisa Drozdov. She is a star and a horsewoman. In short, a star on horseback. And *I* am a man of honour.

SHATOV: Who sells his sister.

LEBYATKIN [*shouting*]: What? The same old calumny! Do you know that I could shame you with a single word?

SHATOV: Say the word.

LEBYATKIN: You think I wouldn't dare.

SHATOV: You may be a captain, but you are a coward. And you would be afraid of your master.

LEBYATKIN: He is provoking me, and you are a witness to it, sir! Well, do you know whose wife this woman is? [GRIGORIEV *steps forward.*]

SHATOV: Whose? You won't dare say.

LEBYATKIN: She is. . . . She is . . .

[MARIA TIMOFEYEVNA *steps forward, her mouth open and speechless.*]

BLACKOUT

THE NARRATOR: Whose wife was that wretched cripple?
Was it true that Dasha had been dishonoured, and by
whom? And who had seduced Shatov's wife? Well, we
shall be told! Indeed, just as the climate of our little city
had become so tense, a newcomer came with a flaming
torch which blew up everything and stripped everyone
naked. And, take my word for it, seeing one's fellow
citizens naked is generally a painful experience. So the
son of the humanist, the offspring of the liberal Stepan
Trofimovich, Peter Verkhovensky, to call him by name,
popped up at the moment when he was least expected.

SCENE FOUR

At Varvara Stavrogin's. GRIGORIEV *and* STEPAN TROFI-
MOVICH.

STEPAN: Ah, my friend, everything is about to be decided.
If Dasha accepts, I shall be a married man next Sunday,
and that's not funny. ||But since my very dear Varvara
Stavrogin asked me to come today and settle everything,
I shall obey her. Didn't I behave badly towards her?

GRIGORIEV: No, not at all. You were simply taken by
surprise.

STEPAN: Yes, I did. When I think of that generous and
compassionate woman, so indulgent to all my petty
foibles! I am a spoiled child with all the selfishness of a
child and none of the innocence. She has been taking care
of me for twenty years. And I, at the very moment when
she is receiving these dreadful anonymous letters ...

GRIGORIEV: Anonymous letters?

STEPAN: Yes, just imagine: she is told that Nicholas has given his property to Lebyatkin. That Nicholas is a monster. Poor Lisa! But you are in love with her, I know.

GRIGORIEV: How dare you?

STEPAN: All right, all right, forget it. Maurice Nicolaevich is in love with her too, don't forget. Poor man, I wouldn't want to be in his place. But, then, mine isn't much easier. ‖ In any case, however ashamed of myself I am, I wrote to Dasha.

GRIGORIEV: Good Lord! What did you tell her?

STEPAN: Well ... I wrote to Nicholas too.

GRIGORIEV: Are you crazy?

STEPAN: But my intention was noble. After all, just imagine that something really took place in Switzerland, or that there was a beginning, a little beginning, or even a very little beginning of something. I had to question their hearts first of all. I wanted them to know that I knew, so that they would feel freer. I acted through noble motives.

GRIGORIEV: But it was utterly stupid!

STEPAN: Yes, yes, it was foolish. But how else could I behave? Everything is open and above-board now. I wrote to my son, too. And yet I don't care! I'll marry Dasha even if I am just covering up the sins of others.

GRIGORIEV: Don't say that.

STEPAN: Oh, if only next Sunday would never come! It would be easy for God to perform a miracle and to cross one Sunday off the calendar. If only to prove his power to the atheists once and for all! How I love her! How I've loved her for twenty years! Can she really think for a minute that I am getting married because of fear, or poverty? I am doing it for her alone.

GRIGORIEV: Of whom are you talking?

STEPAN: Why, of Varvara, of course. She is the only woman I have adored for the last twenty years. [ALEXEY YEGOROVICH *comes in, escorting* SHATOV.] Ah, here is our quick-tempered friend. You have come to see your sister, I suppose . . .

SHATOV: No. I have been summoned by Varvara Stavrogin for a matter in which I am involved. That is the way, I believe, that the police word it when they issue a summons.

STEPAN: No, she meant just what she said, although I don't know what the business is, nor whether you are involved. In any case, our very dear Varvara is at Mass. As for Dasha, she is in her room. Do you want me to send for her?

SHATOV: No.

STEPAN: All right. That is probably better, after all. The later, the better. You probably know Varvara's plans for her?

SHATOV: Yes.

STEPAN: Good, good! In that case, let's say no more about it, let's say no more about it. Of course, I can imagine that you were surprised. I was myself. So suddenly . . .

SHATOV: Shut up.

STEPAN: All right. Be polite, my dear Shatov, at least today. Yes, be patient with me. My heart is heavy.

[VARVARA STAVROGIN *and* PRASCOVYA DROZDOV *enter, escorted by* MAURICE NICOLAEVICH.]

PRASCOVYA: What a scandal! And Lisa mixed up in all that!

VARVARA [*ringing for a servant*]: Be quiet! What do you call a scandal? That poor girl has lost her reason. Be a little charitable, my dear Prascovya!

STEPAN: What? What happened?

VARVARA: Nothing. A poor crippled girl threw herself at

my feet as we were leaving Mass and kissed my hand. [ALEXEY YEGOROVICH *comes in.*] Coffee ... and don't unharness the horses.

PRASCOVYA: In front of everybody, and they all crowded around!

VARVARA: Of course, in front of everybody! Thank God the church was well filled! I gave her ten roubles and picked her up. Lisa insisted on taking her to her home. [LISA *enters, holding* MARIA TIMOFEYEVNA *by the hand.*]

LISA: No, I changed my mind. I thought that you would all be pleased to know Maria Timofeyevna better.

MARIA: How beautiful it is! [*She perceives* SHATOV.] What, you are here, Shatoushka! What are you doing in high society?

VARVARA [*to* SHATOV]: Do you know this woman?

SHATOV: Yes.

VARVARA: Who is she?

SHATOV: See for yourself.

[*She looks with anguish at* MARIA TIMOFEYEVNA. ALEXEY YEGOROVICH *comes in with coffee on a tray.*]

VARVARA [*to* MARIA TIMOFEYEVNA]: You were cold a moment ago, my dear. Drink this coffee – it will warm you up.

MARIA [*smiling*]: Yes. Oh, I had forgotten to give you back the shawl you lent me.

VARVARA: Keep it. It is yours. Sit down and drink your coffee. Don't be afraid.

STEPAN: *Chère amie* –

VARVARA: Oh, you, be quiet. The situation is bad enough without your making it any worse! Alexey, ask Dasha to come down.

PRASCOVYA: Lisa, we must leave now. This doesn't concern you. We have no further contact with this house.

VARVARA: You have gone a little too far, Prascovya. Thank God that there's no one but friends here to hear you.

PRASCOVYA: If they are friends, so much the better. But *I* am not afraid of public opinion. You are the one who, despite all your pride, trembles at the thought of what people will say. You are the one who is afraid of the truth.

VARVARA: What truth, Prascovya?

PRASCOVYA: This truth.

[*She points at* MARIA TIMOFEYEVNA, *who, seeing a finger pointing at her, giggles and fidgets.* VARVARA *stands up, white in the face, and mutters something that is not heard.* DASHA *enters upstage, and no one sees her but* STEPAN TROFIMOVICH.]

STEPAN [*after making signals intended to attract* VARVARA STAVROGIN'*s attention*]: Here is Dasha.

MARIA: Oh! How beautiful she is! Well, Shatoushka, your sister doesn't look like you at all.

VARVARA [*to* DASHA]: Do you know this person?

DASHA: I've never seen her. But I suppose she is Lebyatkin's sister.

MARIA: Yes, he is my brother. But, above all, he is my lackey. I didn't know you either, dearie. And yet I wanted very much to meet you, especially after my lackey told me that you had given him money. Now I am happy – you are charming. . . .Yes, charming, I tell you.

VARVARA: What money is she talking about?

DASHA: Nicholas Stavrogin had asked me in Switzerland to hand over a certain sum to Maria Lebyatkin.

VARVARA: Nicholas?

DASHA: Nicholas himself.

VARVARA [*after a silence*]: All right. Since he did so without mentioning it to me, he must have had reasons for doing so. But in the future I shall ask you to be more careful. That Lebyatkin has not a good reputation.

MARIA: Oh, no! And if he comes, you must send him to the kitchen. That's his place. You can give him coffee if you wish. But I hold him in utter contempt.

ALEXEY YEGOROVICH [*coming in*]: A certain Mr Lebyatkin is very insistent about being announced.

MAURICE: Allow me to say, madame, that he is not the kind of man to be received in good society.

VARVARA: Yet I am going to receive him. [*To* ALEXEY YEGOROVICH] Tell him to come up. [ALEXEY YEGOROVICH *leaves*.] Since you must know, I received anonymous letters informing me that my son is a monster and warning me against a crippled woman destined to play a large part in my life. I want to get to the bottom of the matter.

PRASCOVYA: I, too, have received those letters. And you know what they say about this woman and Nicholas ...

VARVARA: I know.

[LEBYATKIN *comes in, titillated without being quite drunk. He goes towards* VARVARA STAVROGIN.]

LEBYATKIN: I have come, madame –

VARVARA: Sit down in that chair, sir. You can be heard just as well from there. [*He wheels about and goes and sits down.*] Now, will you introduce yourself?

LEBYATKIN [*rising*]: Captain Lebyatkin. I have come, madame –

VARVARA: Is this person your sister?

LEBYATKIN: Yes, madame. She eluded my vigilance for ... I wouldn't want you to think that I was saying anything bad about my sister, but ... [*He taps his forehead with his finger.*]

VARVARA: Did this misfortune happen long ago?

LEBYATKIN: On a certain day, madame, yes, a certain day.

... I have come to thank you for having taken her in. Here are twenty roubles. [*He goes towards her as the others all bestir themselves as if to protect* VARVARA STAVROGIN.]

VARVARA: Why, you must be mad, my man.

LEBYATKIN: No, madame. Rich is your dwelling and poor is the dwelling of the Lebyatkins, but Maria my sister, née Lebyatkin, the nameless Maria would not have accepted from anyone but you the ten roubles you gave her. From you, madame, and from you alone she will accept anything. But while she accepts with one hand, she gives with the other to one of your charities.

VARVARA: That is done through my porter, sir, and you may do so as you leave. I beg you therefore to put your money away and not to wave it in my face. I shall thank you also to sit down again. Now explain yourself and tell me why your sister can accept anything from me.

LEBYATKIN: Madame, that is a secret that I shall carry to the grave with me.

VARVARA: Why?

LEBYATKIN: May I ask you a question openly, in the Russian manner, from the depths of my heart?

VARVARA: I am listening.

LEBYATKIN: Is it possible to die just because of too noble a soul?

VARVARA: That is a question I have never asked myself.

LEBYATKIN: Really never? Well, if that's the way it is ... [*He strikes his chest vigorously.*] Be silent, heart; there is no hope!

[MARIA TIMOFEYEVNA *bursts out laughing.*]

VARVARA: Stop talking in conundrums, sir, and answer my question. Why can she accept anything from me?

LEBYATKIN: Why? Oh, madame, every day for millennia the whole of nature has been asking the Creator 'Why?'

and we are still awaiting the reply. Is Captain Lebyatkin to be the only one to answer? Would that be fair? I should like to be named Paul and yet I am named Ignatius. Why? I am a poet, with the soul of a poet, and yet I live in a pigsty. Why?

VARVARA: You are expressing yourself bombastically, and I look upon that as insolent.

LEBYATKIN: No, madame, not insolent. I am just an infinitesimal insect, but the insect does not complain. A man is sometimes forced to put up with the dishonour of his family rather than to speak the truth. So Lebyatkin will not complain; he will not say one word too many. You must, madame, admit his greatness of soul!

[ALEXEY YEGOROVICH *comes in, showing great emotion.*]

ALEXEY YEGOROVICH: Nicholas Stavrogin has come.

[*All turn towards the door. Hasty steps are heard and* PETER VERKHOVENSKY *enters.*]

STEPAN: But . . .

PRASCOVYA: But it's . . .

PETER: Greetings, Varvara Stavrogin.

STEPAN: Peter! Why, it's Peter, my son! [*He rushes up and embraces* PETER.]

PETER: All right. All right. Don't get excited. [*He breaks away.*] Just imagine, I rush in expecting to find Nicholas Stavrogin. He left me a half-hour ago at Kirilov's and asked me to meet him here. He will be here any minute, and I am happy to announce this good news.

STEPAN: But I haven't seen you for ten years.

PETER [*moving from one person to another in the room*]: All the more reason for not going all to pieces. Behave yourself! Oh, Lisa, how happy I am! And your esteemed mother hasn't forgotten me? How are your legs? Dear Varvara Stavrogin, I had told my father, but naturally he forgot . . .

STEPAN: *Mon enfant, quelle joie!*

PETER: Yes, you love me. But leave me alone. Ah! Here is Nicholas!

[STAVROGIN *enters.*]

VARVARA: Nicholas! [*At the tone of her voice,* STAVROGIN *stops dead.*] I beg you to tell me at once, before you take even one step, whether it is true that this woman here is your legitimate wife.

[STAVROGIN *stares at her, smiles, then walks towards her and kisses her hand. With the same calm stare he walks towards* MARIA TIMOFEYEVNA. MARIA *gets up with an expression of painful delight on her face.*]

STAVROGIN [*with extraordinary gentleness and affection*]: You must not stay here.

MARIA: May I, here and now, kneel down before you?

STAVROGIN [*smiling*]: No, you may not. I am not your brother or your fiancé or your husband, am I? Take my arm. With your permission, I shall take you home to your brother. [*She casts a frightened look towards* LEBYATKIN.] Fear nothing. Now that I am here, he will not touch you.

MARIA: Oh, I fear nothing. At last you have come. Lebyatkin, call for the carriage.

[LEBYATKIN *leaves.* STAVROGIN *gives his arm to* MARIA TIMOFEYEVNA, *who takes it with a radiant expression on her face. But as she walks she stumbles and would fall but for* STAVROGIN *holding her. He leads her towards the exit, showing her great consideration, amid an absolute silence.* LISA, *who has risen from her chair, sits down again with a shudder of disgust. As soon as they have left, everyone stirs.*]

VARVARA [*to* PRASCOVYA DROZDOV]: Well, did you hear what he just said?

PRASCOVYA: Of course. Of course! But why didn't he answer you?

PETER: Why, he couldn't, I assure you!

VARVARA [*suddenly looking at him*]: Why not? What do you know about it?

PETER: I know all about it. But the story was too long for Nicholas to relate just now. I can tell it to you, for I saw it all.

VARVARA: If you give me your word of honour that what you say will not hurt Nicholas in any way ...

PETER: Quite the contrary! He will even be grateful to me for having spoken. You see, we were together in St Petersburg five years ago and Nicholas was leading – how shall I put it? – an ironic life. Yes, that's the word. He was bored then, but did not want to fall into despair. Hence he did nothing and went out with anyone at all. Through nobility of soul, you might say, like a man above all that sort of thing. In short, he spent his time with knaves. Thus it is that he knew that Lebyatkin, a fool and parasite. He and his sister were living in abject poverty. One day in a cabaret someone insulted that lame girl. Nicholas got up, seized the insulter by the collar, and with a single blow threw him out. That's all.

‖VARVARA: What do you mean, 'that's all'?

PETER: Yes, that's where it all started. The lame girl fell in love with her Knight, who spoke two sentences to her. People made fun of her. Nicholas was the only one who didn't laugh and treated her with respect.‖

STEPAN: Why, that is very chivalrous.

‖PETER: Yes, you see, my father feels the same way that the lame girl did. Kirilov, on the other hand, did not.

VARVARA: Why not?

PETER: He used to say to Nicholas: 'It's because you treat her like a duchess that she is losing all self-possession.'

LISA: And what did the Knight reply?

PETER: 'Kirilov,' he said, 'you think I am making fun of her, but you are wrong. I respect her, for she is worth more than all of us.'

STEPAN: Sublime! And even, you might say, chivalrous...‖

PETER: Yes, chivalrous. Unfortunately, the lame girl eventually came to imagine that Nicholas was her fiancé. Finally, when Nicholas had to leave Petersburg, he arranged to leave behind an annual allowance for the lame girl.

LISA: Why that?

PETER: I don't know. A whim perhaps – the kind a man indulges in when he is prematurely tired of existence. Kirilov, on the other hand, claimed that it was the fancy of a blasé young man who wanted to see how far he could lead a half-crazy cripple. But I am sure that's not true.

VARVARA [in a state of rapture]: Why, of course not! It's just like Nicholas! It's just like me! Being carried away like that, blind generosity taking up the defence of anything weak, infirm, perhaps even unworthy ... [She looks at STEPAN TROFIMOVICH] ... protecting the creature for years on end.... Why, it's me all over again! Oh, I have been guilty towards Nicholas! As for that poor creature, it's very simple; I shall adopt her.

PETER: And you will be doing right. For her brother persecutes her. He got it into his head that he had a right to dispose of her allowance. Not only does he take everything she has, not only does he beat her and take her money, but he drinks it all up, he insults her benefactor, threatens to drag him before the law if the allowance is not paid to him directly. In fact, he considers Nicholas's gift as if it were a sort of tribute.

LISA: A tribute for what?

PETER: Well, how should I know? He talks of his sister's

honour, of his family. But honour is a vague word, isn't it? Very vague.

SHATOV: Is it a vague word, really? [*All look at him.*] Dasha, is it a vague word to you? [DASHA *looks at him.*] Answer me.

DASHA: No, brother, honour exists.

> [STAVROGIN *enters.* VARVARA *rises and goes rapidly towards him.*]

VARVARA: Oh, Nicholas, will you forgive me?

STAVROGIN: I am the one to be forgiven, Mother. I should have explained to you. But I was sure that Peter Verkhovensky would inform you.

VARVARA: Yes, he did. And I am happy.... You were chivalrous.

STEPAN: Sublime is the word.

STAVROGIN: Chivalrous, indeed! So that's how you see it? I suppose I owe this compliment to Peter Verkhovensky. And you must believe him, Mother. He lies only in exceptional circumstances. [PETER VERKHOVENSKY *and* STAVROGIN *look at each other and smile.*] Good, but I beg your forgiveness once more for my attitude. [*In a harsh, crisp voice*] In any case, the subject is closed now. There's no point in bringing it up again. [LISA *bursts out with a hysterical laugh.*]

STAVROGIN: Good day, Lisa. I hope you are well.

LISA: Please forgive me. I believe you know Maurice Nicolaevich. Good Lord, Maurice, how is it possible to be so tall?

MAURICE: I don't understand.

LISA: Oh, nothing ... I was just thinking.... Supposing that I were lame, you would lead me through the streets, you would be chivalrous, wouldn't you? You would be devoted to me?

MAURICE: Most certainly, Lisa. But why talk of such a misfortune?

LISA: Most certainly you would be chivalrous. Well, you so tall and I crippled and deformed, we'd make a ridiculous couple.

[VARVARA STAVROGIN *and* PRASCOVYA DROZDOV *go towards* LISA. *But* STAVROGIN *turns and goes towards* DASHA.]

STAVROGIN: I've heard of your marriage, Dasha, and I want to congratulate you. [DASHA *turns her head away.*] My congratulations are sincere.

DASHA: I know it.

PETER: Why these congratulations? Am I to assume that there is some good news?

PRASCOVYA: Yes, Dasha is getting married.

PETER: Why, it's wonderful! Accept my congratulations too. But you have lost your bet. You told me in Switzerland that you would never get married. Decidedly, it's an epidemic. Do you know that my father is getting married too?

STEPAN: Peter!

PETER: Well, didn't you write me so? To be sure, you weren't very clear. First you declare yourself to be delighted and then you ask me to save you; you tell me that the girl is a pure diamond, but that you must get married to cover sins committed in Switzerland; you ask my consent – what a topsy-turvy world this is! – and you beg me to save you from this marriage. [*To the others, laughing*] What on earth could he mean? But that's the way his generation is – big words and vague ideas! [*He seems suddenly to become aware of the effect of his words.*] Well, what's the matter? ... It looks as if I've dropped a brick. ...

VARVARA [*stepping towards him with flushed face*]: Did Stepan Trofimovich write you that in so many words?

PETER: Yes, here is his letter. It is long, like all of his letters. I never read them all the way through, I must confess. Besides, he doesn't care, for he writes them especially for posterity. But there's no harm in what he says.

VARVARA: Nicholas, was it Stepan Trofimovich who informed you of this marriage? In the same manner, I suppose?

STAVROGIN: He did write me, in fact, but a very noble letter.

VARVARA: That's enough! [*She turns towards* STEPAN TROFIMOVICH.] Stepan Trofimovich, I expect a great service of you. I expect you to leave this house and never appear in my presence again.

[STEPAN TROFIMOVICH *steps towards her and bows with great dignity, then goes over towards* DASHA.]

STEPAN: Dasha, forgive me for all this. I thank you for having accepted.

DASHA: I forgive you, Stepan Trofimovich. I feel nothing but affection and esteem for you. You, at least, continue to respect me.

PETER [*striking his forehead*]: Now I understand! Why, he meant with Dasha! Forgive me, Dasha. I didn't know. If only my father had had the sense to tell me instead of indulging in innuendo!

STEPAN [*looking at him*]: Is it possible that you knew nothing! Is it possible that you are not putting on an act?

PETER: Well, you see, Varvara Stavrogin, he's not only an aged child, he's also an aged naughty child. How could I have understood? A sin committed in Switzerland! Just try to make out what he means!

STAVROGIN: Be quiet, Peter, your father acted nobly. And

you have insulted Dasha, whom all of us here respect. [SHATOV *gets up and walks towards* STAVROGIN, *who smiles at him but ceases to smile when* SHATOV *is close to him. Everyone stares at them. Silence. Then* SHATOV *slaps him as hard as he can.* VARVARA *screams.* STAVROGIN *seizes* SHATOV *by the shoulders, then lets him go and puts his hands behind his back.* SHATOV *backs up as* STAVROGIN *stares at him.* STAVROGIN *smiles, bows, and leaves.*]

LISA: Maurice, come here. Give me your hand! [*Pointing to* STAVROGIN] You see that man? You won't see any better. Maurice, before all let me declare that I have agreed to be your wife!

MAURICE: Are you sure, Lisa, are you sure?

LISA [*staring at the door through which* STAVROGIN *has gone out, her face bathed in tears*]: Yes, yes, I am sure!

CURTAIN

SECOND PART

SCENE FIVE

At Varvara Stavrogin's. ALEXEY YEGOROVICH *holds on his arm a coat, a scarf, and a hat. In front of him* STAVROGIN *is dressing to go out.* PETER VERKHOVENSKY, *looking sullen, is near the table.*

STAVROGIN [*to* PETER]: And if you speak to me again like that, you will feel my cane.

PETER: There was nothing insulting in my proposition. If you really think of marrying Lisa ...

STAVROGIN: ... you can free me from the only obstacle separating me from her. I know it, but don't say it again. I'd rather not have to use my cane on you. My gloves, Alexey.

ALEXEY: It is raining, sir. At what time shall I expect you?

STAVROGIN: At two o'clock at the latest.

ALEXEY: Very well, sir. [STAVROGIN *takes his cane and is about to leave by the small door.*] May God bless you, sir. But only if you are planning a good deed.

STAVROGIN: What?

ALEXEY: May God bless you. But only if you are planning a good deed.

STAVROGIN [*after a silence and with his hand on* ALEXEY's *arm*]: My good Alexey, I remember the time when you used to carry me in your arms.

[*He goes out.* ALEXEY *leaves by a door upstage.* PETER VERKHOVENSKY *looks around him, then goes over and*

285

*ransacks the drawer of a writing-desk. He takes out some letters
and reads them.* STEPAN TROFIMOVICH *enters.* PETER
hides the letters.]

STEPAN: Alexey Yegorovich told me you were here, son.

PETER: Why, what are you doing in this house? I thought
you had been driven out.

STEPAN: I came to get the last of my things, and I am going
to leave without hope of returning and without recrimi-
nations.

PETER: Oh, you'll come back! A parasite is always a
parasite.

STEPAN: I don't like the way you talk to me.

‖PETER: You have always said that truth was paramount.
The truth is that you pretended to be in love with Varvara
Petrovna and that she pretended not to see that you were
in love with her. As a reward for such silliness, she was
keeping you. Hence you are a parasite. I advised her
yesterday to put you in a suitable home.

STEPAN: You spoke to her about me?

PETER: Yes, she told me that tomorrow she would have a
conversation with you to settle everything. The truth is
that she wants to see you squirm once more. She showed
me your letters. How I laughed – good Lord, how
I laughed!

STEPAN: You laughed. Have you no heart!‖ Do you know
what a father is?

PETER: You taught me what a father is. You never provided
for me. I wasn't even weaned when you shipped me off to
Berlin by the post. Like a parcel.

STEPAN: Wretch! Although I sent you by the post, my
heart continued to bleed!

PETER: Mere words!

STEPAN: Are you or aren't you my son, monster?

PETER: You must know better than I. To be sure, fathers are inclined to have illusions about such things.

STEPAN: Shut up!

PETER: I will not. And don't whimper. You are a patriotic, snivelling, whimpering old woman. Besides, all Russia whimpers. Fortunately, we are going to change all that.

STEPAN: Who is 'we'?

PETER: Why, we normal men. We are going to remake the world. We are the saviours.

STEPAN: Is it possible that anyone like you aims to offer himself up to men in the place of Christ? But just look at yourself!

PETER: Don't shout. We shall destroy everything. We'll not leave a stone standing, and then we'll begin all over again. Then there will be true equality. You preached equality, didn't you? Well, you shall have it! And I bet that you won't recognize it.

STEPAN: I shall not recognize it if it looks like you. No, it was not of such things that we used to dream! I don't understand anything any more. I have given up understanding.

PETER: All that comes from your sick old nerves. *You* made speeches. *We* act. What are you complaining about, scatterbrained old man?

STEPAN: How can you be so insensitive?

PETER: I followed your teachings. According to you, the thing to do was to treat injustice harshly and to be sure of one's rights, to go ever forwards towards the future! Well, that's where we're going, and we shall strike hard. A tooth for a tooth, as in the Gospels!

STEPAN: You poor fellow, it's not in the Gospels!

PETER: The devil take it! I have never read that confounded

book. Nor any other book. What's the use? What matters is progress.

STEPAN: No, you're crazy! Shakespeare and Hugo don't stand in the way of progress. Quite the contrary, I assure you!

PETER: Don't get excited! Hugo is an old pair of buttocks. As for Shakespeare, our peasants working in the fields don't need him. They need shoes instead. They will be given them as soon as everything is destroyed.

STEPAN [*trying to be ironic*]: And when will this be?

PETER: In May. In June everyone will be making shoes. [STEPAN TROFIMOVICH *falls into a chair, crushed*.] Rejoice, ancestor, for your ideas are going to be put into practice.

STEPAN: They are not my ideas. You want to destroy everything; you don't want to leave a single stone standing. But *I* wanted people to love one another.

PETER: No need for love! Science will take its place.

STEPAN: But that will be boring.

PETER: Why should it be boring? That's an aristocratic idea. When men are equal, they are not bored. They don't have a good time either. Nothing matters and everything is on the same plane. When we have justice plus science, then both love and boredom will be done away with. People will forget.

STEPAN: No man will ever be willing to forget his love.

PETER: Again you're indulging in words. Just remember, ancestor, that you forgot; you got married three times.

STEPAN: Twice. And after a long interval.

PETER: Long or short, people forget. Consequently, the sooner they forget, the better. Oh, but you get on my nerves, never knowing what you want! *I* know what I want. Half the heads will have to be cut off. Those that remain will be taught to drink.

STEPAN: It is easier to cut off heads than to have ideas.

PETER: What ideas? Ideas are nonsense. Nonsense has to be suppressed to achieve justice. Nonsense was good enough for old men like you. A man has to choose. If you believe in God, you are forced to talk nonsense. If you don't believe in Him and yet refuse to admit that everything must be razed, you will still talk nonsense. You're all in the same boat, and consequently you can't keep yourselves from talking nonsense. *I* say that men must act. I'll destroy everything and others will construct. No more reform and no more improvement. The more things are improved and reformed, the worse it is. The sooner people begin to destroy, the better it is. Let's begin by destroying. What happens afterwards doesn't concern us. The rest is nonsense, nonsense!

STEPAN [*rushing out of the room, terrified*]: He's mad, he's mad....

[PETER VERKHOVENSKY *laughs uproariously.*]

BLACKOUT

THE NARRATOR: Well, so much for that! I have forgotten to tell you two facts. The first is that the Lebyatkins had mysteriously moved while Stavrogin was bedridden and had settled in a little house in the suburbs. The second is that a convicted murderer had escaped and was prowling among us. As a result, rich people did not go out at night.

The street at night. STAVROGIN *is walking in the dark, unaware that* FEDKA *is following him.*

SCENE SIX

The common room of the Filipov lodging-house in Epiphany Street.
KIRILOV *is on all fours to retrieve a ball that has rolled under a*
piece of furniture. While he is in that position, STAVROGIN *opens*
the door. KIRILOV, *with the ball in his hand, gets up as he sees*
him come in.

STAVROGIN: You are playing ball?

KIRILOV: I bought it in Hamburg to throw it up and catch
   it; nothing strengthens the back like that. Besides, I play
   with the landlady's boy.

STAVROGIN: Do you like children?

KIRILOV: Yes.

STAVROGIN: Why?

KIRILOV: I like life. You want tea?

STAVROGIN: Yes.

KIRILOV: Sit down. What do you want of me?

STAVROGIN: A service. Read this letter. It is a challenge
   from the son of Gaganov, whose ear I bit some time back.
   [KIRILOV *reads it and then places it on the table and looks at*
   STAVROGIN.] ‖Yes, he has already written me several
   times to insult me. In the beginning I answered to assure
   him that if he was still suffering from the insult I had done
   his father, I was ready to offer him every apology. I
   insisted that my deed had not been premeditated and
   that I was ill at the time. Instead of calming him, this
   seemed to irritate him even more, if I can believe what
   he said about me. Today I am handed this letter.‖ Have
   you read what he says at the end?

KIRILOV: Yes, he speaks of a 'face I'd like to smack'.

STAVROGIN: That's it. Hence I have to fight him, although I don't want to. I have come to ask you to be my second.

KIRILOV: I'll go. What should I say?

STAVROGIN: Begin by repeating my apologies for the offence done to his father. Tell him that I am ready to forget his insults if only he will cease writing me this kind of letter, especially with such vulgar expressions.

KIRILOV: He won't accept. It's clear that he wants to fight you and kill you.

STAVROGIN: I know it.

KIRILOV: Good. Tell me your conditions for the duel.

STAVROGIN: I want everything to be over tomorrow. Go and see him tomorrow morning at nine o'clock. We can be on the field at about two. ‖The weapon will be the pistol. The barriers will be ten yards apart. Each of us shall take his stand ten paces from his barrier. At the signal we shall walk towards each other. Each may shoot as he walks. We shall shoot three times. That's all.

KIRILOV: Ten yards between the barriers isn't much.

STAVROGIN: Twelve, if you prefer. But no more.‖ Have you pistols?

KIRILOV: Yes. You want to see them?

STAVROGIN: Certainly.

[KIRILOV *kneels down in front of a travelling bag and takes out a pistol case, which he places on the table in front of* STAVROGIN.]

KIRILOV: I also have a revolver I bought in America. [*He shows it to him.*]

STAVROGIN: You have many guns. And very handsome ones.

KIRILOV: They are my sole wealth.

[STAVROGIN *looks at him fixedly, then closes the pistol case without ceasing to look at him.*]

STAVROGIN [*with a slight hesitation*]: Are you still firm in your intention?

KIRILOV [*immediately and with a most natural manner*]: Yes.

STAVROGIN: I mean in regard to suicide.

KIRILOV: I understood what you meant. Yes, I have the same intentions.

STAVROGIN: Ah! And when will it be?

KIRILOV: Soon.

STAVROGIN: You seem very happy.

KIRILOV: I am.

STAVROGIN: I understand that. I have sometimes thought of it. Just imagine that you have committed a crime, or, rather, a particularly cowardly, shameful deed. Well, a bullet in the head and everything ceases to exist! What does shame matter then!

KIRILOV: That's not why I am happy.

STAVROGIN: Why, then?

KIRILOV: Have you ever looked at the leaf of a tree?

STAVROGIN: Yes.

KIRILOV: Green and shiny, with all its veins visible in the sunlight? Isn't it wonderful? Yes, a leaf justifies everything. Human beings, birth and death – everything one does is good.

STAVROGIN: And even if ... [*He stops.*]

KIRILOV: Well?

STAVROGIN: If a man harms one of those children you love ... a little girl, for instance. ... If he dishonours her, is that good too?

KIRILOV [*staring at him in silence*]: Did you do that? [STAVROGIN *shakes his head oddly in silence.*] If a man commits such a crime, that is good too. And if someone splits open the head of a man who dishonoured a child or if, on the other hand, he is forgiven, all that is good.

When we know that once and for all, then we are happy.

STAVROGIN: When did you discover that you were happy?

KIRILOV: Last Wednesday. During the night. At two thirty-five. [STAVROGIN *rises suddenly*.]

STAVROGIN: Was·it you who lighted the lamp in front of the icon?

KIRILOV: It was I.

||STAVROGIN: Do you pray?

KIRILOV: Constantly. Do you see that spider? I watch her and am grateful to her for climbing. That's my way of praying.

STAVROGIN: Do you believe in a future life?

KIRILOV: Not in eternal life in the future. But in eternal life here below.

STAVROGIN: Here below?

KIRILOV: Yes. At certain moments. Such a joy that one would die if it lasted more than five seconds. ||

[STAVROGIN *looks at him with a sort of comtempt*.]

STAVROGIN: And you claim not to believe in God!

KIRILOV [*quite simply*]: Stavrogin, I beg you not to use irony in talking to me. Just remember what you were for me, the part you played in my life.

STAVROGIN: It's late. Be in time tomorrow morning at Gaganov's. Remember . . . nine o'clock.

KIRILOV: I am punctual. I can wake up when I want to. When I go to bed I tell myself 'Seven o'clock', and I awaken at seven o'clock.

STAVROGIN: That is a very valuable trait.

KIRILOV: Yes.

STAVROGIN: Go and sleep. But first tell Shatov that I want to see him.

KIRILOV: Just a minute. [*He takes a stick from the corner and knocks on the side wall.*] There, he'll come now. But what about you; won't you sleep? You are duelling tomorrow.

STAVROGIN: Even when I am tired, my hand never trembles.

KIRILOV: That's a valuable trait. Good night.

[SHATOV *appears in the doorway upstage.* KIRILOV *smiles at him and leaves by the side door.* SHATOV *stares at* STAVROGIN *and then enters slowly.*]

SHATOV: How you worried me! Why were you so slow in coming?

STAVROGIN: Were you so sure that I would come?

SHATOV: I couldn't imagine that you would forsake me. I can't get along without you. Just remember the part you played in my life.

STAVROGIN: Then why did you strike me? [SHATOV *says nothing.*] Was it because of my affair with your wife?

SHATOV: No.

STAVROGIN: Because of the rumour that started about your sister and me?

SHATOV: I don't think so.

STAVROGIN: Good. It hardly matters anyway. As I don't know where I'll be tomorrow evening, I came merely to give you a warning and to ask you a service. Here is the warning: you may be murdered.

SHATOV: Murdered?

STAVROGIN: By Peter Verkhovensky's group.

‖SHATOV: I knew it. But how did you find out?

STAVROGIN: I belong to their group. Like you.

SHATOV: You, Stavrogin, are a member of their society? You joined up with those vain and idiotic flunkeys? How could you? Is that worthy of Nicholas Stavrogin?

STAVROGIN: Forgive me, but you ought to get out of the habit of looking upon me as the Tsar of all the Russias and yourself as just a speck of dust.

SHATOV: Oh, don't talk to me that way! You know very well that they are knaves and flunkeys and that you don't belong among them!

STAVROGIN: Indubitably they are knaves. But what does that matter? To tell the truth, I don't belong altogether to their society. Whenever I helped them in the past, I did so as a dabbler and because I had nothing better to do.

SHATOV: Is it possible to do such things as a dabbler?

STAVROGIN: People sometimes get married as dabblers, or have children and commit crimes as dabblers! But, speaking of crimes, you are the one running the risk of being killed. Not I. At least not by them. ‖

SHATOV: They have nothing against me. I joined their organization. But my ideas changed when I was in America. I told them so when I got back. I was very fair in telling them that we disagreed on all points. That's my privilege, the right of my conscience. I will not accept —

STAVROGIN: Don't shout. [KIRILOV *comes in, picks up the pistol case, and leaves*.] Verkhovensky won't hesitate to liquidate you if he gets the idea that you might compromise their organization.

SHATOV: They make me laugh. Their organization doesn't even exist.

STAVROGIN: I suppose in fact that it's all a figment of Verkhovensky's brain. ‖The others think he is a delegate of an international organization and so they follow him. But he has the talent to make them accept his myth. That's the way you form a group. And then some day, starting from the first group, he may succeed in creating the international organization. ‖

SHATOV: That insect, that poor fool, that idiot who doesn't know anything about Russia!

STAVROGIN: It is true that such people don't know anything about Russia. But, after all, they know only a little
less about it than we do. Besides, even an idiot can shoot
a revolver. Which is why I came to warn you.

SHATOV: Thank you. And I thank you particularly for
doing so after I struck you.

STAVROGIN: Not at all. I return good for evil. [*He laughs.*]
Don't worry, I am a Christian. Or, rather, I should be if
I believed in God. But ... [*He gets up.*] ... there is no hare.

SHATOV: No hare?

STAVROGIN: Yes, to make jugged hare you need a hare. To
believe in God you need a God. [*He laughs again, but icily
this time.*]

SHATOV [*greatly excited*]: Don't blaspheme like that! Don't
laugh! And get rid of that pose; take on a normal human
manner. Speak simply and humanly, if only for once in
your life! And remember what you used to say before
I left for America.

STAVROGIN: I don't remember.

SHATOV: I'll tell you. It's high time for someone to tell you
the truth about yourself, to strike you if need be and
remind you of what you are. Do you recall the time when
you used to tell me that the Russian people alone would
save the universe in the name of a new God? Do you
remember your words: 'A Russian atheist is an impossibility'? You didn't say then that the hare doesn't
exist.

STAVROGIN: I seem indeed to remember our conversations.

SHATOV: The devil take your conversations! ‖There *were* no
conversations! There was simply a master proclaiming
great truths and a disciple rising from the dead. I was the
disciple and you were the master.

STAVROGIN: Great truths, really?

SHATOV: Yes, really. ‖ Wasn't it you who told me that if it were mathematically proven that truth stood apart from Christ, you would rather be with Christ than with truth? ‖Wasn't it you who used to say that the blind life-force driving a nation in search of its god is greater than reason and science and that it alone determines good and evil, and that hence the Russian nation, if it is to march in the van of humanity, must follow its Christ?‖ I believed you. The seed germinated in me, and –

STAVROGIN: I am happy for your sake.

SHATOV: Drop that pose! Drop it at once or I'll.... Yes, you told me all that. And at the same time you used to say just the opposite to Kirilov, as I learned from him in America. You were pouring falsehood and negation into his heart. You were driving his reason towards madness. Have you seen him since? Have you contemplated your handiwork?

STAVROGIN: Let me point out to you that Kirilov himself has just told me he was utterly happy.

SHATOV: That is not what I am asking you. How could you tell him one thing and me the opposite?

STAVROGIN: Probably I was trying, in both cases, to persuade myself.

SHATOV [*with a note of despair*]: And now you are an atheist and don't believe what you taught me?

STAVROGIN: And you?

SHATOV: I believe in Russia, in its orthodoxy, in the body of Christ.... I believe that the second coming will take place in Russia. I believe –

STAVROGIN: And in God?

SHATOV: I ... I *shall* believe in God one day.

STAVROGIN: That's just it. You don't believe. Besides, can anyone be intelligent and still believe? It's an impossibility.

SHATOV: No, I didn't say that I didn't believe. We are all dead or half dead and incapable of believing. But men must rise up, and you must be the first. I am the only one who knows your intelligence, your genius, the breadth of your culture, of your conceptions. In the whole world each generation produces but a handful of superior men, two or three. You are one of them. You are the only one, yes, the only one who can raise the flag.

STAVROGIN: I note that everyone at the moment wants to thrust a flag into my hands. Verkhovensky, too, would like me to bear their flag. But he does so because he admires what he calls my 'extraordinary aptitude for crime'. What should I make of all this?

SHATOV: I know that you are also a monster. That you have been heard to assert that you saw no difference between any bestial act and a great deed of sacrifice. ‖It is even said that in St Petersburg you belonged to a secret society that indulged in revolting debauches.‖ They say, they also say – but I can't believe this – that you used to attract children to your house to defile them.... [STAVROGIN *suddenly rises*.] Answer. Tell the truth. Nicholas Stavrogin cannot lie to Shatov, who struck him in the face. Did you do that? If you did it, you could not bear the flag and I should understand your despair and your helplessness.

STAVROGIN: Enough. Such questions are unseemly. [*He stares at* SHATOV.] What does it matter anyway? *I* am interested only in more ordinary questions. Such as: should one live or should one destroy oneself?

SHATOV: Like Kirilov?

STAVROGIN [*with a sort of melancholy*]: Like Kirilov. But he will go all the way. He is a Christ.

SHATOV: And you.... Would you be capable of destroying yourself?

STAVROGIN [*painfully*]: I ought to! I ought to! But I am afraid of being too cowardly. Perhaps I shall do so tomorrow. Perhaps never. That is the question ... the only question I ask myself.

SHATOV [*hurling himself at* STAVROGIN *and seizing him by the shoulder*]: That's what you are seeking. You are seeking punishment. Kiss the ground, water it with your tears, beg for mercy!

STAVROGIN: Hands off, Shatov. [*He holds him at a distance, and with an expression of pain*] Just remember: I could have killed you the other day and I folded my hands behind my back. So don't persecute me.

SHATOV [*leaping backwards*]: Oh, why am I condemned to believe in you and to love you? I cannot tear you from my heart, Nicholas Stavrogin. I shall kiss your footprints on the floor when you have left.

STAVROGIN [*with the same expression*]: I regret to have to tell you, but I cannot love you, Shatov.

SHATOV: I know it. You cannot love anyone because you are a man without roots and without faith. ‖Only men who have roots in the soil can love and believe and build. The others destroy. And you destroy everything without intending to, and you are even drawn to idiots like Verkhovensky who want to destroy for their own comfort, simply because it is easier to destroy than not to destroy.‖ But I shall lead you back to your former way. You will find peace and I shall cease being alone with what you have taught me.

STAVROGIN: Thank you for your good intentions. But until you have a chance to help me find the hare, you could do me the more modest service I came to ask of you.

SHATOV: And what is it?

STAVROGIN: If I happened to disappear in one way or another, I should like you to take care of my wife.

SHATOV: Your wife? Are you married?

STAVROGIN: Yes, to Maria Timofeyevna. ‖I know that you have considerable influence over her. You are the only one who can ... ‖

SHATOV: So it is true that you married her?

STAVROGIN: Four years ago in Petersburg.

SHATOV: Were you obliged to marry her?

STAVROGIN: Obliged? No.

SHATOV: Have you a child by her?

STAVROGIN: She has never had a child and couldn't have one. Maria Timofeyevna is still a virgin. But I ask you simply to take care of her.

> [SHATOV, *dazed, watches him leaving. Then he runs after him.*]

SHATOV: Ah! I understand. I know you. I know you. You married her to punish yourself for a dreadful crime. [STAVROGIN *makes a gesture of impatience.*] Listen, listen, go and see Tihon.

STAVROGIN: Who is Tihon?

SHATOV: A former bishop who has retired here to the Monastery of St Euthymia. He will help you.

STAVROGIN [*staring at him*]: Who in this world could help me? Not even you, Shatov. And I'll never ask you anything again. Good night.

SCENE SEVEN

A bridge at night. STAVROGIN *is walking in another direction under the rain, having opened his umbrella.* FEDKA *pops up behind him.*

FEDKA: Might I, sir, take advantage of your umbrella? [STAVROGIN *stops. He and* FEDKA *face each other under the umbrella.*]

STAVROGIN: Who are you?

FEDKA: No one important. But you, you are Mr Stavrogin, a noble lord!

STAVROGIN: You are Fedka, the convict!

FEDKA: I am not a convict any more. I was sent up for life, to be sure. But I found time dragging and changed my status.

STAVROGIN: What are you doing here?

FEDKA: Nothing. I need a passport. In Russia it's impossible to make a move without a passport. Fortunately, a man you know, Peter Verkhovensky, promised me one. Meanwhile, I was lying in wait for you in the hope that Your Grace would give me three roubles.

STAVROGIN: Who gave you the order to lie in wait for me?

FEDKA: No one, no one! Although Peter Verkhovensky told me incidentally that perhaps with my talents I could do a service for Your Grace, in certain circumstances, by ridding you of people who are in your way. As he told me also that you would go over this bridge to see a certain party on the other side of the river, I have been waiting for you the past three nights. You see that I deserve my three roubles.

STAVROGIN: Good. Listen. I like to be understood. You will not receive a kopeck from me and I neither have nor shall have need of you. If I ever find you in my way again on this bridge or anywhere else, I'll bind you and hand you over to the police.

FEDKA: Yes, but *I* need you.

STAVROGIN: Begone or I'll strike you.

FEDKA: Please take into consideration, sir, that I am a poor defenceless orphan and that it is raining!

STAVROGIN: I give you my word of honour that if I meet you again, I'll bind you up.

FEDKA: I'll wait for you anyhow. You never know!

[*He disappears.* STAVROGIN *stares in his direction for a moment.*]

BLACKOUT

SCENE EIGHT

The Lebyatkins' dwelling. STAVROGIN *is already in the room.* LEBYATKIN *is relieving him of his umbrella.*

LEBYATKIN: What frightful weather! Oh, you are all wet. [*He pushes up an armchair.*] I beg you, I beg you. [*He straightens up.*] Ah, you are looking at this room. You see, I live like a monk. Abstinence, solitude, poverty, according to the three vows of the knights of old.

STAVROGIN: Do you think the knights of old took such vows?

LEBYATKIN: I don't know. I am perhaps confusing things.

STAVROGIN: You are certainly confusing things. I hope that you haven't been drinking.

LEBYATKIN: Hardly at all.

STAVROGIN: I asked you not to get drunk.

LEBYATKIN: Yes. Odd request!

STAVROGIN: Where is Maria Timofeyevna?

LEBYATKIN: In the next room.

STAVROGIN: Is she sleeping?

LEBYATKIN: Oh, no, she is telling her fortune. She is expecting you. As soon as she heard the news, she got all dressed up.

STAVROGIN: I shall see her in a moment. But first I have something to settle with you!

LEBYATKIN: I hope so. So many things have piled up in my heart. I should like to be able to talk freely with you, as I used to do. Oh, you have played such a great part in my life. And now I am treated so cruelly.

STAVROGIN: I see, Captain, that you haven't changed at all in the past four years. [*He stares at him silently.*] ‖So they are right, those who claim that the second half of a human life is determined by the habits acquired during the first half.

LEBYATKIN: Oh! what sublime words! Why, the enigma of life is solved! And yet‖ I insist that I am casting my skin like a serpent. Besides, I have written my will.

STAVROGIN: That's odd. To bequeath what and to whom?

LEBYATKIN: I want to leave my skeleton to the medical students.

‖STAVROGIN: And you hope for payment during your lifetime?

LEBYATKIN: And why not? You see, I read the biography of an American in the newspapers. He bequeathed his huge fortune to scientific foundations, his skeleton to the medical students of the city, and his skin to be made into a drum on which the American national anthem would

be beaten night and day. But, alas, we are merely
pygmies in comparison to the Americans and their
boldness of thought. If I tried to do the same, I'd be
accused of being a socialist and my skin would be confiscated. Consequently, I had to be satisfied with the
students. I want to leave them my skeleton on condition
that a label will be stuck to my skull saying: 'A repentant
freethinker'. ‖

STAVROGIN: So you know that you are in danger of death.

LEBYATKIN [*giving a start*]: No, not at all. What do you
mean? What a joke!

STAVROGIN: Didn't you write a letter to the governor to
denounce Verkhovensky's group, to which you belong
nevertheless?

LEBYATKIN: I don't belong to their group. I agreed to
hand out proclamations, but only to do a service, as it
were. I wrote to the governor to explain something of the
sort to him. But if Verkhovensky really thinks.... Oh, I
must get to St Petersburg. That's why I was waiting for
you. Anyway, my dear benefactor, I need money to go
there.

STAVROGIN: You will have nothing from me. I have already
given you too much.

LEBYATKIN: That's true. But *I* accepted the shame of it.

STAVROGIN: What shame is there in the fact that your sister
is my legitimate wife?

LEBYATKIN: But the marriage is kept secret! It is kept
secret and there is a fatal mystery about it! I receive
money from you – all right, that's normal. Then I am
asked: 'Why do you receive that money?' I am bound
by my word and cannot answer, thus wronging my sister
and the honour of my family.

STAVROGIN: I have come to tell you that I am going to

make up for that outrage done to your noble family. Tomorrow, probably, I shall announce our marriage officially. Hence the question of the family dishonour will be settled. And likewise, of course, the question of the allowance that I shan't have to pay you.

LEBYATKIN [*panic-stricken*]: But it's not possible. You can't make this marriage public. She is half crazy.

STAVROGIN: I'll take care of that.

LEBYATKIN: What will your mother say? You will have to take your wife into your house.

STAVROGIN: That doesn't concern you.

LEBYATKIN: But what shall *I* become? You are casting me off like an old worn-out shoe.

STAVROGIN: Yes, like an old shoe. That's the correct expression. Now call Maria Timofeyevna.

[LEBYATKIN *goes out and brings back* MARIA TIMO-FEYEVNA, *who stands in the middle of the room.*]

STAVROGIN [*to* LEBYATKIN]: Leave now. No, not that way. I'm afraid you would listen to us. I mean outside.

LEBYATKIN: But it's raining.

STAVROGIN: Take my umbrella.

LEBYATKIN [*bewildered*]: Your umbrella – really, am I worthy of that honour?

STAVROGIN: Every man is worthy of an umbrella.

LEBYATKIN: Yes, yes, of course, that's a part of the rights of man! [*He goes out.*]

MARIA: May I kiss your hand?

STAVROGIN: No. Not yet.

MARIA: All right. Sit down in the light so that I can see you.

[*To reach the armchair,* STAVROGIN *walks towards her. She crouches down with her arm raised as if to protect herself, an expression of fright on her face.* STAVROGIN *stops.*]

STAVROGIN: I frightened you. Forgive me.

MARIA: Never mind. No, I was wrong.

[STAVROGIN *sits down in the light.* MARIA TIMOFE-YEVNA *screams.*]

STAVROGIN [*with a touch of impatience*]: What's the matter?

MARIA: Nothing. Suddenly I didn't recognize you. It seemed to me that you were someone else. What are you holding in your hand?

STAVROGIN: What hand?

MARIA: Your right hand. It's a knife?

STAVROGIN: But look, my hand is empty.

MARIA: Yes. Last night I saw in a dream a man who looked like my Prince, but it wasn't he. He was coming towards me with a knife. Ah! [*She screams.*] Are you the murderer from my dream or my Prince?

STAVROGIN: You are not dreaming. Calm yourself.

MARIA: If you are my Prince, why don't you kiss me? To be sure, he never kissed me. But he was affectionate. I don't feel anything affectionate in you. On the other hand, there's something stirring in you that threatens me. He called me his dove. He gave me a ring. He said: 'Look at it in the evening and I'll come to you in your sleep.'

STAVROGIN: Where is the ring?

MARIA: My brother drank it up. And now I am alone at night. Every night ... [*She weeps.*]

STAVROGIN: Don't weep, Maria Timofeyevna. From now on we shall live together.

[*She stares at him fixedly.*]

MARIA: Yes, your voice is soft now. And I recall. I know why you are telling me we shall live together. The other day in the carriage you told me that our marriage would be made public. But I'm afraid of that, too.

STAVROGIN: Why?

MARIA: I'll never know how to handle guests. I don't suit
you at all. I know, there are lackeys. But I saw your
family – all those ladies – at your house. They are the ones
I don't suit.

STAVROGIN: Did they do anything to hurt you?

MARIA: Hurt? Not at all. I was watching you all. There you
were, getting excited and bickering. You don't even know
how to laugh freely when you are together. So much
money and so little joy! It's dreadful. No, I wasn't hurt.
But I was sad. It seemed to me that you were ashamed of
me. Yes, you were ashamed, and that morning you began
to be more remote. Your very face changed. My Prince
went away, and I was left with the man who scorned me,
who perhaps hated me. No more kind words – just
impatience, anger, the knife ... [*She gets up, trembling.*]

STAVROGIN [*suddenly beside himself*]: Enough! You are mad,
mad!

MARIA [*in a meek, little voice*]: Please, Prince, go outside and
come back in.

STAVROGIN [*still trembling and impatiently*]: Come back in?
Why come back in?

MARIA: So that I'll know who you are. For those five years
I was waiting for him to come, I constantly imagined
the way he would come in. Go outside and come back in
as if you had just returned from a long absence, and then
perhaps I'll recognize you.

STAVROGIN: Be quiet. Now, listen carefully. I want all
your attention. Tomorrow, if I'm still alive, I shall make
our marriage public. We shall not live in my house. We
shall go to Switzerland, to the mountains. We shall spend
our whole life in that gloomy, deserted spot. That is how
I see things.

MARIA: Yes, yes, you want to die, you are already burying

yourself. But when you come to want to live again, you will want to get rid of me. No matter how!

STAVROGIN: No, I shall not leave that place; I'll not leave you. Why do you talk to me like this?

MARIA: Because now I have recognized you and I know that you are not my Prince. *He* would not be ashamed of me. He would not hide me in the mountains. He would show me to everyone – yes, even to that young lady who couldn't take her eyes off me the other day. No, you look very much like my Prince, but it's all over.... I have seen through you. *You* want to make an impression on that young lady. You covet her.

STAVROGIN: Will you listen to me? Cease this madness!

MARIA: *He* never told me I was mad. He was a Prince, an eagle. He could fall at the feet of God if he wanted to, and not fall at the feet of God if he didn't want to. As for you, Shatov slapped you. You are a lackey too.

STAVROGIN [*taking her by the arm*]: Look at me. Recognize me. I am your husband.

MARIA: Let go of me, impostor. I don't fear your knife. *He* would have defended me against the whole world. *You* want my death because I am in your way.

STAVROGIN: What have you said, you wretch! What have you said?

[*He flings her backwards. She falls and he rushes towards the door. She stumbles after him. But* LEBYATKIN *suddenly appears and holds her down while she screams.*]

MARIA: Assassin! Anathema! Assassin!

BLACKOUT

SCENE NINE

The bridge. STAVROGIN *is walking rapidly while muttering to himself. When he has gone beyond the middle of the bridge,* FEDKA *pops up behind him.* STAVROGIN *turns around suddenly, seizes him by the neck, and pins him face downwards on the ground, without seeming to make an effort. Then he lets go of him. At once* FEDKA *is on his feet with a broad short knife in his hand.*

STAVROGIN: Put away that knife! [FEDKA *hides the knife.* STAVROGIN *turns his back and continues walking.* FEDKA *follows him. A long walk. The bridge has now been replaced by a long, deserted street.*] I almost broke your neck, I was so angry.

FEDKA: You are strong, Excellency. The soul is weak, but the body is vigorous. Your sins must be great.

STAVROGIN [*laughing*]: So you've gone in for preaching? Yet I have heard that you robbed a church last week.

FEDKA: To tell the truth, I had gone in to pray. And then it occurred to me that Divine Grace had led me there and that I should take advantage of it because God was willing to give me a little help.

STAVROGIN: You slaughtered the watchman too.

FEDKA: You might say we cleaned out the church together. But in the morning, down by the river, we fell to disputing as to who should carry the big bag. And then I sinned.

STAVROGIN: Superb. Go on slaughtering and robbing!

FEDKA: That's what little Verkhovensky told me. I'm quite willing. There are plenty of opportunities. Why, at Captain Lebyatkin's, where you went this evening ...

STAVROGIN [*suddenly stopping*]: Well?

FEDKA: Now, don't hit me again! I mean that that drunkard leaves the door open every night, he is so drunk. Anyone could go in and kill everyone in the house, both brother and sister.

STAVROGIN: Did you go in?

FEDKA: Yes.

STAVROGIN: Why didn't you kill everybody?

FEDKA: I made a little calculation.

STAVROGIN: What?

FEDKA: I could steal a hundred and fifty roubles after having killed him – after having killed *them*, I mean. But if I am to believe little Verkhovensky, I could get fifteen hundred roubles from you for the same work. So ... [STAVROGIN *looks at him in silence*.] I am turning to you as to a brother or father. ||Nobody will ever know anything about it, not even young Verkhovensky.|| But I need to know whether you want me to do it: just give me the word or a little down payment. [STAVROGIN *begins to laugh as he looks at him*.] Now, wouldn't you like to give me the three roubles I asked you for earlier?

[STAVROGIN, *still laughing, takes notes out of his pocket and drops them on the ground one by one*. FEDKA *picks them up uttering 'ahs' which go on after the light has dimmed to* BLACKOUT.]

THE NARRATOR: The man who kills, or plans to kill, or lets others be killed, often wants to die himself. He is a comrade of death. Perhaps that is what Stavrogin's laugh meant. But it is not certain that Fedka understood it thus.

BLACKOUT

‖SCENE TEN*

The Forest of Brykovo. It is wet and windy. The trees are bare, the ground is soaking wet. On the stage are two barriers. In front of one of them, STAVROGIN, *wearing a light coat and a white beaver hat, and in front of the other,* GAGANOV – *thirty-three years old, tall, fat, well fed, blond. In the middle are the seconds,* MAURICE NICOLAEVICH *on Gaganov's side and* KIRILOV. *The opponents already hold their pistols.*

KIRILOV: And now for the last time I propose a reconciliation. I say this only to observe the rules; it is my duty as a second.

MAURICE: I wholeheartedly approve Mr Kirilov's words. The idea that there can be no reconciliation on the field is merely a prejudice which we can leave to the French. Besides, there's no sense in this duel, since Mr Stavrogin is ready to offer his apologies again.

STAVROGIN: I confirm once more my proposal to offer every possible apology.

GAGANOV: But this is unbearable! We're not going to go through the same comedy again. [*To* MAURICE NICOLAEVICH] If you are my second and not my enemy, explain to this man ... [*He points at him with his pistol.*] ... that his concessions only aggravate the insult. He always seems to consider that my offensive remarks can't touch him and that there is no shame in dodging me. He insults me constantly, I tell you, and you are only irritating me so that I'll miss him.

KIRILOV: That's enough. I beg you to follow my orders.

*The whole scene of the duel was cut in production.

Back to your places. [*The opponents go back to their places behind the barriers, almost in the wings.*] One, two, three, go. [*The opponents walk towards each other.* GAGANOV *shoots, stands still for a moment, and, seeing that he missed* STAVROGIN, *goes and takes his place at his barrier.* STAVROGIN *walks towards him and shoots above* GAGANOV. *Then he takes out a pocket handkerchief and wraps it around his little finger.*]

KIRILOV: Are you wounded?

STAVROGIN: The bullet scraped me.

KIRILOV: If your opponent does not declare himself satisfied, your duel must continue.

GAGANOV: I declare that that man shot intentionally in the air. It's one more insult.

STAVROGIN: I give you my word of honour that I have no intention of insulting you. I shot in the air for reasons that concern no one but me.

MAURICE: It seems to me, however, that if one of the opponents declares in advance that he will shoot in the air, the duel cannot go on.

STAVROGIN: I never said that I would shoot in the air each time. You don't know how I shall shoot the second time.

GAGANOV: I repeat that he did it on purpose. But I want to shoot a second time, according to my right.

KIRILOV [*wryly*]: It is in fact your right.

MAURICE: Since that is the way it is, the duel goes on. [*They start in the same way.* GAGANOV *reaches the barrier and takes aim for a long time at* STAVROGIN, *who stands waiting with his arms at his sides.* GAGANOV'*s hand trembles.*]

KIRILOV: You are aiming too long. Shoot. Shoot quickly. [GAGANOV *shoots.* STAVROGIN'*s hat flies off.* KIRILOV *picks it up and gives it to* STAVROGIN. *Together they examine the hat.*]

MAURICE: Your turn to shoot. Don't keep your opponent waiting.

[STAVROGIN *looks at* GAGANOV *and shoots his pistol upwards.* GAGANOV, *mad with rage, runs offstage.* MAURICE NICOLAEVICH *follows him.*]

KIRILOV: Why didn't you kill him? You have insulted him even more seriously.

STAVROGIN: What should I have done?

KIRILOV: Either not provoke him to a duel or else kill him.

STAVROGIN: I didn't want to kill him. But if I had not provoked him, he would have slapped me in public.

KIRILOV: Well, then, you would have been slapped!

STAVROGIN: I'm beginning to feel as if I didn't understand. Why does everybody expect of me what no one expects of anyone else? Why must I endure what no one endures and accept burdens that no one could carry?

KIRILOV: You go out of your way to seek those burdens, Stavrogin.

STAVROGIN: Ah! [*A pause.*] You noticed that?

KIRILOV: Yes.

STAVROGIN: Is it as obvious as that?

KIRILOV: Yes.

[*Silence.* STAVROGIN *puts on his hat and arranges it carefully. He resumes his distant manner, then looks at* KIRILOV.]

STAVROGIN [*slowly*]: One tires of burdens, Kirilov. It is not my fault that that idiot missed me.

BLACKOUT

SCENE ELEVEN

At Varvara Stavrogin's. STAVROGIN, *in the centre, is asleep bolt upright on the sofa, with a bandage on his finger. He scarcely seems to be breathing. His face is pale and severe, as if petrified, and he is frowning.*

DASHA *comes in and rushes to him, stops, and stares at him. She makes the sign of the cross over him. He opens his eyes and remains motionless, staring fixedly at the same point in front of him.*

DASHA: Are you wounded?

STAVROGIN [*looking at her*]: No.

DASHA: Did you draw blood?

STAVROGIN: No, I killed no one and, above all, no one killed me, as you see. The duel took place quite stupidly. I shot in the air and Gaganov missed me. I have no luck. But I am tired and should like to be alone.

DASHA: All right. I shall stop seeing you, since you constantly run away from me. I know that at the end I'll find you.

STAVROGIN: At the end?

DASHA: Yes. When all is over, call me and I'll come.

[*He looks at her and seems to wake up completely.*]

STAVROGIN [*in a natural manner*]: I am so vile and cowardly, Dasha, that I believe I shall actually call you at the very end. And you, despite all your prudence, will come running in fact. But, tell me, will you come, whatever the end is? [DASHA *is silent.*] Even if in the meantime I have committed the worst of crimes?

DASHA [*looking at him*]: Are you going to bring about your wife's death?

STAVROGIN: No. No. Neither hers nor anyone's. I don't

want to. Perhaps I shall bring about the death of the other one, the girl. . . . Perhaps I shall not be able to keep myself from doing so. Oh, leave me, Dasha. Why destroy yourself by following me? [*He gets up.*]

DASHA: I know that at the end I'll be alone with you, and I'm waiting for that moment, I pray for it.

STAVROGIN: So you pray?

DASHA: Yes. Ever since a certain day, I haven't ceased praying.

STAVROGIN: And suppose I don't call you? Suppose I take flight. . . .

DASHA: That can't be. You will call me.

STAVROGIN: There is great contempt in what you are saying.

DASHA: There is not only contempt.

STAVROGIN [*laughing*]: So, there *is* contempt. That doesn't matter. I don't want to cause your ruin.

DASHA: You won't cause my ruin. If I don't come with you, I shall become a nun and take care of the sick.

STAVROGIN: A nurse! That's it. That's it. You are interested in me just as a nurse would be. After all, that's probably what I need the most.

DASHA: Yes, you are ill.

STAVROGIN *suddenly takes a chair and flings it without apparent effort across the room.* DASHA *screams.* STAVROGIN *turns his back on her and goes and sits down. Then he talks quite naturally, as if nothing had happened.*]

STAVROGIN: You see, Dasha, I constantly have visions now. They're a kind of little demon. There is one, above all . . .

DASHA: You already told me about him. You are ill.

STAVROGIN: Last night he sat down very close to me and didn't leave me. He is stupid and insolent. And second-rate. Yes, second-rate. I am furious that my personal demon should be second-rate.

DASHA: You talk about him as if he really existed. Oh, may God save you from that.

STAVROGIN: No, no. I don't believe in the devil. Yet last night the demons came out of every swamp and swooped down upon me. Why, a little devil on the bridge offered to cut the throats of Lebyatkin and his sister, Maria Timofeyevna, to get rid of my marriage. He asked for a down payment of three roubles, but he calculated the cost of the operation at fifteen hundred roubles. He was a book-keeper devil.

DASHA: Are you sure he was a vision?

STAVROGIN: No, he was not a vision. It was Fedka, the escaped convict.

DASHA: What did you reply?

STAVROGIN: Why, nothing at all. To get rid of him, I gave him the three roubles and even more. [DASHA *exclaims*.] Yes. He must think I am in agreement. But don't let your kind heart worry. For him to act, I shall have to give him the order. Perhaps, after all, I shall give it!

DASHA [*clasping her hands*]: Good Lord, good Lord, why do you torment me like this?

STAVROGIN: Forgive me. It was only a joke. Besides, I've been like this since last night – I have a terrible impulse to laugh, to laugh without stopping, endlessly... [*He gives her a forced, hollow laugh.* DASHA *stretches out her hand towards him.*] I hear a carriage. It must be my mother.

DASHA: May God preserve you from your demons. Call me. I shall come.

STAVROGIN: Listen, Dasha. If I were to go and see Fedka and give him the order, would you come, would you come even after the crime?

DASHA [*in tears*]: Oh, Nicholas, Nicholas, I beg you, don't stay alone like this. . . . Go and see Tihon at the seminary; he will help you.

STAVROGIN: You too!

DASHA: Yes, Tihon. And afterwards I shall come. . . . I shall come . . . [*She flees, weeping.*]

STAVROGIN: Of course she'll come. With delight. [*With disgust*] Ah! . . .

‖ALEXEY YEGOROVICH [*coming in*]:* Maurice Nicolaevich wishes to see you.

STAVROGIN: He? What can he . . . [*He has a smug smile.*] I'll see him.

> [MAURICE NICOLAEVICH *enters and* ALEXEY YEGOROVICH *leaves.* MAURICE NICOLAEVICH *sees* STAVROGIN's *smile and stops, as if he were about to wheel around and leave. But* STAVROGIN's *expression changes, and, with a look of sincere surprise, he holds out his hand, which* MAURICE NICOLAEVICH *does not shake.* STAVROGIN *smiles again, but courteously this time.*]

STAVROGIN: Sit down.

> [MAURICE NICOLAEVICH *sits on a chair and* STAVROGIN *at an angle on the sofa. For a minute* STAVROGIN *looks silently at his visitor, who seems to hesitate and then suddenly speaks.*]

MAURICE: If you can, marry Lisa Nicolayevna.

> [STAVROGIN *stares at him without any change of expression.* MAURICE NICOLAEVICH *stares back.*]

STAVROGIN [*after a pause*]: If I am not wrong, Lisa Nicolayevna is your fiancée.

MAURICE: Yes, we are officially engaged.

*The scene between Maurice Nicolaevich and Stavrogin was cut in production

317

STAVROGIN: Have you had a quarrel?

MAURICE: No. She loves and esteems me, in her own words. And her words are the most precious thing in the world to me.

STAVROGIN: I can understand that.

MAURICE: I know that if you were to call her, though she stood at the altar in her wedding veil, she would forsake me and everyone else to follow you.

STAVROGIN: Are you sure of that?

MAURICE: Yes, she says she hates you, and she is sincere. But in reality she loves you insanely. And although she says she loves me, there are moments when she hates me cordially.

STAVROGIN: Yet I am surprised that you can dispose of Lisa Nicolayevna. Did she authorize you to do so?

MAURICE: You have just made a vulgar remark, a remark full of vengeance and scorn. But I'm not afraid to humiliate myself even more. No, I have no right, nor any authority. Lisa doesn't know what I am doing. Without her knowing it, I have come to tell you that you alone can make her happy and that you must take my place at the altar. Moreover, after saying this, I could never marry her. I could never live with myself.

STAVROGIN: If I married her, would you kill yourself after the ceremony?

MAURICE: No. Much later. Perhaps never ...

STAVROGIN: You are saying that to set my mind at rest.

MAURICE: To set your mind at rest! A little blood more or less – what does that matter to you!

STAVROGIN [*after a pause*]: I assure you that I am deeply touched by your proposition. However, what makes you think that my feelings for Lisa are such that I want to marry her?

MAURICE [*rising suddenly*]: What? Don't you love her? Didn't you try to win her hand?

STAVROGIN: I can't ever talk to anyone of my feelings for a woman, except to the woman herself. Forgive me, but that's a quirk of my nature. However, I can tell you the truth as to everything else: I am married, and hence it is not possible for me to marry another woman or to try to win her hand, as you say. [MAURICE NICOLAEVICH *looks at him as if petrified, grows pale, and strikes the table violently with his fist.*]

MAURICE: If after such a confession you don't leave Lisa alone, I'll take a club and beat you to death like a dog. [*He leaps up and rushes out, at the door bumping into* PETER VERKHOVENSKY, *who is on the point of coming in.*] ‖

PETER: Why, he's crazy! What did you do to him?

STAVROGIN [*laughing*]: Nothing. Besides, it doesn't concern you.

PETER: I am sure he came to offer you his fiancée. Eh? I am the one who indirectly pushed him into it, if you want to know. And if he refuses to give her to us, we'll take her ourselves, won't we? She's a juicy morsel.*

STAVROGIN: You still intend to help me take her, I see.

PETER: As soon as you decide to. We'll get rid of your responsibilities for you. It won't cost you anything.

STAVROGIN: Oh, yes it will. Fifteen hundred roubles. . . . By the way, what have you come for?

*After omitting the preceding scene, the following text was substituted for the last three lines:

ALEXEY [*coming in*]: Peter Verkhovensky insists on seeing you.

PETER [*following him closely*]: I have just met Maurice Nicolaevich. He wanted to give you his fiancée. I advised him to wait. Besides, we don't really need him; she is crazy to come. We'll go and get her ourselves, won't we? She's a juicy morsel.

319

PETER: What? Have you forgotten? What about our meeting? I have come to remind you that it takes place in an hour.

STAVROGIN: Oh, to be sure! Excellent idea. You couldn't have picked a more opportune moment. I feel like having a good time. What part am I supposed to play?

PETER: You are one of the members of the Central Committee and you know all about the whole secret organization.

STAVROGIN: What am I to do?

PETER: Just assume a mysterious look, that's all.

STAVROGIN: But there is no Central Committee?

PETER: Yes, there is. You and I.

STAVROGIN: In other words, you. And there is no organization?

PETER: There will be one if I can manage to organize those idiots into a group, to weld them into a single unit.

STAVROGIN: How will you go about it?

PETER: Well, to begin with, titles and functions – secretary, treasurer, president – you know the kind of thing! Then sentimentality. For them justice is a matter of sentimentality. Hence, they must be given plenty of opportunity to talk, especially the stupider ones. In any case, they are united by fear of opinion. That is the motivating force, the real cement. The thing they fear most of all is being taken for reactionaries. Consequently, they are obliged to be revolutionaries. They would be ashamed of thinking for themselves, of having an individual idea. As a result, they will think as I want them to.

STAVROGIN: Excellent programme! But I know a much better way of cementing this pretty group together. Force four members to kill the fifth on the pretext that he is a stool pigeon, and they will be bound by blood.

But how stupid I am – it's precisely your idea, isn't it, since you want to have Shatov killed?

PETER: I! Why ... what makes you think of such a thing!

STAVROGIN: No, *I'm* not thinking of it. But *you* are. And if you want my opinion, it's not at all stupid. ||In order to bind men together, there is something stronger than sentimentality or fear of opinion; it is dishonour.|| The best way of attracting our fellow citizens and of sweeping them along with you is to preach publicly the right to dishonour.

PETER: Yes, I know it. Hurrah for dishonour and everybody will come to us; no one will want to lag behind. Ah, Stavrogin, you understand everything! You will be the leader and I'll be your secretary. We shall set sail on a noble ship. The masts will be of polished wood, the sails silken, and on the high stern we shall put Lisa Nicolayevna.

STAVROGIN: There are only two objections to that prophecy. The first is that I shall not be your leader –

PETER: You will; I'll explain to you.

STAVROGIN: The second is that I'll not help you kill Shatov to bind your idiots together. [*He laughs uproariously.*]

PETER [*bursting with wrath*]: I ... I must go and tell Kirilov. [*He rushes out. The moment he is gone,* STAVROGIN *ceases laughing and sits down on the sofa, silent and sinister-looking.*]

BLACKOUT

The street. PETER VERKHOVENSKY *is walking towards Kirilov's.*

THE NARRATOR [*suddenly appearing as* VERKHOVENSKY *disappears*]: At the same time that Peter Verkhovensky arrived, something began spreading over the town. Mysterious fires broke out; the number of thefts doubled. A second lieutenant who had got into the habit of lighting candles in his room in front of books expounding materialist ideas suddenly scratched and bit his commanding officer. A lady of the highest society began beating her children at fixed intervals and insulting the poor whenever she had an opportunity. And another wanted to practise free love with her husband. 'That's impossible,' she was told. 'What do you mean?' she exclaimed; 'we're free, aren't we?' We were free indeed, but of what?

SCENE TWELVE

KIRILOV, FEDKA, *and* PETER VERKHOVENSKY *in the living-room of the Filipov lodging-house. Shatov's room is dimly lighted.*

PETER [*to* FEDKA]: Mr Kirilov will hide you.

FEDKA: You are a vile little insect, but I'll obey you, I'll obey you. Just remember what you promised me.

PETER: Go and hide.

FEDKA: I'll obey. Just remember. [FEDKA *disappears*.]

KIRILOV [*as if noting a fact*]: He loathes you.

PETER: He doesn't have to like me; all he has to do is obey me. Sit down. I have something to say to you. I came to remind you of the agreement binding us.

KIRILOV: I am not bound by anything or to anything.

PETER [*giving a start*]: What, have you changed your mind?

KIRILOV: I have not changed my mind. But I act according to my own will. I am free.

PETER: All right, all right. I am willing to admit that it is your own free will, provided that your will hasn't changed. You get excited about a word. You have become very irritable of late.

KIRILOV: I am not irritable, but I don't like you. Yet I shall keep my word.

PETER: But it must be very clear between us. You still intend to kill yourself?

KIRILOV: Still.

PETER: Fine. Admit that no one is forcing you to it.

KIRILOV: You are expressing yourself stupidly.

PETER: All right, all right. I expressed myself very stupidly. Beyond a shadow of a doubt, no one can force you. Let me go on. You belonged to our organization and you confessed your plan to one of its members?

KIRILOV: I did not confess anything; I simply said what I would do.

PETER: Good, good. Indeed, there was no reason to confess anything. You simply made a statement. Fine.

KIRILOV: No, it's not fine. You're just talking. I made up my mind to kill myself because I want to. You saw that my suicide could help the organization. If you commit a crime here and the guilty are pursued, I blow out my brains, leaving a letter in which I declare that I am the guilty one. So you asked me to wait a while before killing myself. I answered that I would wait, since it didn't matter to me.

PETER: Good. But you gave your word to write the letter with my help and to wait for my orders. Only in this matter, of course, for in everything else you are free.

KIRILOV: I didn't give my word. I agreed because it was a matter of indifference to me.

PETER: If you wish. Do you still feel the same?

KIRILOV: Yes. Will it be soon?

PETER: In a few days.

KIRILOV [*rising as if reflecting*]: Of what should I declare myself guilty?

PETER: You'll know in time.

KIRILOV: Good. But don't forget this: I'll not help you in any way against Stavrogin.

PETER: All right, all right.

[SHATOV *enters from an inner room.* KIRILOV *sits down in a corner.*]

PETER: It's good of you to have come.

SHATOV: I don't need your approval.

PETER: You are wrong. In the fix you are in, you will need my help, and I have already used up considerable breath in your favour.

SHATOV: I don't have to answer to anyone. I am free.

PETER: Not altogether. Many things were entrusted to you. You have no right to break off without warning.

SHATOV: I sent a very clear letter.

PETER: We didn't understand it clearly. They say that you might denounce them now. I defended you.

SHATOV: Yes, just as there are lawyers who make a business of getting people hanged.

PETER: In any case, they have agreed now for you to be free if only you return the printing press and the papers. Where is the press?

SHATOV: In the forest. Near the Brykovo clearing. I buried everything in the ground.

PETER [*with a sort of smile*]: In the ground? Very good! Why, it's very good indeed!

[*There is a knock at the door. The plotters enter:* LIPUTIN, VIRGINSKY, SHIGALOV, LYAMSHIN, *and a defrocked seminarist. As they settle down, they are already talking.* SHATOV *and* KIRILOV *in a corner.*]

VIRGINSKY [*at the door*]: Ah! Here is Stavrogin.

LIPUTIN: He's just in time.

THE SEMINARIST: Gentlemen, I am not accustomed to waste my time. Since you were so kind as to invite me to this meeting, may I ask a question?

LIPUTIN: Go ahead, comrade, go ahead. Everyone here likes you since you played that practical joke on the woman distributing religious tracts by sticking obscene photographs in her Bibles.

THE SEMINARIST: It wasn't a practical joke. I did it out of conviction, being of the opinion that God must be destroyed.

LIPUTIN: Is that what they teach in the seminary?

THE SEMINARIST: No. In the seminary they suffer because of God. Consequently they hate him. In any case, here is my question: has the meeting begun or not?

SHIGALOV: Allow me to point out that we continue to talk aimlessly. Can the authorities tell us why we are here?

[*All look towards* VERKHOVENSKY, *who changes his position as if he were about to speak.*]

LIPUTIN [*in a hurry*]: Lyamshin, please sit down at the piano.

LYAMSHIN: What? Again! It's the same every time!

LIPUTIN: If you play, no one can hear us. Play, Lyamshin! For the cause!

VIRGINSKY: Why, yes, play, Lyamshin.

[LYAMSHIN *sits down at the piano and plays a waltz haphazardly. All look towards* VERKHOVENSKY, *who, far from speaking, has resumed his somnolent position.*]

LIPUTIN: Verkhovensky, have you no declaration to make?

PETER [*yawning*]: Absolutely none. But I should like a glass of cognac.

LIPUTIN: And you, Stavrogin?

STAVROGIN: No, thanks, I've given up drinking.

LIPUTIN: I'm not talking of cognac. I'm asking you if you want to speak.

STAVROGIN: Speak? What about? No.

[VIRGINSKY *gives the bottle of cognac to* PETER VER-KHOVENSKY, *who drinks a great deal during the evening. But* SHIGALOV *rises, dull and sombre-looking, and lays on the table a thick notebook filled with fine writing, which all look at with fear.*]

SHIGALOV: I request the floor.

VIRGINSKY: You have it. Take it.

[LYAMSHIN *plays louder.*]

THE SEMINARIST: Please, Mr Lyamshin, but really we can't hear ourselves.

[LYAMSHIN *stops playing.*]

SHIGALOV: Gentlemen, in asking for your attention, I owe you a few preliminary explanations.

PETER: Lyamshin, pass me the scissors that are on the piano.

LYAMSHIN: Scissors? For what?

PETER: I forgot to cut my nails, I should have done so three days ago. Go on, Shigalov, go on; I'm not listening.

SHIGALOV: Having devoted myself wholeheartedly to studying the society of the future, I reached the conclusion that from the earliest times down to the present all creators of social systems simply indulged in nonsense. So I had to build my own system or organization. Here it is! [*He strikes the notebook.*] To tell the truth, my system is not completely finished. In its present state, however, it deserves discussion. For I shall have to explain to you also the contradiction to which it leads. Starting from unlimited freedom, I end up in fact with unlimited despotism.

VIRGINSKY: That will be hard to make the people swallow!

SHIGALOV: Yes. And yet – let me insist upon it – there is not and there cannot be any other solution to the social problem than mine. It may lead to despair, but there is no other way.

THE SEMINARIST: If I have understood properly, the agenda concerns Mr Shigalov's vast despair.

SHIGALOV: Your expression is more nearly correct than you think. Yes, I was brought smack up against despair. And yet there was no other way out but my solution. If you don't adopt it, you will do nothing worth while. And some day you'll come round to it.

THE SEMINARIST: I suggest voting to find out just how far Mr Shigalov's despair interests us and whether it is necessary for us to devote our meeting to the reading of his book.

VIRGINSKY: Let's vote! Let's vote!

LYAMSHIN: Yes, yes.

LIPUTIN: Gentlemen! Gentlemen! Let's not get excited. Shigalov is too modest. I have read his book. Certain of its conclusions are debatable. But he started from human nature as we now know it through science and he really solved the social problem.

THE SEMINARIST: Really?

LIPUTIN: Yes, indeed. He proposes dividing humanity into two unequal parts. About a tenth will have absolute freedom and unlimited authority over the other nine tenths, who will have to lose their personality and become like a flock of sheep. Kept in the state of complete submission of sheep, they will, on the other hand, achieve the state of innocence of sheep. In short, it will be Eden, except that men will have to work.

SHIGALOV: Yes. That's how I achieve equality. All men

are slaves and equal in their slavery. They can't be equal otherwise. Hence it is essential to level. For instance, the level of education and talent will be lowered. Since men of talent always tend to rise, Cicero's tongue will have to be torn out, Copernicus's eyes gouged out, and Shakespeare stoned. There is my system.

LIPUTIN: Yes, Mr Shigalov discovered that superior faculties are germs of inequality, hence of despotism. Consequently, as soon as a man is seen to have superior gifts, he is shot down or imprisoned. Even very handsome people are suspect in this regard and must be suppressed.

SHIGALOV: And even fools, if they are very notable fools, for they might lead others into the temptation of glorifying in their superiority, which is a germ of despotism. By these means, on the other hand, equality will be absolute.

THE SEMINARIST: But you have fallen into a contradiction. Such equality is despotism.

SHIGALOV: That's true, and that's what drives me to despair. But the contradiction disappears the moment you say that such despotism is equality.

PETER [*yawning*]: What nonsense!

LIPUTIN: Is it really nonsense? On the contrary, I find it very realistic.

PETER: I wasn't speaking of Shigalov or of his ideas, which bear the mark of genius, of course, but I meant all such discussions.

LIPUTIN: By discussing, one might reach a result. That is better than maintaining silence while posing as a dictator.

[*All approve this direct blow.*]

PETER: Writing and constructing systems is just nonsense. An aesthetic pastime. You are simply bored here, that's all.

LIPUTIN: We are merely provincial, to be sure, and therefore worthy of pity. But up to now you haven't brought out anything sensational either. Those tracts you gave us say that universal society will be improved only by lopping off a hundred million heads. That doesn't seem to me any easier to put into practice than Shigalov's ideas.

PETER: The fact is that by lopping off a hundred million heads you progress faster, obviously.

THE SEMINARIST: You also run the risk of getting your own head lopped off.

PETER: It's a disadvantage. And that's the risk you always run when you try to establish a new religion. But I can very well understand, sir, that you would hesitate. And I consider that you have the right to withdraw.

THE SEMINARIST: I didn't say that. And I am ready to bind myself definitively to an organization if it proves serious and efficient.

PETER: What, you would be willing to take an oath of allegiance to the group we are organizing?

THE SEMINARIST: That is to say.... Why not, if ...

PETER: Listen, gentlemen, I can understand very well that you expect from me explanations and revelations about the workings of our organization. But I cannot give them to you unless I am sure of you unto death. So let me ask you a question. Are you in favour of endless discussions or in favour of millions of heads? Of course, this is merely an image. In other words, are you in favour of wallowing in the swamp or of crossing it at full speed?

LYAMSHIN [*gaily*]: At full speed, of course, at full speed! Why wallow?

PETER: Are you therefore in agreement as to the methods set forth in the tracts I gave you?

THE SEMINARIST: That is to say.... Why, of course.... But they still have to be specified!

PETER: If you are afraid, there is no point in specifying.

THE SEMINARIST: No one here is afraid and you know it. But you are treating us like pawns on a chessboard. Explain things to us clearly and we can consider them with you.

PETER: Are you ready to bind yourself to the organization by oath?

VIRGINSKY: Certainly, if you ask it of us decently.

PETER [*nodding towards* SHATOV]: Liputin, you haven't said anything.

LIPUTIN: I am ready to answer that question and any others. But I should first like to be sure that there is no stool pigeon here.

[*Tumult.* LYAMSHIN *rushes to the piano.*]

PETER [*apparently very much alarmed*]: What? What do you mean? You alarm me. Is it possible that there is a spy among us?

[*All talk at once.*]

LIPUTIN: We would be compromised!

PETER: I'd be more compromised than you. Hence, you must all answer a question which will decide whether we are to separate or go on. If one of you learned that a murder was being prepared for the good of the cause, would he go and warn the police? [*To* THE SEMINARIST] Allow me to ask you first.

THE SEMINARIST: Why me first?

PETER: I don't know you so well.

THE SEMINARIST: Such a question is an insult.

PETER: Be more precise.

THE SEMINARIST [*furious*]: I would not denounce the group, of course not.

PETER: And you, Virginsky?

VIRGINSKY: No, a hundred times no!

LIPUTIN: But why is Shatov getting up?

[SHATOV *has in fact stood up. Pale with wrath, he stares at* PETER VERKHOVENSKY *and then strides towards the door.*]

PETER: Your attitude may harm you greatly, Shatov.

SHATOV: At least it may be useful to the spy and scoundrel that you are. So be satisfied. I shall not stoop to answering your vicious question.

[*He goes out. Tumult. Everyone has got up except* STAVROGIN. KIRILOV *goes slowly back into his room.* PETER VERKHOVENSKY *drinks another glass of cognac.*]

LIPUTIN: Well! The test has done some good. Now we know. [STAVROGIN *gets up.*]

LYAMSHIN: Stavrogin didn't answer either.

VIRGINSKY: Stavrogin, can you answer the question?

STAVROGIN: I don't see the need of it.

VIRGINSKY: But we all compromised ourselves and you didn't!

STAVROGIN: Well, then, you will be compromised and I won't be.

[*Tumult.*]

THE SEMINARIST: But Verkhovensky didn't answer the question either.

STAVROGIN: To be sure. [*He goes out.*]

[PETER VERKHOVENSKY *rushes after him and then returns suddenly.*]

PETER: Listen. Stavrogin is the delegate. You must all obey him, and also me, his second unto death. Unto death, you understand. And remember that Shatov has just clearly taken his stand as a traitor and that traitors must be punished. Take an oath. . . . Come now, take an oath . . .

THE SEMINARIST: To what?

PETER: Are you men or aren't you? And will you hesitate before an oath of honour?

VIRGINSKY [*somewhat bewildered*]: But what must we swear?

PETER: To punish traitors. Quickly, take an oath. Hurry, now. I must catch up with Stavrogin. Take an oath...

[*They all raise their hands very slowly.* PETER VER-KHOVENSKY *rushes outside.*]

BLACKOUT

SCENE THIRTEEN

First in the street and then at Varvara Stavrogin's. STAVROGIN *and* PETER VERKHOVENSKY.

PETER [*running after* STAVROGIN]: Why did you leave?

STAVROGIN: I had had enough. And your comedy with Shatov nauseated me. But I'll not let you get away with it.

PETER: He put the finger on himself.

STAVROGIN [*stopping*]: You are a liar. I have already told you why you needed Shatov's blood. He is to serve you to cement your group together. You've just succeeded very cleverly in getting him to leave. You knew that he would refuse to say 'I shall not denounce the group'. ||And that he would consider it cowardly to answer you.||

PETER: All right, all right! But you shouldn't have left. I need you.

STAVROGIN: I suspect as much, since you want to push me into having my wife slaughtered. But why? How can I be useful to you?

332

PETER: How? Why, in every way.... Besides, you spoke the truth. Be on my side and I shall get rid of your wife for you. [PETER VERKHOVENSKY *grasps* STAVROGIN *by the arm.* STAVROGIN *tears himself away, seizes him by the hair, and flings him to the ground.*] Oh, you are strong! Stavrogin, do what I ask of you and tomorrow I shall bring you Lisa Drozdov. Will you? Answer! Listen, I'll let you keep Shatov too if you ask me to.

STAVROGIN: So it's true that you have made up your mind to kill him?

PETER [*getting up*]: How can that matter to you? Wasn't he mean to you?

STAVROGIN: Shatov is good. *You* are mean.

PETER: I am. But *I* didn't slap you.

STAVROGIN: If you raised a hand against me, I'd kill you on the spot. You know very well that I can kill.

PETER: I know it. But you won't kill me because you despise me.

STAVROGIN: You are perspicacious. [*He walks away.*]

PETER: Listen! Listen ...

[PETER *gives a signal.* FEDKA *appears, and together they follow* STAVROGIN. *The curtain representing the street rises to show Varvara Stavrogin's drawing-room.*

DASHA *is on the stage. Hearing* PETER VERKHOVENSKY'S *voice, she goes out on the right.* STAVROGIN *and* PETER VERKHOVENSKY *enter.*]

PETER: Listen ...

STAVROGIN: You are obstinate.... Tell me once and for all what you expect of me and leave.

PETER: Yes, yes. All right. [*He looks at the door on the side.*] Just a minute. [*He goes towards the door and opens it carefully.*]

STAVROGIN: My mother never listens at doors.

PETER: I'm sure she doesn't. You nobles are far above that.

I, on the contrary, listen at doors. Besides, I thought I heard a sound. But that's not the question. You want to know what I expect of you? [STAVROGIN *is silent.*] Well, this is it.... Together we'll rouse Russia and lift her from the mire.

STAVROGIN: She is heavy.

PETER: Ten more groups like this one and we'll be powerful.

STAVROGIN: Ten groups of idiots like these!

‖PETER: It's idiots who make history. For instance, just look at the governor's wife, Julia Mikhailovna. She is with us. How incredibly stupid!

STAVROGIN: You are not going to tell me that she is plotting?

PETER: No. But her idea is that Russian youth must be kept from heading towards the abyss – and by that she means towards revolution. Her system is simple. The thing to do is to praise revolution, to be on the side of youth, and to show them that it is quite possible to be a revolutionary and the governor's wife. Then youth will realize that this is the best régime, since you can insult it without danger and even be rewarded for planning its destruction.

STAVROGIN: You must be exaggerating. It isn't possible to be all that stupid. ‖

PETER: Oh, they are not so stupid; they're just idealists. Fortunately, *I* am not idealist. But I am not intelligent either. What?

STAVROGIN: I didn't say anything.

PETER: Too bad. I hoped you would say: 'Why yes, you are intelligent.'

STAVROGIN: I never thought of saying anything of the sort.

PETER [*with hatred in his voice*]: You are right; I am stupid.

That's why I need you. My organization does not have a head.

STAVROGIN: You have Shigalov. [*He yawns.*]

PETER [*with the same hatred in his voice*]: Don't make fun of him. Absolute levelling is an excellent idea – not at all ridiculous. It's one of the elements of my plan. We shall have to organize it carefully. People will be forced to spy on one another and to denounce one another. In that way there'll be no more selfishness! From time to time a few convulsions, carefully controlled, just enough to over-come boredom. ||We leaders will take care of that. For there will be leaders, since there must be slaves.|| Hence total obedience, absolute depersonalization, and every thirty years we shall authorize convulsions, and then everyone will fall on one another and devour one another.

STAVROGIN [*looking at him*]: I have wondered for a long time what you resembled. But I made the mistake of looking for my comparison in the animal kingdom. It has just come to me.

PETER [*his mind on other things*]: Yes, yes.

STAVROGIN: You resemble a Jesuit.

PETER: All right, all right. But the Jesuits have the idea. They discovered the formula. The plot, the lie, and a single aim! Impossible to live otherwise in the world. Besides, we shall have to have the Pope on our side.

STAVROGIN: The Pope?

PETER: Yes, but it's very complicated. First the Pope would have to come to an agreement with the International. It's too soon for that. That will come inevitably later on, because it's the same spirit. Then there will be the Pope at the summit, we around him, and beneath us the masses governed by Shigalov's system. But that's an idea for the future. Meanwhile, work must be divided. So in the West there will be the Pope, and among us . . . among us . . . there will be you.

STAVROGIN: Decidedly you are drunk. Get out.

PETER: Stavrogin, you are handsome. Are you aware that you are handsome, and strong, and intelligent? No, you don't know it, for you are also unsophisticated. *I* do know it, and that's why you are my idol. I am a nihilist, and nihilists need idols. ||You are the man we need. You never insult anyone and yet everyone hates you. You treat people as your equals and yet they are afraid of you. But you are afraid of nothing; you can sacrifice your own life as easily as anyone else's. That is excellent. || Yes, you are the man I need, and I can't think of any other. You are the leader, you are the sun. [*He suddenly seizes* STAVRO-GIN's *hand and kisses it.* STAVROGIN *repulses him.*] Don't despise me. Shigalov has found the system, but I alone have discovered the way of putting it into practice. I need you. Without you I am nothing. With you I shall destroy the old Russia and build the new.

STAVROGIN: What Russia? The Russia of spies?

PETER: When we hold power in our hands, we shall be able perhaps to make people more virtuous, if you really insist. But for the moment, to be sure, we need one or two thoroughly immoral generations; we need an exceptional, revolting corruption that will transform man into a filthy, cowardly, and selfish insect. That's what we need. And, on the side, we'll give them a touch of fresh blood so that they'll get a taste for it.

STAVROGIN: I always knew you weren't a socialist. You're a scoundrel.

PETER: All right, all right. A scoundrel. But let me explain my plan. We begin the general upheaval. Fires, crimes, incessant strikes, everything a mockery. You see what I mean? Oh, it will be wonderful! A heavy fog will descend over Russia. The earth will bewail its former gods. And then ... [*He pauses.*]

STAVROGIN: And then ...

PETER: We shall bring forth the new Tsar.

[STAVROGIN *looks at him and moves slowly away from him.*]

STAVROGIN: I see. An impostor.

PETER: Yes. We'll say that he is hiding but that he is about to appear. He exists, but no one has seen him. Just imagine the force of that idea – 'He is in hiding'! He can be shown perhaps to one out of a hundred thousand. And the rumour will spread over the whole country. 'He has been seen.' Will you accept?

STAVROGIN: Accept what?

PETER: Why, being the new Tsar.

STAVROGIN: Ah! So that's your plan!

PETER: Yes. Just listen. With you it will be possible to build up a legend. You will have only to appear and you will be triumphant. At first, 'he is hiding, he is hiding,' and we shall pronounce in your name two or three judgments of Solomon. If one request out of ten thousand is satisfied, all will turn to you. In every village each peasant will know that somewhere there is a box in which he can put his request. And throughout the country the rumour will spread! 'A new law has been passed, a just law.' The seas will rise up and the old wooden hulk will sink. And then we can think of building in steel. Well? [STAVROGIN *laughs in scorn.*] Oh, Stavrogin, don't leave me alone. Without you I am like Columbus without America. Can you imagine Columbus without America? I, in turn, can help you. I'll fix everything for you. Tomorrow I'll bring

you Lisa. You want her; you want Lisa dreadfully, I
know. Just one word and I'll fix everything.

STAVROGIN [*turning towards the window*]: And afterwards,
of course, you will have a hold on me ...

PETER: What does that matter? *You* will have a hold on
Lisa. She is young and pure ...

STAVROGIN [*with an odd expression, as if fascinated*]: She is
pure ...

[PETER VERKHOVENSKY *whistles piercingly.*] What are
you doing? [FEDKA *appears.*]

PETER: Here is a friend who can help us. Just say yes,
Stavrogin – a simple yes – and Lisa is yours, and the
world is ours.

[STAVROGIN *turns towards* FEDKA, *who is smiling calmly.
From another room* DASHA *screams, bursts in, and throws
herself on* STAVROGIN.]

DASHA: Oh, Nicholas, I beg you, don't stay with these men.
Go and see Tihon – yes, Tihon, as I have already told
you. Go and see Tihon.

PETER: Tihon? Who is that?

FEDKA: A holy man. Don't say anything bad about him,
you little sneak; I forbid you.

PETER: Why? Did he help you kill someone? Does he too
belong to the Church of Blood?

FEDKA: No. *I* kill. But *he* forgives crime.

BLACKOUT

THE NARRATOR: Personally, I didn't know Tihon. I simply
knew what was said of him in our town. The humble
people attributed great holiness to him. But the
authorities disapproved of his library, in which works of
piety stood side by side with plays and perhaps even worse.

Offhand, I'd say there was no chance Stavrogin would pay him a visit.

SCENE FOURTEEN

Tihon's cell in the Convent of the Virgin. TIHON *and* STAVROGIN *are standing.*

STAVROGIN: Did my mother tell you I was mad?

TIHON: No. She didn't talk of you exactly as of a madman. But she told me of a slap you received and of a duel ... [*He sits down with a groan.*]

STAVROGIN: Are you ill?

TIHON: I have pains in my legs. And I don't sleep very well.

STAVROGIN: Do you want me to leave you?

TIHON: No. Sit down! [STAVROGIN *sits down with his hat in his hand, like a man observing ceremony. But he seems to have trouble breathing.*] You too look ill.

STAVROGIN [*with the same manner*]: I am. You see, I have hallucinations. I often see or feel near me a sort of creature who is mocking, wicked, rational, and who takes on different aspects. But it's always the same creature. He drives me wild. I shall have to consult a doctor.

TIHON: Yes. Do so.

STAVROGIN: No, it's useless. I know who it is. And you do too.

TIHON: You mean the Devil?

STAVROGIN: Yes. You believe in him, don't you? A man of your calling is obliged to believe in him.

TIHON: Well, I'd say that in your case it is more probably an ailment.

STAVROGIN: You are sceptical, I see. Do you at least believe in God?

TIHON: I believe in God.

STAVROGIN: It is written: 'If you believe and if you command the mountain to be removed, you shall be obeyed.' Can you move a mountain?

TIHON: Perhaps. With the help of God.

STAVROGIN: Why 'perhaps'? If you believe, you must say yes.

TIHON: My faith is imperfect.

STAVROGIN: Well, it's a pity. Do you know the answer that a certain bishop made? With the knife at his throat, a barbarian asked him if he believed in God. 'Very little, very little,' the bishop replied. That's not worthy, is it?

TIHON: His faith was imperfect.

STAVROGIN [smiling]: Yes, yes. But, in my opinion, faith must be perfect or there is no faith. That's why I'm an atheist.

TIHON: The complete atheist is more respectable than the man who is indifferent. He is on the last rung preceding perfect faith.

STAVROGIN: I know it. Do you remember the passage from the Apocalypse about the lukewarm?

TIHON: Yes. 'I know thy works, that thou art neither cold nor hot: I would thou wert cold or hot. So then because thou art lukewarm, and neither cold nor hot, I will spew thee out of my mouth. Because thou sayest ...'

STAVROGIN: That will do. [A silence. Without looking at him] You know, I like you very much.

TIHON [in a whisper]: I like you too. [Rather long silence. Stroking STAVROGIN's elbow with his finger] Don't be annoyed.

STAVROGIN [giving a start]: How did you know ... [He

resumes his normal tone of voice.] Indeed, yes, I was annoyed because I told you that I liked you.

TIHON [*firmly*]: Don't be annoyed, and tell me everything.

STAVROGIN: So you are sure that I came with an ulterior motive?

TIHON [*lowering his eyes*]: I read it on your face when you came in.

[STAVROGIN *is pale and his hands tremble. He takes several sheets of paper out of his pocket.*]

STAVROGIN: All right. I wrote a story about myself which I am going to publish. Whatever you may say to me about it won't change my decision in any way. However, I should like you to be the first to know this story, and I'm going to tell it to you. [TIHON *slowly nods his head.*] Stop up your ears. Promise not to listen to me and I shall speak. [TIHON *doesn't answer.*] From 1861 to 1863 I lived in Petersburg indulging in debaucheries that provided no pleasure. I was living with nihilist comrades who adored me because of my money. I was dreadfully bored. So much so that I might have hanged myself. ‖The reason that I didn't hang myself then is that I was hoping for something, I didn't know just what.‖ [TIHON *says nothing.*] I had three apartments.

TIHON: Three?

STAVROGIN: Yes. One in which I had set up Maria Lebyatkin, who later became my legitimate wife. And two others in which I used to receive my mistresses. One of them was rented to me by shopkeepers, who occupied the rest of the apartment and worked elsewhere. Hence I was alone there, rather often, with their twelve-year-old daughter named Matriocha. [*He stops.*]

TIHON: Do you want to go on or stop there?

STAVROGIN: I'll go on. She was a very gentle and calm child, pale blonde and freckled. One day I couldn't find my pocket knife. I mentioned it to the mother, who accused her daughter and beat her, in my presence, until she bled. That evening I found the pocket-knife in the folds of my blanket. I put it into my waistcoat pocket and, once outside, threw it away in the street so that no one would know about it. Three days later I went back to Matriocha's house. [*He stops.*]

TIHON: Did you tell her parents?

STAVROGIN: No. They weren't there. Matriocha was alone.

TIHON: Ah!

STAVROGIN: Yes. Alone. She was sitting in a corner on a little bench. She had her back turned. For some time I watched her from my room. Suddenly she began to sing softly, very softly. My heart began beating violently. I got up and slowly approached Matriocha. ‖The windows were decorated with geraniums; the sun was hot.‖ I sat down silently beside her on the floor. She was frightened and suddenly stood up. I took her hand and kissed it; she laughed like a child; I made her sit down again, but she again got up with a frightened look. I kissed her hand again. I drew her on to my lap. She withdrew a bit and smiled again. I was laughing too. Then she threw her arms around my neck and kissed me ... [*He stops.* TIHON *looks at him.* STAVROGIN *stares back at him and then, showing a blank sheet*] At this point in my story I left a blank.

TIHON: Are you going to tell me what followed?

STAVROGIN [*laughing awkwardly, his face distorted*]: No, no. Later on. When you become worthy of it ... [TIHON *stares at him.*] But nothing happened at all; what are you thinking? Nothing at all. ... It would be better if you didn't look at me. [*In a whisper*] And don't try my patience.

[TIHON *lowers his eyes*.] When I returned two days later, Matriocha fled into the other room as soon as she saw me. But it was clear to me that she hadn't said anything to her mother. Yet I was afraid. During that whole time I was horribly afraid that she would talk. Finally, one day her mother told me, before leaving us alone, that the girl was in bed with a fever. I sat down in my room and, without stirring, watched the bed in the darkness of the other room. An hour later she moved. She came out of the darkness, emaciated in her nightgown, came to the door of my room, and there, tossing her head, shook her frail little fist at me. Then she fled. I heard her run along the inner balcony. I got up and saw her disappear into a nook where wood was kept. I knew what she was going to do. But I sat down again and forced myself to wait twenty minutes. ‖Someone was singing in the courtyard; a fly was buzzing near me. I caught it, held it in my hand a moment, and then let it go.‖ I recall that on a geranium near me a tiny red spider was walking slowly. When the twenty minutes were up, I forced myself to wait a quarter of an hour more. Then, as I left, I looked into the nook through a crack. Matriocha had hanged herself. I left and spent the evening playing cards, with the feeling that a weight had been lifted from me.

TIHON: A weight lifted from you?

STAVROGIN [*with a change in manner*]: Yes. But at the same time I knew that the feeling was based on a horrible cowardice and that never again, never again, could I feel noble in this life, or in another life, never . . .

TIHON: Is that why you acted so strangely here?

STAVROGIN: Yes. I should have liked to kill myself. But I didn't have the courage. So I ruined my life in the stupidest way possible. I led an ironic life. It occurred to me that it would be a good idea – quite stupid, really – to marry a crazy woman, a cripple, and so I did. I even accepted a duel and kept from shooting in the hope of being killed foolishly. Finally I accepted the heaviest responsibilities, without believing in them. But all that was in vain! And now I live between two dreams. In one of them there are happy islands surrounded by a sun-drenched sea where men wake up and go to bed innocent, and in the other I see an emaciated Matriocha tossing her head and shaking her little fist at me. . . . Her little fist. . . I should like to erase a deed from my life, and I cannot.

[*He hides his head in his hands. Then, after a silence, he straightens up.*]

TIHON: Are you really going to publish this story?

STAVROGIN: Yes. Yes!

TIHON: Your intention is noble. The spirit of penitence can go no further. It would be an admirable action to punish oneself this way if only . . .

STAVROGIN: If?

TIHON: If only it were a true penance.

STAVROGIN: What do you mean?

TIHON: You express directly in your narrative the need felt by a heart mortally wounded. This is why you wanted to be spat upon, to be slapped, and to be shamed. But at the same time there is pride and defiance in your confession. ‖Sensuality and idleness have made you insensitive, incapable of loving, and you seem to be proud of that insensitivity. You are proud of what is shameful. ‖ That is despicable.

STAVROGIN: I thank you.

TIHON: Why?

STAVROGIN: Because, although you are annoyed with me,

you don't seem to feel any disgust and you talk to me as to an equal.

TIHON: I was disgusted. But you have so much pride that you didn't notice it. Yet your words 'You talk to me as an equal' are beautiful words. They show that your heart is great and your strength tremendous. But that great useless strength in you frightens me because it seeks to express itself only in foul deeds. You have negated everything, you no longer love anything, and a punishment pursues all those who break away from their native soil, from the truth belonging to their own people and their own time.

STAVROGIN: I don't fear that punishment, or any other.

TIHON: One must fear, on the contrary. Or else there is no punishment but only delight. Listen. If someone, someone you didn't know, whom you would never see again, read that confession and forgave you silently in his heart, would that bring you peace?

STAVROGIN: That would bring me peace. [*In a whisper*] If you forgave me, that would do me great good. [*He stares at him and then breaks out in violent passion.*] No! I want to win my own forgiveness! That is my principal and sole aim. Only then will the vision disappear! That is why I long for an exceptional suffering; that is why I seek it myself! Don't discourage me or I shall burst with rage!

TIHON [*rising*]: If you believe that you can forgive yourself, and that you will achieve your forgiveness in this world through suffering, if you seek solely to obtain that forgiveness – oh, then you have complete faith! God will forgive you ‖your absence of faith, for you venerate the Holy Ghost without knowing it‖.

STAVROGIN: There can be no forgiveness for me. It is

written in your books that there is no greater crime than to offend one of these little ones.

TIHON: If you forgive yourself, Christ will forgive you likewise.

STAVROGIN: No. No. Not He. There can be no forgiveness! Never again, never again ...

[STAVROGIN *takes his hat and strides towards the door like a madman. But he turns back towards* TIHON *and resumes his ceremonious manner. He seems exhausted.*] I shall return. We shall talk of all this again. I assure you that I'm very happy to have met you. I appreciate your welcome and your understanding.

TIHON: Are you leaving already? I wanted to ask you a favour.... But I fear ...

STAVROGIN: Please do. [*He negligently picks up a little crucifix from the table.*]

TIHON: Don't publish that story.

STAVROGIN: I warned you that nothing will stop me. I shall make it known to the whole world!

TIHON: I understand. But I propose to you an even greater sacrifice. Give up your intention and in this way you will overcome your pride, you will crush your demon, and you will achieve liberty. [*He clasps his hands.*]

STAVROGIN: You take all this too much to heart. If I listened to you, I'd just settle down, have children, become a member of a club, and come to the monastery on holy days.

TIHON: No. I am suggesting a different penance. In this monastery there is an ascetic, an old man of such Christian wisdom that neither I nor even you can imagine it. Go to him, submit to his authority for five or seven years, and you will obtain, I promise you, everything for which you thirst.

346

STAVROGIN [*in a bantering tone of voice*]: Enter the monastery?
Why not? After all, I am convinced that I could live like
a monk, although I am gifted with a bestial sensuality.
[TIHON *cries out, with his hands stretched in front of him.*]
What's the matter?

TIHON: I see, I see clearly that you have never been closer
to committing another crime even more heinous than the
one you have just related.

STAVROGIN: Calm yourself. I can promise you not to
publish this story immediately.

TIHON: No. No. There will come a day, an hour, before that
great sacrifice, when you will look for a way out in a new
crime, and you will commit it only to avoid publication
of these pages! [STAVROGIN *stares at him fixedly, breaks
the crucifix, and drops the pieces on the table.*]

CURTAIN

THIRD PART

SCENE FIFTEEN

At Varvara Stavrogin's. STAVROGIN *comes in, his face distorted, hesitates, wheels around, and then disappears through the door upstage.* GRIGORIEV *and* STEPAN TROFIMOVICH *come in, greatly excited.*

STEPAN: But, after all, what does she want of me?

GRIGORIEV: I don't know. She asked you to come at once.

STEPAN: It must be the house search. She heard of it. She will never forgive me.

GRIGORIEV: But who came to search you?

STEPAN: I don't know, *une espèce d'Allemand,* who directed everything. I was excited. He talked. No, I was the one who talked. I told him my whole life – from the political point of view, I mean. I was excited but dignified, I assure you. Yet . . . I fear I may have wept.

GRIGORIEV: But you should have demanded his search warrant. You should have shown a little arrogance.

STEPAN: Listen, Anton, don't criticize me. When you are unhappy, there is nothing more unbearable than having friends tell you that you have made a mistake. In any case, I have taken my precautions. I have had warm clothing packed.

GRIGORIEV: For what reason?

STEPAN: Well, if they come to get me. . . . That's the way it is now: they come, they seize you, and then Siberia or worse. Consequently I sewed thirty-five roubles into the lining of my waistcoat.

GRIGORIEV: But there's no question of your being arrested.

STEPAN: They must have received a telegram from St Petersburg.

GRIGORIEV: About you? But you haven't done anything.

STEPAN: Yes, yes, I'll be arrested. And off to prison, or else they forget you in a dungeon. [*He bursts into sobs.*]

GRIGORIEV: Come, come, calm yourself. You haven't anything on your conscience. Why are you afraid?

STEPAN: Afraid? Oh, I'm not afraid! I mean, I'm not afraid of Siberia. There's something else I fear. I fear shame.

GRIGORIEV: Shame? What shame?

STEPAN: The whip!

GRIGORIEV: What do you mean, the whip? You frighten me, my friend.

STEPAN: Yes, they flog you too.

GRIGORIEV: But why should they flog you? You haven't done anything.

STEPAN: That's just it. They'll see that I haven't done anything and they'll flog me.

GRIGORIEV: You should take a rest after you have seen Varvara Stavrogin.

STEPAN: What will she think? How will she react when she learns of my shame? Here she is. [*He makes the sign of the cross.*]

GRIGORIEV: You make the sign of the cross?

STEPAN: Oh, I've never believed in that. But, after all, it's better not to take any chances.

[VARVARA STAVROGIN *comes in. They rise.*]

VARVARA [*to* GRIGORIEV]: Thank you, Anton. Would you be so kind as to leave us alone? ... [*To* STEPAN TROFI-MOVICH] Sit down. [GRIGORIEV *leaves. She goes to the*

desk and writes a note rapidly. Meanwhile, STEPAN TROFI-
MOVICH *squirms on his chair. Then she turns around towards
him.*] Stepan Trofimovich, we have questions to settle
before separating definitively. I shall be blunt. [*He cringes
on his chair.*] Don't say a word. Let me do the talking.
I consider myself committed to continuing your allowance
of twelve hundred roubles. I am adding eight hundred
roubles for exceptional expenses. Is that enough for you?
It seems to me that it is not negligible. So you will take
this money and go to live, as you will, in Petersburg, in
Moscow, abroad, but not in my house. Do you understand?

STEPAN: Not long ago you made another arbitrary demand,
just as urgent and just as categorical. I submitted to it.
I disguised myself as a fiancé and danced the minuet for
love of you . . .

VARVARA: You didn't dance. You came to my house
wearing a new necktie, pomaded and perfumed. You had
an urgent desire to get married; it could be seen on your
face, and, take my word for it, it was not pretty to see.
Especially with an innocent young girl, almost a child . . .

STEPAN: Please let's not talk about it any more. I shall go
to a home for the aged.

VARVARA: People don't go to a home for the aged when
they have an income of two thousand roubles. ‖You say
that because your son, who, by the way is more intelligent
than you say he is, joked one day about a home. But there
are all sorts of homes and there are even some that take in
generals. So you could have a game of whist there . . . ‖

STEPAN: *Passons.* Let's not mention it.

VARVARA: *Passons?* So you are becoming rude now? In
that case, let's end our conversation right here. You are
forewarned: henceforth we shall live apart.

STEPAN: And that's all? That's all that remains of our twenty years together? Is that our final farewell?

VARVARA: Yes, what about those twenty years! Twenty years of vanity and posturing! Even the letters you sent me were written for posterity. You are not a friend; you are a stylist!

STEPAN: You talk like my son. I see that he has influenced you.

VARVARA: So, you don't think I'm big enough to think for myself? What have you done for me during these twenty years? You even refused me the books that I ordered for you. You wouldn't give them to me until you had read them yourself, and since you never read them I had to wait for them twenty years. The truth is that you were jealous of my intellectual development.

STEPAN [in despair]: But is it possible to break off everything for so little reason!

VARVARA: When I came back from abroad and wanted to tell you my impressions of the Sistine Madonna, you didn't even listen to me; you simply smiled with an air of superiority.

STEPAN: I smiled, yes, but I didn't feel superior.

VARVARA: There was no reason to, in any case! No one is interested in that Sistine Madonna except a few old simpletons like you. That's obvious.

STEPAN: What is obvious, after all these cruel words, is that I must leave. Mark my words: I shall take up my beggar's staff and bag; I shall leave all your gifts and I'll start out on foot to end my life as a tutor in the home of some shopkeeper or die of hunger in a ditch. Farewell.

[VARVARA STAVROGIN rises, exploding.]

VARVARA: I was sure of it. I have known for years that you were simply waiting for the chance to dishonour me. You are capable of dying just so that my house will be slandered.

STEPAN: You have always despised me. But I shall end my life like a knight faithful to his lady. From this minute forward, I shall accept nothing more from you and shall honour you in a disinterested way.

VARVARA: *That* will be new.

STEPAN: I know, you have never had any regard for me. Yes. I was your parasite and I was occasionally weak. But to live as a parasite never was the ruling principle of my conduct. It just happened, I don't know how. I always thought there was something between us over and above eating and drinking, and I never was vulgar. Well, now I'll take to the road to right my wrongs! It is very late, the autumn is well along, the countryside is thick in fog, the frost of old age covers my way, and in the howling of the wind I can hear the call of the grave. *En route, cependant!* Oh, I say farewell to you, my dreams! *Vingt ans!* [*His face is covered with tears.*] *Allons!*

VARVARA [*she is deeply moved, but stamps her foot*]: ‖This is just one more bit of childishness. You will never be capable of carrying out your selfish threats. You won't go anywhere, you won't find any shopkeepers, and you will remain on my neck, continuing to draw your allowance and to receive your dreadful friends every Tuesday.‖ Farewell, Stepan Trofimovich!

STEPAN: *Alea jacta est.* [*He rushes out*].

VARVARA: Stepan!

[*But he has disappeared. She walks in circles, tearing her muff to pieces, then flings herself on the sofa in tears. Outside, vague noises.*]

GRIGORIEV [*coming in*]: Where was Stepan Trofimovich going? And there is an uprising in town!

VARVARA: An uprising?

GRIGORIEV: Yes. The workers from Spigulin's factory are holding a demonstration in front of the governor's house. The governor himself is reported to have gone mad.

VARVARA: Good Lord, Stepan may get caught in the uprising!

[*There enter, ushered in by* ALEXEY YEGOROVICH: PRASCOVYA DROZDOV, LISA, MAURICE NICOLAE-VICH *and* DASHA.]

PRASCOVYA: Oh! Good heavens! It's the revolution! And my poor legs that can't drag me any further.

[*There enter* VIRGINSKY, LIPUTIN, *and* PETER VER-KHOVENSKY.]

PETER: Things are stirring, things are stirring. That idiot of a governor had an attack of brain fever.

VARVARA: Have you seen your father?

PETER: No, but he's not running any risk. He might be flogged, but that will do him good.

[STAVROGIN *appears. His necktie is twisted out of place. He looks a bit mad, for the first time.*]

VARVARA: Nicholas, what's the matter with you?

STAVROGIN: Nothing. Nothing. It seemed to me that someone was calling me. No. . . . No. . . . Who would call me?

[LISA *takes a step forward.*]

LISA: Nicholas Stavrogin, a certain Lebyatkin, who calls himself your wife's brother, is sending me improper letters claiming to have revelations to make about you. If he is really your relative, keep him from bothering me.

[VARVARA *rushes towards* LISA.]

STAVROGIN [*with strange simplicity*]: I have in fact the misfortune of being related to that man. It is four years now since I married his sister, née Lebyatkin, in Petersburg.

[VARVARA *lifts up her right arm as if to shield her face and falls in a faint. All rush towards her except* LISA *and* STAVROGIN.]

STAVROGIN [*in the same tone of voice*]: Now is the time to follow me, Lisa. We shall go to my country house at Skvoreshniki.

[LISA *walks towards him like an automaton.* MAURICE NICOLAEVICH, *who was paying attention to* VARVARA PETROVNA, *rises and rushes towards her.*]

MAURICE: Lisa!

[*A gesture on her part stops him.*]

LISA: Have pity on me. [*She follows* STAVROGIN.]

BLACKOUT

THE NARRATOR [*in front of a curtain lighted by the burning city*]: The fire that had been smouldering for so long finally burst forth. It first burst out in reality the night that Lisa followed Stavrogin. The fire destroyed the suburb separating Stavrogin's country house from the town. In that suburb stood the house lived in by Lebyatkin and his sister, Maria. But the fire burst forth likewise in people's souls. After Lisa's flight misfortune followed misfortune.

SCENE SIXTEEN

The drawing-room of the country house at Skvoreshniki. Six a.m. LISA, *wearing the same dress, which is now rumpled and badly hooked up, is standing by the french window watching the fires of the city. She shudders.* STAVROGIN *comes in from the outside.*

354

STAVROGIN: Alexey has gone on horseback to get news. In a few minutes we shall know all. It is said that a part of the suburb has already burned down. The fire broke out between eleven and midnight.

[LISA *turns around suddenly and goes over and sits down in an armchair.*]

LISA: Listen to me, Nicholas. We haven't much longer to be together and I want to say all I have to say.

STAVROGIN: What do you mean, Lisa? Why haven't we much longer to be together?

LISA: Because I am dead.

STAVROGIN: Dead? Why, Lisa? You must live.

LISA: You have forgotten that as we arrived here yesterday I told you that you had brought a dead woman. I have lived since then. I have had my hour of life on earth, and that is enough. I don't want to be like Christofor Ivanovich. You remember?

STAVROGIN: Yes.

LISA: He bored you dreadfully, didn't he, at Lausanne? He always used to say: 'I have come just for a minute' and then he would stay all day. I don't want to be like him.

STAVROGIN: Don't talk like that. You are hurting yourself and hurting me too. I swear to you that I love you more at this moment than I did yesterday when we arrived here.

LISA: What an odd declaration!

STAVROGIN: We shan't separate again. We shall leave together.

LISA: Leave? Why? To be reborn together, as you said. No, all that is too sublime for me. If I were to leave with you, it would be for Moscow, to have a home and live among friends. That is my ideal, a very middle-class ideal. But, as you are married, all this is pointless.

STAVROGIN: But, Lisa, have you forgotten that you gave yourself to me?

LISA: I haven't forgotten it. I want to leave you now.

STAVROGIN: You are taking revenge on me for your whim of yesterday.

LISA: That is a thoroughly vulgar thought.

STAVROGIN: Then why did you do it?

LISA: What do you care? You are guilty of nothing; you don't have to answer to anyone.

STAVROGIN: Don't despise me like that. I fear nothing except losing the hope you gave me. I was lost, like a drowning man, and I thought that your love would save me. Do you have any idea what that new hope cost me? I paid for it with life itself.

LISA: Your life or someone else's?

STAVROGIN [*thoroughly upset*]: What do you mean? Tell me at once what you mean!

LISA: I simply asked you if you had paid for that hope with your life or mine. Why do you stare at me so? What did you think? You look as if you were afraid, as if you had been afraid for some time.... You are so pale now ...

STAVROGIN: If you know something, *I* know nothing, I swear. That's not what I meant.

LISA [*terrified*]: I don't understand you.

STAVROGIN [*sitting down and hiding his face in his hands*]: A bad dream.... A nightmare.... We were talking of two different things.

LISA: I don't know what you were talking about ... [*She stares at him.*] Nicholas ... [*He raises his head.*] Is it possible that you didn't guess yesterday that I would leave you today? Did you know it – yes or no? Don't lie: did you know it?

STAVROGIN: I knew it.

LISA: You knew it and yet you took me.

STAVROGIN: Yes, condemn me. You have the right to do so. I knew also that I didn't love you and yet I took you. I have never felt love for anyone. I desire, that's all. And I took advantage of you. But I have always hoped that some day I could love, and I have always hoped that it would be you. The fact that you were willing to follow me gave strength to that hope. I shall love, yes, I shall love you . . .

LISA: You will love me! And I imagined. . . . Ah! I followed you through pride, in order to rival you in generosity; I followed you to ruin myself with you and to share your misfortune. [*She weeps.*] But, despite everything, I imagined that you loved me madly. And you. . . . You hope to love me some day. What a little fool I was! Don't make fun of these tears. I love being sentimental about myself. But that is enough! I am not capable of anything and you are not capable of anything either. Let us console ourselves by sticking out our tongues at each other. Like that our pride at least will not suffer.

STAVROGIN: Don't weep. I can't endure it.

LISA: I am calm. I gave my life for an hour with you. Now I am calm. As for you, you will forget. You will have other hours and other moments.

STAVROGIN: Never, never! No one but you . . .

LISA [*looking at him with a wild hope*]: Ah! You . . .

STAVROGIN: Yes, yes. I shall love you. Now I am sure of it. Some day my heart will relax at last, I shall bow my head and forget myself in your arms. You alone can cure me . . .

LISA [*who has recovered possession of herself, with a dull tone of despair*]: Cure you! I don't want to. I don't want to be a Sister of Charity for you. Ask Dasha instead; she will follow you everywhere like a dog. And don't worry about

357

me. I knew in advance what was in store for me. I always knew that if I followed you, you would lead me to a spot inhabited by a monstrous spider as big as a man, that we would spend our life watching the spider and trembling with fear, and that our love would go no farther ...
[ALEXEY YEGOROVICH *comes in.*]

ALEXEY: Sir, sir, they have found ... [*He stops as he sees* LISA.] I ... Sir, Peter Verkhovensky wishes to see you.

STAVROGIN: Lisa, wait in this room. [*She goes towards it.* ALEXEY YEGOROVICH *goes out.*] Lisa ... [*She stops.*] If you hear anything, you might as well know now that *I* am the guilty one.

[*She looks at him in fright and slowly backs into the study.* PETER VERKHOVENSKY *comes in.*]

PETER: Let me tell you first of all that none of us is guilty. It was a mere coincidence. Legally, you are not involved ...

STAVROGIN: They were burned? Assassinated?

PETER: Assassinated. Unfortunately, the house only half burned and the bodies were found. Lebyatkin's throat was slit. His sister had been slashed over and over again with a knife. But it was a prowler, most certainly. I have heard that, the night before, Lebyatkin was drunk and showed everybody the fifteen hundred roubles I had given him.

STAVROGIN: You had given him fifteen hundred roubles?

PETER: Yes. Quite deliberately. And from you.

STAVROGIN: From me?

PETER: Yes. I was afraid he would denounce us and I gave him the money so that he could get to St Petersburg ... [STAVROGIN *takes a few steps with an absent-minded stare.*] But listen at least to the way things turned out ... [*He grasps* STAVROGIN *by the lapel of his Prince Albert.* STAVROGIN *gives him a violent blow.*] Oh, you might have broken my arm! Of course, he boasted of having that money. Fedka saw it, that's all. I'm sure now that it was Fedka. He must not have understood your true intentions ...

STAVROGIN [*oddly absent-minded*]: Was it Fedka who lighted the fire?

PETER: No. No. You know that such fires were planned in our group action. It's a very Russian way of starting a revolution.... But it came too soon! I was disobeyed, that's all, and I'll have to take steps. But don't forget that this misfortune has its advantages. For instance, you are a widower and you can marry Lisa tomorrow. Where is she? I want to give her the good news. [STAVROGIN *laughs suddenly, but with a sort of wild laugh.*] You are laughing?

STAVROGIN: Yes. I am laughing at one who apes me, I am laughing at you. Good news, indeed! But don't you think that those corpses will upset her somewhat?

PETER: Not at all! Why? Besides, legally.... And she's a young lady who isn't daunted by anything. You'll be amazed to see the way she steps over those corpses. Once she's married, she'll forget.

STAVROGIN: There will be no marriage. Lisa will remain alone.

PETER: No? As soon as I saw you together, I realized that it hadn't worked. Ah! A complete flop? ||I'll bet you spent the whole night seated on different chairs, wasting precious time discussing very serious things.|| Besides, I was sure that it would all end in nonsense.... Good. I shall easily marry her off to Maurice Nicolaevich, who must be waiting for her outside now in the rain. As for the others – the ones who were killed – it's better not to tell her anything about that. She'll find out soon enough. [LISA *comes in.*]

LISA: What shall I find out soon enough? Who has killed

someone? What did you say about Maurice Nicolaevich?

PETER: Well, young lady, so we listen at doors!

LISA: What did you say about Maurice Nicolaevich? Has he been killed?

STAVROGIN: No, Lisa. It was only my wife and her brother who were killed.

PETER [*in a hurry*]: A strange, a monstrous coincidence! Someone took advantage of the fire to kill and rob them. It must have been Fedka.

LISA: Nicholas! Is he telling the truth?

STAVROGIN: No. He is not telling the truth.

[LISA *moans.*]

PETER: But don't you see that this man has lost his reason! Besides he spent the night with you. Hence –

LISA: Nicholas, talk to me as if you stood before God at this moment. Are you guilty or not? I will trust your word as I would God's word. And I shall follow you, like a dog, to the end of the world.

STAVROGIN [*slowly*]: I did not kill and I was against that murder, but I knew they would be assassinated and I did not keep the murderers from doing it. Now, leave me.

LISA [*looking at him with horror*]: No! No! No! [*She rushes off, shouting.*]

PETER: So I have wasted my time with you!

STAVROGIN [*in a dull voice*]: Me. Oh! Me ... [*He laughs madly all of a sudden; then, getting up, shouts in a thunderous voice*] I loathe and detest everything that exists in Russia, the people, the Tsar, and you and Lisa. I hate everything that lives on earth, and myself first of all. So let destruction reign and crush them all, and with them all those who ape Stavrogin, and Stavrogin himself. . .

BLACKOUT

‖SCENE SEVENTEEN*

In the street. LISA *is running.* PETER VERKHOVENSKY *is running after her.*

PETER: Wait, Lisa, wait. I'll take you home. I have a fiacre.

LISA [*bewildered*]: Yes, yes, you are good. Where are they? Where is the blood?

PETER: Stop! What can you do? It's raining, you see. Come. Maurice Nicolaevich is here.

LISA: Maurice! Where is he? Oh, my God, he's waiting for me! He knows!

PETER: What does that matter? Surely he doesn't have any prejudices!

LISA: Wonderful, wonderful! Ah, he mustn't see me. Let's flee in the woods, in the fields . . .

[PETER *leaves and* LISA *continues running.* MAURICE *appears and pursues her. She falls. He bends over her, weeping, takes off his coat, and covers her with it. She kisses his hand, weeping.*]

MAURICE: Lisa! I am nothing compared to you, but don't reject me!

LISA: Maurice, don't abandon me! I'm afraid of death. I don't want to die.

MAURICE: You are soaked! Good Lord! And it's still raining!

LISA: It doesn't matter. Come, lead me. I want to see the blood. They killed his wife, I've heard. And he says he was the one who killed her. But it's not true, is it? Oh, I must see with my own eyes those who were killed

*This scene was cut in production.

because of me.... Hurry! Hurry! Oh, Maurice, don't forgive me. I was wicked. Why should anyone forgive me? Why are you weeping? Strike me and kill me, right here!

MAURICE: No one has the right to judge you, and I least of all. May God forgive you!

[*Little by little the curtain is lighted by the flames of the fire, and the sound of the crowd can be heard.* STEPAN TROFIM-OVICH *appears in travelling costume with a travelling bag in his left hand, a staff and an umbrella in his right hand.*]

STEPAN [*in delirium*]: Oh, you! *Chère, chère,* is it possible? In this fog.... You can see the fire!... You are unhappy, aren't you? I can see it. We are all unhappy, but we must forgive them all. To shake off the world and become free, *il faut pardonner, pardonner, pardonner ...*

LISA: Oh! Get up! Why are you kneeling?

STEPAN: At the moment of saying farewell to the world, I want to say farewell to you – and so to my whole past. [*He weeps.*] I am kneeling down before everything that was beautiful in my life. I dreamed of scaling the heights to heaven, and here I am in the mud, a crushed old man.... See their crime in all its red horror. They couldn't do otherwise. I am fleeing their delirium, their nightmare, and I am going in search of Russia. But you are both soaked. Here, take my umbrella. [MAURICE *automatically takes the umbrella.*] I'll find a cart of some kind. But, dear Lisa, what did you just say? Has someone been killed? [LISA *starts to swoon.*] Oh, my God, she is fainting!

LISA: Quick, quick, Maurice. Give this child back his umbrella! At once! [*She turns back towards* STEPAN TROFIMOVICH.] I want to make the sign of the cross over you, poor man. You, too, pray for poor Lisa!

[STEPAN TROFIMOVICH *goes off, and they walk towards the*

flames. *The noise increases. The flames are becoming brighter. The crowd is now shouting.*]

VOICES: It's Stavrogin's wench. It's not enough for them to kill people. They also want to see the bodies.

[*A man strikes* LISA. MAURICE NICOLAEVICH *throws himself on him. They fight.* LISA *picks herself up. Two other men strike her, one of them with a stick. She falls. Everything becomes calm.* MAURICE NICOLAEVICH *takes her in his arms and drags her towards the light.*]

MAURICE: Lisa, Lisa, don't forsake me. [LISA *falls back dead.*] Lisa, dear Lisa, now it's my turn to join you!

BLACKOUT‖

THE NARRATOR: While they were looking everywhere for Stepan Trofimovich, who was wandering on the road like a deposed king, events were precipitated. Shatov's wife returned after three years' absence. But what Shatov took for a new beginning was in reality to be an end.

SCENE EIGHTEEN

Shatov's room. MARIA SHATOV *is standing with a travelling bag in her hand.*

MARIA: I'll not stay long, just long enough to find work. But if I am in your way, I beg you to tell me at once quite honestly. I'll sell something and go to the hotel. [*She sits down on the bed.*]

SHATOV: Maria, you mustn't talk of a hotel. You are at home here.

363

MARIA: No, I am not at home here. We separated three years ago. Don't get it into your head that I am repenting and coming back to begin over again.

SHATOV: No, no, that would be pointless. But it doesn't matter anyway. You are the only person who ever told me she loved me. That's enough. You are doing what you want, and now you are here.

MARIA: Yes, you are good. I have come back under your roof because I have always considered you a good man — so far above all those scoundrels . . .

SHATOV: Listen, Maria, you look exhausted. Please don't get annoyed. . . . If you'd only take a little tea, for instance. Tea always does one good. If you would only . . .

MARIA: Yes, I would. You are still just as much a child. Give me some tea if you have any. It's so cold here.

SHATOV: Yes, yes, you shall have tea.

MARIA: You don't have any here?

HATOV: There will be some. There will be some. [*He steps out and knocks at Kirilov's door.*] Can you lend me some tea?

KIRILOV: Come in and drink it!

SHATOV: No. My wife has come back. . .

KIRILOV: Your wife!

SHATOV [*sputtering and half weeping*]: Kirilov, Kirilov, we suffered together in America.

KIRILOV: Yes, yes, wait. [*He disappears and reappears with a tea tray.*] Here it is. Take it. And a rouble too — take it.

SHATOV: I'll give it back to you tomorrow! Ah, Kirilov!

KIRILOV: No, no, I am glad she has come back and that you still love her. I am glad that you turned to me. If you need anything, just call me at any time whatever. I shall be thinking of you and her.

SHATOV: Oh, what a man you would be if you could only get rid of your dreadful ideas.

[KIRILOV *disappears suddenly.* SHATOV *stares after him. There is a knock at the door.* LYAMSHIN *comes in.*]

SHATOV: I can't receive you now.

LYAMSHIN: I have something to tell you. I have come to tell you from Verkhovensky that everything is arranged. You are free.

SHATOV: Is that true?

LYAMSHIN: Yes, absolutely free. You will just have to show Liputin the place where the press is buried. I shall come to get you tomorrow at exactly six o'clock, before dawn.

SHATOV: I'll come. Now go. My wife has come back. [LYAMSHIN *leaves.* SHATOV *goes back towards the room.* MARIA *has gone to sleep. He places the tray on the table and watches her.*] Oh, how beautiful you are!

MARIA [*waking up*]: Why did you let me go to sleep? I'm in your bed. Ah! [*She stiffens as if in a sort of attack and grips* SHATOV's *hand.*]

SHATOV: You are suffering, my dear. I shall call the doctor... Where does it hurt? Do you want compresses? I know how to make them...

MARIA: What? What do you mean?

SHATOV: Nothing... I don't understand you.

MARIA: No, it's nothing.... Don't stand still. Tell me something.... Talk to me of your new ideas. What are you preaching now? You can't keep yourself from preaching; it's in your nature.

SHATOV: Yes.... That is... I am preaching God now.

MARIA: And yet you don't believe in Him. [*New attack.*] Oh, how unbearable you are! [*She repulses* SHATOV, *who is bending over the bed.*]

SHATOV: Maria, I'll do what you want.... I'll keep moving.... I'll talk.

MARIA: But don't you see that it's begun?

SHATOV: Begun? What has?

MARIA: Don't you see that I'm about to give birth? Oh! Cursed be this child! [SHATOV *gets up.*] Where are you going, where are you going? I forbid you!

SHATOV: I'll be back, I'll be back. We need money and a midwife. . . . Oh, Maria! . . . Kirilov! Kirilov!

[BLACKOUT. *Then the light gradually increases in the room.*]

SHATOV: She's in the next room with him.

MARIA: He is beautiful.

SHATOV: What a great joy!

MARIA: What shall I name him?

SHATOV: Shatov. He is my son. Let me fix your pillows.

MARIA: Not like that! How awkward you are! [*He does his best.*]

MARIA [*without looking at him*]: Lean over me! [*He leans towards her.*] Closer! Closer! [*She slips her arm around his neck and kisses him.*]

SHATOV: Maria! My love!

[*She rolls on her side.*]

MARIA: Ah! Nicholas Stavrogin is a wretch. [*She bursts into sobs. He caresses her and talks to her softly.*]

SHATOV: Maria. It's over now. The three of us will live together calmly, and we shall work.

MARIA [*reaching out and grasping him in her arms*]: Yes, we shall work, we shall forget everything, my love . . .

[*There is a knock at the door of the living-room.*]

MARIA: What's that?

SHATOV: I had forgotten it. Maria, I must leave you. I'll be gone a half-hour.

MARIA: You are going to leave me alone? We have just found each other after all these years and you are leaving me . . .

SHATOV: But this is the last time. After this we shall be together for ever. Never, never again shall we think of the horror of the past.

[*He kisses her, takes up his cap, and gently closes the door. In the living-room* LYAMSHIN *is waiting for him.*]

SHATOV: Lyamshin, have you ever been happy in your life?

[BLACKOUT. *Then* LYAMSHIN *and* SHATOV *step around the curtain representing the street.* LYAMSHIN *stops and hesitates.*]

SHATOV: Well! What are you waiting for? [*They continue walking.*]

BLACKOUT

SCENE NINETEEN

The Forest of Brykovo. SHIGALOV *and* VIRGINSKY *are already there when* PETER VERKHOVENSKY *arrives with* THE SEMINARIST *and* LIPUTIN.

PETER [*lifts his lantern and looks at them all in the face*]: I hope you haven't forgotten what was agreed.

VIRGINSKY: Listen. I know that Shatov's wife came back to him last night and that she gave birth to a child. Anyone who knows human nature knows that he will not denounce us now. He is happy. Perhaps we could postpone this for the present.

PETER: If you suddenly became happy, would you postpone accomplishing an act of justice that you considered just and necessary?

VIRGINSKY: Certainly not. Certainly not. But ...

PETER: You would prefer to be unhappy rather than to be cowardly?

VIRGINSKY: Certainly ... I should prefer it.

PETER: Well, let me point out to you that Shatov now considers this denunciation just and necessary. Besides, what happiness could there possibly be in the fact that his wife, after an escapade of three years, has returned to him to give birth to a child by Stavrogin?

VIRGINSKY [*interrupting*]: Yes, but I protest. We'll ask him to give his word of honour. That's all.

PETER: You can't talk of honour unless you're in the pay of the government.

LIPUTIN: How dare you? Which of us here is in the pay of the government?

PETER: You, perhaps. ... Traitors are always afraid at the moment of danger.

SHIGALOV: Enough, I must speak up. Since last night I have scrupulously examined the question of this assassination and have reached the conclusion that it was useless, frivolous, and petty. You hate Shatov because he despises you and he insulted you all. That is a personal question. But personal questions lead to despotism. Hence I am leaving you. Not out of fear of danger nor out of friendship for Shatov, but because this assassination contradicts my system. Farewell. As for denouncing you, you know that I won't do it. [*He wheels about and goes away.*]

PETER: Stay here! ... We'll catch up with that madman. Meanwhile, I must tell you that Shatov already told Kirilov of his intention of denouncing us. It was Kirilov who told me, because he was shocked by it. Now you know everything. And, furthermore, you have taken an oath. [*They look at one another.*] Good. Let me remind you that we are to throw him into the pond afterwards and then scatter. Kirilov's letter will cover all of us. Tomorrow I am leaving for St Petersburg. You will have news from me soon. [*A shrill whistle. After a hesitation* LIPUTIN *answers it.*] Let's hide.

[*They all hide except* LIPUTIN. LYAMSHIN *and* SHATOV *come on stage.*]

SHATOV: Well! You are silent? Where is your pickaxe? Don't be afraid. There's not a soul here. You could shoot a cannon off here and no one would hear a thing in the suburb. Here it is. [*He strikes the ground with his foot.*] Right here.

[THE SEMINARIST *and* LIPUTIN *leap on him from the rear, seize his arms, and pin him to the ground.* PETER VERKHOVENSKY *puts his revolver to* SHATOV's *forehead.* SHATOV *utters a brief, desperate cry:* 'Maria!' VERKHOVENSKY *shoots.* VIRGINSKY, *who has not taken part in the murder, suddenly begins to tremble and to scream.*]

VIRGINSKY: That's not the way. No, no. That's not the way at all.... No ... [LYAMSHIN, *who has stood behind him all the time without taking part in the murder either, suddenly grabs him from behind and begins screaming.* VIRGINSKY, *in fright, tears himself away.* LYAMSHIN *throws himself on* PETER VERKHOVENSKY, *screaming likewise. He is seized and silenced.* VIRGINSKY *weeps.*] No, no, that's not the way ...

PETER [*looking at them with scorn*]: Filthy cowards!

BLACKOUT

SCENE TWENTY

The street. VERKHOVENSKY, *hastening towards the Filipov lodging-house, encounters* FEDKA.

PETER: Why the hell didn't you stay hidden, as I had ordered you to?

FEDKA: Don't talk that way to me, you little sneak. I didn't want to compromise Mr Kirilov, who is an educated man.

PETER: Do you or don't you want a passport and money to go to Petersburg?

FEDKA: You are a louse. That's what I think you are. You promised me money in the name of Mr Stavrogin to shed innocent blood. I know now that Mr Stavrogin was not informed. So that the real murderer is neither me nor Mr Stavrogin: it's you.

PETER [*beside himself*]: You wretch, I'll hand you over to the police at once! [*He takes out his revolver. Quicker than he,* FEDKA *strikes him four times on the head.* PETER *falls.* FEDKA *runs away with a burst of laughter.* PETER *picks himself up.*] I'll find you at the other end of the world. I'll crush you. As for Kirilov!... [*He runs towards the Filipov lodging-house.*]

BLACKOUT

SCENE TWENTY-ONE

The Filipov lodging-house.

KIRILOV [*in complete blackness*]: You killed Shatov! You killed him! You killed him! [*The lights come up gradually.*]

PETER: I have explained it a hundred times. Shatov was on the point of denouncing us all.

KIRILOV: Shut up. You killed him because he spat in your face in Geneva.

PETER: For that. And for many other things too. What's the matter with you? Oh ...

[KIRILOV *has taken out a revolver and is aiming at him.* PETER VERKHOVENSKY *takes out his revolver too.*]

KIRILOV: You had got your weapon ready in advance because you were afraid I would kill you. But I'll not kill. Although ... although ... [*He continues taking aim. Then he lowers his arm, laughing.*]

PETER: I knew you wouldn't shoot. But you took a big risk. *I* was going to shoot ...

[*He sits down again and pours himself some tea with a trembling hand.* KIRILOV *lays his revolver on the table, starts walking up and down, and stops in front of* PETER VERKHOVENSKY.]

KIRILOV: I'm sorry about Shatov.

PETER: So am I.

KIRILOV: Shut up, you wretch, or I'll kill you.

PETER: All right. I don't regret him. ... Besides, there's not much time. I must take a train at dawn and cross the frontier.

KIRILOV: I understand. You are leaving your crimes behind and taking shelter yourself. Filthy swine!

PETER: Filth and decency are just words. Everything is just words.

KIRILOV: All my life I wanted there to be something other than words. That's what I lived for, so that words have a meaning, so that they would be deeds also ...

PETER: And so?

KIRILOV: So ... [*He looks at* PETER VERKHOVENSKY.] Oh, you're the last man I shall ever see. I don't want us to separate in hatred.

PETER: I assure you that I have nothing against you personally.

KIRILOV: We are both miserable wretches, and I am going to kill myself and you will go on living.

PETER: Of course I shall go on living. *I* am a coward. It's despicable, I know.

KIRILOV [*with increasing excitement*]: Yes, yes, it's despicable. Listen. Do you remember what Christ Crucified said to the thief who was dying on his right hand? 'Today shalt thou be with me in Paradise.' The day ended, they died, and there was neither Paradise nor Resurrection. And yet He was the greatest man on earth. Without that man the whole planet and everything on it is simply meaningless. Well, if the laws of nature did not even spare such a man, if they forced Him to live in lies and to die for a lie, then this whole planet is but a lie. What is the good of living, then? Answer, if you are a man.

PETER: Yes, what is the good of living! I have understood your point of view completely. If God is a lie, then we are alone and free. You kill yourself and prove that you are free and there is no God. But for that you must kill yourself.

KIRILOV [*more and more excited*]: You have understood. Ah! Everyone will understand if even a low scoundrel like you can understand. But someone has to begin and kill himself to prove to others the terrible freedom of man. I am unfortunate because I am the first and because I am dreadfully frightened. I am Tsar only for a short time. But I shall begin and open the door. And all men will be happy; they will all be Tsars and for ever. [*He rushes to the table.*] Ah! Give me the pen. Dictate and I'll sign anything. Even that I killed Shatov. Dictate. I don't fear anyone; everything is a matter of indifference. All that is hidden will be known, and you will be crushed. I believe. I believe. Dictate.

PETER [*leaps up and places paper and pen in front of* KIRILOV]:
I, Alexey Kirilov, declare . . .

KIRILOV: Yes. To whom? To whom? I want to know to
whom I'm making this declaration.

PETER: To no one, to everyone. Why specify? To the whole
world.

KIRILOV: To the whole world! Bravo. And without
repenting. I don't want any repenting. I don't want to
address myself to the authorities. Go ahead, dictate. The
universe is evil. I'll sign.

PETER: Yes, the universe is evil. And down with the
authorities! Write.

KIRILOV: Wait a minute! I want to draw on the top of the
page a face sticking out its tongue.

PETER: No. No drawing. The tone is enough.

KIRILOV: The tone – yes, that's it. Dictate the tone.

PETER: 'I declare that this morning I killed the student
Shatov in the woods for his betrayal and his denunciation
in the matter of the proclamation.'

KIRILOV: Is that all? I want to insult them too.

PETER: That's enough. Give it to me. But you haven't dated
it or signed. Sign it now.

KIRILOV: I want to insult them.

PETER: Put down 'Long live the Republic.' That'll get
them.

KIRILOV: Yes. Yes. No, I'm going to put: 'Liberty,
equality, fraternity, or death.' There. And then in
French: '*gentilhomme, séminariste russe et citoyen du monde
civilisé.*' There! There! It's perfect. Perfect. [*He gets up,
takes the revolver, and runs and turns out the lamp. The stage is in
complete darkness. He shouts in the darkness at the top of his
lungs*] At once! At once!

[*A shot rings out. Silence. Someone can be heard groping in the darkness.* PETER VERKHOVENSKY *lights a candle and casts a light on* KIRILOV's *body.*]

PETER: Perfect! [*he goes out.*]

MARIA SHATOV [*shouting on the landing*]: Shatov! Shatov!

BLACKOUT

THE NARRATOR: Denounced by the weak Lyamshin, Shatov's murderers were arrested, except for Verkhovensky, who at that moment, comfortably installed in a first-class carriage, was crossing the frontier and outlining new plans for a better society. But if such as Verkhovensky are immortal, it is not certain that such as Stavrogin are.

SCENE TWENTY-TWO

At Varvara Stavrogin's. VARVARA STAVROGIN *is putting on a cape. Beside her,* DASHA *is wearing mourning.* ALEXEY YEGOROVICH *is at the door.*

VARVARA: Prepare the carriage! [ALEXEY *leaves.*] To run away like that at his age, and in the rain! [*She weeps.*] The fool! The fool! But he is ill now. Oh! I'll bring him back dead or alive! [*She starts towards the door, stops, and comes back towards* DASHA.] My dear, my dear! [*She kisses her and leaves.* DASHA *watches her from the window, then goes and sits down.*]

DASHA: Protect them all, good Lord, protect them all before protecting me too. [STAVROGIN *suddenly enters.* DASHA *stares at him fixedly. Silence.*] You have come to get me, haven't you?

374

STAVROGIN: Yes.

DASHA: What do you want with me?

STAVROGIN: I have come to ask you to leave with me tomorrow.

DASHA: I will! Where shall we go?

STAVROGIN: Abroad. We shall settle there for good. Will you come?

DASHA: I'll come.

STAVROGIN: The place I am thinking of is lugubrious. At the bottom of a ravine. The mountain cuts off the view and crushes one's thoughts. It is the one place in the world that is most like death.

DASHA: I'll follow you. But you will learn to live, to live again.... You are strong.

STAVROGIN [*with a wry smile*]: Yes, I am strong. I was capable of being slapped without saying a word, of overpowering a murderer, of living in dissipation, of publicly confessing my downfall. I can do anything. I have infinite strength. But I don't know where to apply it. Everything is foreign to me.

DASHA: Ah, may God give you just a little love, even if I am not the object of it!

STAVROGIN: Yes, you are courageous; you will be a good nurse! But, let me repeat, don't let yourself be taken in. I have never been able to hate anything. Hence, I shall never love. I am capable only of negation, of petty negation. If I could believe in something, I could perhaps kill myself. But I can't believe.

DASHA [*trembling*]: Nicholas, such a void is faith or the promise of faith.

STAVROGIN [*looking at her after a moment of silence*]: Hence, I have faith. [*He straightens up.*] Don't say anything. I have something to do now. [*He gives a strange little laugh.*]

What weakness to have come for you! You were dear to me, and in my sorrow it was pleasant to be with you.

DASHA: You made me happy by coming.

STAVROGIN [*stares at her with an odd look*]: Happy? All right, all right. . . . No, it isn't possible. . . . I bring nothing but evil. . . . But I'm not accusing anyone.

[*He goes out on the right. Hubbub outside.* VARVARA *comes in upstage. Behind her,* STEPAN TROFIMOVICH *is carried like a child by a tall, stalwart peasant.*]

VARVARA: Quick, put him on this sofa. [*To* ALEXEY YEGOROVICH] Go and get the doctor. [*To* DASHA] You, get the room warmed up. [*After laying* STEPAN *on the sofa, the peasant withdraws.*] Well! You poor fool, did you have a good walk? [*He faints. Panic-stricken, she sits down beside him and taps his hands.*] Oh, calm yourself, calm yourself! My dear! Oh, tormentor, tormentor!

STEPAN [*lifting his head*]: Ah, *chère!* Ah, *chère!*

VARVARA: No, just wait, keep quiet.

[*He takes her hand and squeezes it hard. Suddenly he lifts* VARVARA's *hand to his lips. Gritting her teeth,* VARVARA STAVROGIN *stares at a corner of the room.*]

STEPAN: I loved you . . .

VARVARA: Keep quiet.

STEPAN: I loved you all my life, for twenty years . . .

VARVARA: But why do you keep repeating: 'I loved you, I loved you'? Enough. . . . Twenty years are over, and they'll not return. I'm just a fool! [*She rises.*] If you don't go to sleep again, I'll . . . [*With a sudden note of affection*] Sleep. I'll watch over you.

STEPAN: Yes. I shall sleep. [*He begins raving, but in an almost reasonable way.*] *Chère et incomparable amie*, it seems to me . . . yes, I am almost happy. But happiness doesn't suit me, for right away I begin to forgive my enemies.... If only I could be forgiven too.

VARVARA [*deeply moved and speaking bluffly*]: You will be forgiven. And yet ...

STEPAN: Yes. I don't deserve it, though. We are all guilty. But when you are here, I am innocent as a child. *Chère*, I have to live in the presence of a woman. And it was so cold on the road.... But I got to know the people, I told them my life.

VARVARA: You spoke about me in your taverns!

STEPAN: Yes ... but only by allusion ... you see. And they didn't understand a word. Oh, let me kiss the hem of your frock!

VARVARA: Stay still. You will always be impossible.

STEPAN: Yes, strike me on the other cheek, as in the Gospels. I have always been a wretch. Except with you.

VARVARA [*weeping*]: With me too.

STEPAN [*getting excited*]: No, but all my life I've lied ... even when I told the truth. I never spoke with the truth in mind, but solely with myself in mind. Do you realize that I am lying even now, perhaps?

VARVARA: Yes, you are lying.

STEPAN: That is.... The only true thing is that I love you. As for all the rest, yes, I am lying, that's certain. The trouble is that I believe what I say when I lie. The hardest thing is to go on living and not to believe in one's own lies. *Mais vous êtes là, vous m'aiderez* ... [*He swoons.*]

VARVARA: Come back to life! Come back to life! Oh, he is burning hot! Alexey!

[ALEXEY YEGOROVICH *enters.*]

ALEXEY: The doctor is coming, madame.

[ALEXEY *goes out on the right.* VARVARA *turns back towards* STEPAN.]

STEPAN: *Chère, chère, vous voilà!* I reflected on the road and I understood many things ... that we should give up negating. We should never negate anything again.... It's too late for us, but for those to come, the young who will take our place, *la jeune Russie* ...

VARVARA: What do you mean?

STEPAN: Oh! Read me the passage about the swine.

VARVARA [*frightened*]: About the swine?

STEPAN: Yes, in St Luke, you know, when the devils enter into the swine. [VARVARA *goes to get the Gospels on her desk and leafs through them.*] Chapter VIII, verses 32 to 36.

VARVARA [*standing near him and reading*]: '... Then went the devils up out of the man, and entered into the swine: and the herd ran violently down a steep place into the lake, and were choked.

'And when they that fed them saw what was done, they fled, and went and told this in the city and in the country.

'Then they went out to see what was done; and came to Jesus, and found the man, out of whom the devils were departed, sitting at the feet of Jesus, clothed, and in his right mind: and they were afraid.'

STEPAN: Ah, yes! Yes.... Those devils who depart from the sick man, *chère*, you see – well, you recognize them.... They are our defects, our impurities, of course, and the sick man is Russia.... But the impurities leave him, they enter into the swine. I mean us, my son, the others, and we run violently down a steep place as if possessed of the devil, and we shall perish. But the sick man will be cured and he will sit at the feet of Jesus and all will be cured.... Yes, Russia will be cured some day!

VARVARA: You're not going to die. You say that just to torment me a little more, cruel man ...

STEPAN: No, *chère*, no.... Besides, I shall not die altogether.

We shall be raised from the dead, we shall be raised from the dead, won't we? If God is, we shall be raised. . . . That is my profession of faith. And I make it to you whom I loved . . .

VARVARA: God *is*, Stepan Trofimovich. I assure you that he exists.

STEPAN: I realized that on the road . . . amidst my people. I have lied all life long. Tomorrow, tomorrow, *chère,* we shall live again together . . . [*He falls back dead.*]

VARVARA: Dasha! [*Then, standing stiffly*] *O, mon Dieu,* have pity on this child!

ALEXEY [*rushing out of the room on the right*]: Madame, madame! . . . [DASHA *comes on.*] There! Look there! [*He points to the room.*] Mr Stavrogin!

    [DASHA *runs towards the room. A gasp is heard from her. Then she comes out slowly.*]

DASHA [*falling on her knees*]: He has hanged himself.

    [*The* NARRATOR *enters.*]

THE NARRATOR: Ladies and gentlemen, one word more. After Stavrogin's death the doctors conferred and pronounced that he showed not the slightest sign of insanity.

CURTAIN

Discover more about our forthcoming books through Penguin's FREE newspaper...

Penguin Quarterly

It's packed with:

- exciting features
- author interviews
- previews & reviews
- books from your favourite films & TV series
- exclusive competitions & much, much more...

Write off for your free copy today to:
Dept JC
Penguin Books Ltd
FREEPOST
West Drayton
Middlesex
UB7 0BR
NO STAMP REQUIRED

READ MORE IN PENGUIN

In every corner of the world, on every subject under the sun, Penguin represents quality and variety – the very best in publishing today.

For complete information about books available from Penguin – including Puffins, Penguin Classics and Arkana – and how to order them, write to us at the appropriate address below. Please note that for copyright reasons the selection of books varies from country to country.

In the United Kingdom: Please write to *Dept. JC, Penguin Books Ltd, FREEPOST, West Drayton, Middlesex UB7 OBR*

If you have any difficulty in obtaining a title, please send your order with the correct money, plus ten per cent for postage and packaging, to *PO Box No. 11, West Drayton, Middlesex UB7 OBR*

In the United States: Please write to *Penguin USA Inc., 375 Hudson Street, New York, NY 10014*

In Canada: Please write to *Penguin Books Canada Ltd, 10 Alcorn Avenue, Suite 300, Toronto, Ontario M4V 3B2*

In Australia: Please write to *Penguin Books Australia Ltd, 487 Maroondah Highway, Ringwood, Victoria 3134*

In New Zealand: Please write to *Penguin Books (NZ) Ltd,182–190 Wairau Road, Private Bag, Takapuna, Auckland 9*

In India: Please write to *Penguin Books India Pvt Ltd, 706 Eros Apartments, 56 Nehru Place, New Delhi 110 019*

In the Netherlands: Please write to *Penguin Books Netherlands B.V., Keizersgracht 231 NL–1016 DV Amsterdam*

In Germany: Please write to *Penguin Books Deutschland GmbH, Friedrichstrasse 10–12, W–6000 Frankfurt/Main 1*

In Spain: Please write to *Penguin Books S. A., C. San Bernardo 117–6° E–28015 Madrid*

In Italy: Please write to *Penguin Italia s.r.l., Via Felice Casati 20, I–20124 Milano*

In France: Please write to *Penguin France S. A., 17 rue Lejeune, F–31000 Toulouse*

In Japan: Please write to *Penguin Books Japan, Ishikiribashi Building, 2–5–4, Suido, Bunkyo-ku, Tokyo 112*

In Greece: Please write to *Penguin Hellas Ltd, Dimocritou 3, GR–106 71 Athens*

In South Africa: Please write to *Longman Penguin Southern Africa (Pty) Ltd, Private Bag X08, Bertsham 2013*

BY THE SAME AUTHOR

'Probably no European writer of his time left so deep a mark on the imagination, and at the same time on the moral and political consciousness of his generation, and of the next' Conor Cruise O'Brien

'Few French writers of this century have been more versatile or more influential than Camus ... No one in his lifetime wrote better prose than he, no one better blended conviction and grace of style' – *The Times*

'Of all available modern prophets, M. Camus seems to be the most enlightened, the most perceptive, the most helpful' – Philip Toynbee

Novels

The Fall
A Happy Death
The Plague
The Rebel
The Outsider

Short Stories

Exile and the Kingdom

and

The Myth of Sisyphus
Selected Essays and Notebooks
Youthful Writings